City Magick

City Magick

Urban rituals, spells, and shamanism

Christopher Penczak

WEISERBOOKS

Boston, MA/York Beach, ME

First published in 2001 by
Red Wheel/Weiser, llc
York Beach, ME
With offices at
368 Congress Street
Boston, MA 02210
www.redwheelweiser.com

Library of Congress Cataloging-in-Publication Data

Penczak, Christopher.
  City Magick: urban rituals, spells, and shamanism / Christopher Penczak.
    p. cm.
  Includes bibliographical references and index.
    1. Cities and towns—Miscellanea. 2. Magic. 3. Shamanism. 4. City dwellers—
  Religious life. I. Title.

  BF1623.C5 P46 2001
  133.4'3'091732—dc21   00–068577

VG

Typeset in Kennerly
Cover design by Kathryn Sky-Peck
Interior design by Jill Feron/Feron Design

Photographs on pages 185, 186, and 189 are by William Michie.
Photographs on pages 187 and 199 are by Lena Jenkins.

Printed in the United States of America

08 07 06 05 04 03
8 7 6 5 4 3 2

The paper used in this publication meets the minimum requirements of the
American National Standard for Information Sciences—Permanence of Paper
for Printed Library Materials Z39.48-1992 (R1997).

To Steve, Rosalie, and Ronald, for all their love and support;
and to all my unseen helpers near and far. . .

Contents

List of Figures

List of Exercises

Introduction

"THAT'S JUST WRONG! CITIES ARE EVIL,"
said a very good friend of mine when I first mentioned this book to
her. She's a pagan too, and although we come from different traditions, I respect her opinions and beliefs. Her thoughts on any matter
hold a lot of weight for me. For a moment, I was bruised–but for just
a moment. I was immediately impressed with her precognitive powers, exceeding the bounds of most psychics, to divine the content of
the book before it was even written. Then I thought, these words
came from a woman who has running water, electricity, heat, a computer, a television, a stereo, two VCRs, a Jeep, a refrigerator, a
banana rack, wireless speakers, and an ice cream maker! I asked her
to bring those thoughts to the next logical step. She said, "What?
That I should blow all the cities up?" She can get passionate about
things at times. I reminded her of her household conveniences. If you
followed those thoughts to their logical conclusion, you would be living
in a tent in the forest, foraging and hunting for your own food. There
would be no e-mail or television shows. And she would probably love
it too. She's very primal. And perhaps that is the better way to live.

My friend then proceeded to tell me, however, that the things I
had mentioned were different. You could have them without cities.
Cities cause too many problems. She also refers to her vehicle as a
"she," and truly communicates with its animating spirit. Pretty strange
behavior for someone who sees cities as evil. Wisely, she chalked her

City Magick

opinions up to knowing what was good for her and commented that her beliefs weren't for everybody else. I agreed.

Honoring another path is what it's all about. I honor hers and she honors mine. This book is all about honor. My goal was to present a possible path for those not living off the beaten paths, near the forests, mountains, and waters–and particularly for those who choose not to move there. Many of those in rural settings think they have a monopoly on what is natural, magical, and spiritual. They don't. Everything is natural. Many in the city think they are confined to a nonspiritual setting, filled with unnatural and harmful forces. I thought so for a while. I felt very disconnected from the world in the city, until I learned to forge new connections with the world around me. Again, everything is natural. There is spirit in all things, and we are part of spirit regardless of where we are.

Hopefully, city magick can open the doors to a new urban magical world. Magick is hiding everywhere, waiting to be found. Cities do have their problems. They have a lot of problems. I would love to create a "shining bright city, perfect and clean," as mentioned in an obscure song called "Mysteries of the Unexplained" by pop singer Tanya Donelly. We have a collective archetype of a Utopian city in our minds, and are constantly reminded of it by our artists, our true visionaries of what was, is, and will be. I might never have heard that song if I had not worked for Ms. Donelly's manager in a recording studio/management company in Cambridge, Massachusetts. There, in the turmoil of the music business, working in the city, I felt disconnected from nature, my roots, and my magick. I had the ideal of Utopia in my mind, but the reality fell somewhat short. There, I started the practices described in this book to reclaim my daily magick, my daily spirituality, regardless of where I lived or worked.

Many writers, musicians, artists, and generally unusual folk–magical and otherwise– have been my wisest teachers in creating this book. Those on the fringe have provoked new thoughts, techniques, and ways to look at things. I owe a particular debt to the new and daring generation of comic book writers (believe it or not) who face reality with new lenses. Grant Morrison, chaos magician and writer of *The Invisibles,* was a tremendous source and perhaps the inspiration for the book. Leave it to Mr. Morrison to demonstrate an actual magical initiation and adventure through his comic books. His creations are like the grand adventures of Carlos Castenada–fantastic, but very real on a different level of reality. These things only seem crazy to the uninitiated, those who work in only one world. Morrison gives us sorcerers like Tom O'Bedlam, living on the streets, teaching the upstart young hero how to walk between the worlds of the city. Together, they visit Luan-Dun, the city of the Moon in the sunless shadows of London. The unlikely hero, the mundane boy or future Buddha, is initiated reluctantly into the mysteries of the world and takes up the cause as his own. As demonstrated by the work of Joseph Campbell, the story is an age-old one, told again and again in our ancient myths, through our science fiction trilogies like *Star Wars,* and even through our comic books. Grant Morrison would probably be less than thrilled to find his work inspiring another New Age book, but it's the core of the work that counts, not necessarily the medium, and I hope he'd appreciate that. He and his peers inspire me greatly. They, along with other writers, musicians, and artists, are creating the new myths. I hope some last as long as the classics that I grew up learning. Their work is worth checking out, as entertainment and as a thought-provoking new mythos.

There is a mythological ideal of the city that we have not really achieved in this world. Did it exist on forgotten continents? If so, we have no evidence of it. We will never know how to create it if we do not honor the energy and spirits in the cities we have already built. Even modern science is coming to the conclusion that there is more to us than the merely physical. We have an energy component. Not only people, but the entire world, has an energy aspect. Perhaps by honoring it and working with it, we can transform our urban dwellings from potential engines of destruction to bright and shining centers of learning and prosperity. I'm sure it's not that easy, but it may well be. Some things are much simpler than we think. We need to honor the spirit in all things to find out. We need to try and work with what we have. The world may not be changed with a wave of the magick wand, but if we work collectively toward something, our power to transform is great. It works in our mystical lives and in our daily living.

Honoring starts at home. Start with yourself, your family, your home, and your tools. All are sacred. If you have only been an arm-chair practitioner till this point—interested in magick, but never taking the leap because you weren't close enough to the natural forces—then get up off the sofa and open your eyes. You are a natural force—one with all the other forces around you. Open the door, walk down the street, and let the adventure begin.

City Magick

Chapter 1
Welcome to the Concrete Jungle

BRIGHT LIGHTS AND BIG CITIES are taking over the world. Little hamlets are filling up, growing dangerously close to urban Meccas. Quaint little towns are birthing strip malls and quickie marts. Noise and light pollution dominate a formerly untainted land. Established metropolises, already vast, are brimming full and quickly swallowing up all the areas around them. New York, Los Angeles, London, and Hong Kong are capitals of industry and finance, and homes to the great world machine connecting everyone. Many of us find ourselves surrounded in these jungles of concrete, glass, and steel. They can be a bit overwhelming.

I have to imagine it's much like what ancient people felt, surrounded by the dark forests of Europe or the jungles of South America and Africa. As strange as it may sound, the two are very similar. Both are vast, overwhelming places that surround you on all sides. Familiar trails change daily, taking you into unknown territory. Perils may await you at any turn. If you know the landscape and the predators, you will probably survive, but there is always an element of danger. You have to put your natural fears on hold, because this is your home. This is all you know. You deal with it. Both city dwellers and forest folk live in the wild. The city, however, is of our own making. As modern society has destroyed so much natural landscape to build our so-called civilization, it has, in essence, re-created what it destroyed in these concrete jungles. Some of these archetypal images, tapping the forces of the unknown, are needed. We can't escape them. Even though we think we are conquering the land, subduing it as decreed by whatever collective gods we follow—the gods of industry and supposed progress—we are really being sucked in to a trap. Our creations try to subdue us in the name of the land. And they are doing a very good job, because we don't understand what they've become.

The city is the new primordial forest. Like the land, it is filled with danger, but can bring sustenance. People live there quite effectively and happily, finding what they need by living in harmony with and honoring all things. Both the concrete and natural jungles are filled with their own beauty. The theaters have plays unparalleled in the surrounding communities. Art and history are respected. Those who revere it create exhibits in museums to share the culture with everyone. Merchants peddle their unusual items from around the world. Cities are like the groves of the forest and the oasis in the desert. Like the land, they are full of power.

Those of us in pagan and New Age communities find ourselves in an era that can usher us all back to the land. We are disconnected from the source spirit. We are separated into little compartments, like office cubicles, and have no sense of unity. We are stuck in a polarity of consciousness—"me vs. them," instead of "all of us together." We're all on one ship called Earth, sink or swim. All our fates are bound together. So get back to the land, we are told. Get away from the hustle and bustle of the city. Listen to your inner child. Commune with nature spirits. Commune with the living Earth. Find your totem animal. Hug a tree today. The slogans are endless, and there is much truth to them, but I hate being preached to by any one group that claims to know the way. I trust groups more if they encourage me to find answers within or inspire me to search for my own. I am encouraging you do to that, no matter where you are. If you personally need to change your environment, then do so. Don't feel you have to move, however, to connect with natural forces. Finding them wherever you are may be the stronger lesson for you.

Nature is the heart of magick. The untouched forest is a place of high prana, or life energy. When we are close to it, we can attune ourselves to the natural cycles and hear the secret voices from the forest. These voices bring us knowledge, power, and wisdom. There, in the wild, it is easier to shut out the distractions of our normal lives. Our normal lives, however, are actually filled with nature. Nature comes in many forms. It finds a voice in anything created. All things are sacred. Everything—including concrete, glass, steel, and even plastic—come from the same source. Don't be fooled into thinking things are unnatural. Why is one thing, like honey, made from materials found on Earth natural, while another, like a compact disc, made from different materials found on the same planet, not natural? Both are made by other beings, bees and people respectively, from natural resources. The original materials go through a great change. You can argue the merits of use, need, consumption, chemical change, and biodegradability, but neither item is more sacred than the other. Both bring enjoyment. Both are valued.

Prana is all around us, in different ways and amounts. Unsettled land does have a large amount of this spirit energy, but the city has its own flow of prana. The very creation of the city and its buildings diverts and redirects the prana streams as boulders divert a river. They may divert the flow, but they will not stop it. The pathways and side streets between skyscrapers feel almost riverlike as you walk them. Sidewalks are like the banks of a vast river. People flow, traffic flows, and even warm and cold currents of air flow through them. Spirit flows there, too. It flows with everything.

The city is a powerful landscape of magick, filled with secrets and energy for those who know where to look. Some people, longing for the woods to connect to spirit, put off exploring their magical path because they live in the city. They need to stay at their current job in the city to make enough money to buy that car, or house, or whatever. Then they will find someplace nice and quiet, where they can relax, meditate, set up an altar, and grow their own herb garden. Until then, they will hang out in New Age shops and read lots of books on magick, witchcraft, and crystals. They'll remain convinced, however, that magick won't work if they are distracted by the cars going by or the people in the apartment above, or are surrounded by "unliving" material. They won't try these practices in the comfort of their own apartments. It's not the desire to be all-natural that is talking here, however. Rather it is fear or laziness that has taken command. If you don't want to change your habits or practices, or even if you feel you are not ready, be honest with yourself. Don't make up an excuse. Don't think about what stops you. Don't blame your location. Just do it. You can be spiritual, magical, and pagan living in the city. You can recognize the sacred around you all the time. That is the true magick. This book helps you know where to look in the confused street mazes. You can start your sacred journey from your living room. Then you can bring it to the park. Soon, you will discover you can bring it anywhere, because it is a part of you. Magick is your perception, an active role you take in the creation of your own reality. Your point of view is more a function of magick than your environment. Magick is in every environment.

Our urban dwellings are built on the most natural forces of all—energy vortices. Each center draws people to it, both geographically and spiritually. A settled area may be near resources like fresh water, abundant food, or a port to the sea, but our attraction to it is more than physical. Some other force draws us there. Each city is a sacred site, whether we treat it that way or not. We should start to treat them this way, however. The planet is covered with different sets of energy lines and grids. They are like the nervous system and acupuncture meridians of Earth. Many of the lines cross at certain points in each grid, creating an energy zone, or vortex. Perhaps it is the other way around and the vortex creates the energy lines. The vortices of Sedona, Arizona, have become a popular New Age vacation spot, to the extent that many people believe it is the only such site on the planet. It is a wonderful energy site, but you can find a vortex almost anywhere. They come in all sizes, intensities, and personalities.

Each energy center is like a chakra for the planet, much like our human chakras on the body–the heart, crown, or third eye. Each one has a different personality, characteristics, and function. The quality of the vortex, as well as the way the energy flows through and around our man-made structures, gives each city its uniqueness. I am sure everyone here has noticed a city where they felt at home, or a city that had "bad vibes." Your own nature is reacting to the qualities, the personality–the vibe, if you will–of the city. You can instantly like one and dislike another, just as with people, because, in a sense, cities are alive.

Some cities are generally more inviting. Others seem inherently magical, like New Orleans or London. Psychologically, we feel this is because of our conscious association with magick in these locations–voodoo and ceremonial magick, respectively. We must ask, however, why magical practitioners were drawn there in the first place. I am told that something about New Orleans just promotes psychic abilities. The flow of spirit through the districts opens those with eyes to see the spirit world. More activities occur here because there is more of an opening between worlds. If you know this and feel comfortable there, and if you have a good relationship with the city and this flow of energy, then magick can be powerful indeed. This doesn't mean you have to move to New Orleans, London, or anywhere else to do magick. Every city has magick in it.

Some sacred sites, where a greater number of energy lines converge in a vortex, became temple sites for ancient peoples instead of actual cities. These energy centers are places of worship and power–Stonehenge, the pyramids of Egypt and South America, and the temples in Greece, among many others across the globe. No one settles on these sites, but cities gather close to them, even when the beliefs that fostered them have died out. Other energy vortices become our dwellings. The energy and spirit of the place invites human settlers. It is alive and embodies some form of consciousness, even if we do not readily recognize it. People are drawn to it. The physical benefits of food, water, and shelter are added benefits the spirit of the land manifests to make the area more enticing. As these resources have dwindled, however, we have created new reasons to draw others to this land. Our host vortex, in its own consciousness, may not have conceived of the city structure as our dwelling, but we have created it nonetheless. New cities often get built over the remains of older ones because the vortex draws new people there, even after disaster or war. Other vortices shift, move, or cease to be active at the end of a city's life. We, therefore, may have difficulty discovering its remains, because we are not drawn by the swirling energy.

We tend to romanticize ancient cities as beautiful and shining repositories of wisdom, while we demonize the ones we live with here and now. Modern cities are seen as dirty or as dens of corruption, twisting what we value as a society. I wonder how many ancient philosophers of Greece would marvel at Manhattan or Tokyo if we could transport them in time to the end of the 20th century. Quite a few, I think. After a while, however, they would probably begin to recognize problems here similar to those they had in the cities back in their own times. Perhaps they would be saddened that we had not solved them yet. Or they might be happy that if they couldn't find the answers, it appears that no one else could either. The essence of the city, good and bad, would probably have changed little from then to now.

All cities contain extremes. There are the rich and the poor, the safe areas and the places where you wouldn't want to be alone late at night. Even with the modern miracles of running water and plumbing, we still have garbage, sewage problems, and pollution. Many ancient cities that we romanticize had sewage flowing through the streets and animal dung on their doorsteps. Most were overpopulated, since so many people were drawn there. Political conspiracies were much more common in the ancient world, involving the outright assassination of those who stood in the way of the ruling party. We may have character assassination, but very rarely does it cross over to a physical act. They may have had their mystery schools and sacred learning centers, but we have amazing libraries and colleges. Our modern public access to information is vastly greater than that of an Old World commoner to access formal education. Formal education and college tuition can be difficult to attain now, but if you want to read a book, all you really need is a library card. As you can see, there is a certain amount of give and take in all urban worlds. I am sure even mythic cities in the Golden Ages of Atlantis and Lemuria had their problems, or they would still be here as shining examples for us, instead of sunk beneath the waves. On the other hand, perhaps they are myths of our future, of possibilities yet to come.

The cityscape beckoned and we heard the call, mostly through our subconscious and our intuition, but we came. We settled. We created. Others hear the call and continue to come. The vortices continue to draw new people to them, and to the cities. Hopefully we will become more co-creative with the land, instead of trying to dominate it. In our need to control everything, this new dark and mysterious landscape has created its own tricks, traps, and surprises to show us who is boss. Nature, in whatever form it takes, may be our partner, but we are not its master. We have not subdued the city any more than the forest. Make friends with it before it takes you over. Now the concrete jungles are the chosen home for some, evoking a new magical world mythology for our modern psyche. Archetypes have arisen in new forms, retelling ancient stories from our unconscious.

Our new mythic world is based on the popular culture around us. We fall in love with and adore our movie and rock stars, our politicians, and our sports heroes. When our culture is gone, will their names be read as a race of new gods and worshiped by those who follow us? We name Elvis our king, even if only of rock and roll, and mythically expect him to rise from the dead like some Osirian figure, instead of ending his life on the toilet. It is equally hard to believe that our modern-day Dionysus, Jim Morrison, of the Doors, god of poetry and excess, could have met his end in the bathtub. Of course, his death was faked and he's living out his life in some secret hideaway.

His followers leave offerings of empty beer cans and used condoms at his gravesite in France. The rites of rock concerts have become the new sacraments and initiations into ecstatic mysteries. Children screamed hysterically for the Beatles, flailing about madly in a trance-like ceremony. From Alice Cooper, to Ozzy Osborn, and now Marilyn Manson, we have dark figures ushering our children into the primal unknown. Like Persephone, they take them to the lands where we tell them not to play. That earlier famous Marilyn, Marilyn Monroe, is the temptress goddess and minor figure in the downfall of the beloved leader of Camelot, John F. Kennedy. His spirit, however, will return, like King Arthur's, when we need the good king again. Sports figures turned wife-beaters and murderers haunt our television sets, our mighty oracle. We are told by this box to get magick shoes with a special name on them and we will run, jump, and play just like the sports gods. If we drink the right soda and eat the right candy, we will live forever, as if we imbibed a magical elixir. Urban legends leave us frightened that we will awaken someday in a hotel bathtub with a kidney removed, another victim of organ pirates. Bloody Mary will appear in our bathroom mirror if we summon her by chanting her name three times. Or very real irate wives will chop off their husbands' penises and be cheered onward, reliving the mythos of Set and Osiris in a slightly altered fashion. We have created new monsters to replace the ghosts and nosferatu. Undying maniacs in hockey masks will murder us at summer camp. Muamar Kadaffi, Sadam Hussein, or the next would-be conqueror of the Middle East become the devil incarnate, the root of all evil in this world, instead of just ordinary people trying to do what they think is right for themselves and their people. Our desert strikes and wars become the millennium's holy crusades, rallying the faithful as we wait for alien visitors to swoop down from the sky, finally revealing themselves and bringing us either our much-deserved enlightenment or our equally deserved destruction, depending on which book you read.

Our mythology is very rich and dark. There is a hope, however, from within. Although it appears that many of us are giving away our personal power, at the same time, we are going through such an amazing shift that it's hard to believe. I think of it as a "shamanizing" of the culture. Although the term originally referred to the medicine men of Siberian tribes, in general, a shaman is one who heals the spirit through making contact with the spirits of plants, animals, minerals, and other worlds. In modern lands and cultures, bereft as they are of true spirit healers who make contact with other worlds, we are reclaiming those powers little by little.

The most striking of these cultural changes appears in the NDEs, or Near Death Experiences, so many people seem to be having. Through these miraculous stories, ordinary people are finding out that there is life beyond death, and that it is not anything to fear. Most experiences are loving, filled with tunnels of light, glowing beings, and people who have passed on before. The mainstream religious imagery of punishment or reward does not seem to apply. Not many report either hellfire and damnation or pearly gates. Most important, as these seekers discover wonderful new worlds and make striking changes in the way they live their lives, they come back and share this information with the rest of us. We all gain comfort from their stories. They are the modern-day shamans. Through a spirit sickness or near death experience, they gain entry into the land of the dead. They return with knowledge of this world and a power they did not have before. They may use this knowledge and gift to return there, or their experience may be unique. They bring back, however, much-needed spirit medicine for their people. They reclaim our natural power as human beings to travel far and wide, and share that power with all of us.

Are the repeated images of the spirit floating above the body, often hearing what other people in the room are saying, and then traveling to the white light to meet their families who have passed, a cliché of our new mythology? Perhaps, but does that make it any less real? I don't think so. It's no more imaginary than going to the underworld to have your heart weighed against a single feather, as in the ancient Egyptian beliefs. Both are real.

Hopefully, the result of these NDEs will be the transformation of modern society and the world. By turning back to spirit, we may be able to simplify many of our world's problems. We must make sure, however, that the pendulum does not swing too far away from advances and bring about the opposite extreme. Ideally, spirit and science will both be honored by those well-versed in both subjects. Technology alone is not inherently "evil," and ancient tradition is not the only "good" way. Thoughtless technology, used without looking at a larger, holistic picture, is dangerous, as we are learning to the detriment of the planet. Tradition hinders us when it completely blinds a society to new information, experimentation, or change. A synthesis of both–the best of both worlds–is needed. We must never forget our roots, nor should we fear change.

The New Age movement, for all its inconsistencies, is largely responsible for people consciously reclaiming their power. Magick is a choice. People are researching their ethical and spiritual roots to take back their lost traditions. Others are taking new and bold steps in that direction, combing other worlds as well as their familiar surroundings. New interest in shamanism grows steadily. Neopaganism and witchcraft have grown by leaps and bounds, stressing the ability to change your reality for the better. More people believe that angels, spirit guides, or dead relatives are aiding them in their lives and looking after them. Magick is afoot in many forms.

Meditation and introspection are the first steps. Alternative care systems are gaining acceptance. Acupuncture, herbalism, flower essences, Reiki, past-life regressions, and crystal healing are making strides, each in its own way. Things considered "on the fringe" years ago are more accepted as alternative treatments by the mainstream. Knowing someone who is from a nontraditional spiritual path is more common. Brave pagans are coming out of the broom closet to share their beliefs and their magick with those who have never experienced it before. The spirit worlds, the subtle energies, are making a comeback in all our daily lives.

All these changes are greatly needed today. If we are to survive the changes of the modern-day world, new and very old energies need to be integrated into our lives to transform our species. Magick to change our reality for the better must be available to all who need it. We desperately need our shamans, healers, witches, and mystics and we need them everywhere, including in our cities. Honoring magick, the life force from our source god, goddess, or whatever you choose to call it, is paramount. Take this trip through the urban jungle with me, and discover the magick hidden within it. All jungle tools and totems can heal or hurt. You will never know which are your helpers, however, if you are too afraid to take the journey. Walk through the city's magick. You never know what you may find.

Chapter 2
The Three Rs

MAGICK IS A SKILL AND A DISCIPLINE.
City magick is a peculiar brand of this craft, working with the same natural, ambient energy found all around us, but finding these energy reserves in the most unusual places. To work with the power of the city, you have to understand some basic magical concepts. You need these building blocks before you can create your magical house. You wouldn't attempt to study a particular area of science, like organic chemistry, without understanding the introductory chemistry course. Magick is the same. Magick is an esoteric science, but it is also an art, full of creativity and expression. True craftsmen in this discipline balance art and science with spirituality. Magick embodies all three.

Like reading, writing, and arithmetic from more traditional schools, magick has three basic building blocks–its own three Rs: reality, rapture, and ritual. Not every practitioner of the magical arts will know them by these names, but the concepts are familiar to all who walk between worlds. By understanding these concepts and how they work in more traditional arenas, you can understand how they apply to this brand of urban mysticism.

◎ REALITY ◎

Reality is the form in which we perceive ourselves, our environment, and all those with whom we interact. Reality is our structure. Most people define reality as the physical universe, a place defined and measurable, containing matter, energy, the laws of physics, and linear time. Reality is only the things discovered by the physical senses or those scientific instruments that heighten our physical perceptions. Basic rules apply to reality. Matter is arranged in tiny interlocking particles. What goes up, must come down, thanks to our friend gravity. Earth always revolves around the Sun. Water is two parts hydrogen and one part oxygen. These things are immutable. They are only immutable, however, in this reality.

The physical universe is only one perception of reality. Granted, it has been the dominant perception of people on Earth for several thousand years. Physical, three-dimensional reality is one portion of the reality spectrum. Think of a shadow. Shadows are a part of us. If shadows are conscious, however, and only pay attention to the flat ground and other shadows, they will live in a two-dimensional world of darkness and light. As we do simple movements, we change the shadow's reality. If the shadow doesn't see us, however, it doesn't know why some things are changing. If it looks beyond the shadow realm, it sees a more complex being to which it is connected, and a more complex world of color and three-dimensional form. We are but shadows of something more intricate. This "something" is still us, it just exists on another level. Some people call it the divine or higher self, or Holy Guardian Angel. Many more things exist in these non-physical and nonvisible levels of reality. Some people call them planes, dimensions, or worlds, but they all refer to the same ideas.

Many mystical systems are used to define these levels of reality. The most basic starts with the physical and nonphysical, lumping everything that doesn't fit into physical, linear space-time into the nonphysical, spiritual realm. Shamanic traditions often divide the realms into the physical middle world, the underworld below us, and the upper realm, or sky world. Each is filled with various mythological characters and contains different powers. The tree symbolism is strong here, with the middle world as the trunk, the underworld as the roots, and the sky realm as the branches and leaves. More complex systems, particularly using the tree symbolism, are plentiful. Norse traditions say Odin made the universe by placing the nine worlds of their cosmology in the World Tree. The Hebrews and ceremonial magicians speak of the Kabalah, the Tree of Life, defining reality as a neat map of ten different spheres and the various paths connecting them. More modern concepts of seven, nine, and thirteen dimensions come to us from the lightworkers of the New Age movement. No matter what you choose to call them or how you categorize and characterize them, they are all different areas of reality.

One thing common to all these models is the ability to find new realities. In each of these traditions, someone was able to perceive and even travel to these realms and bring back new information. The information is colored by the tradition's own history and outlook on the world, and the limits of the explorer's experience in them, but so much common ground is shared between them. The mystic of the community is called to traverse these worlds and open perceptions to this new realm. The mystic goes by many names, depending on the culture, tradition, and role. The shaman is the most accepted in these practices, but witches, Druids, seers, priests, and mages play a similar role as intermediaries between the physical and nonphysical realms. The link between these traditions is simple—magick. Magick draws them together. Each one relies on a form of magick, making changes through their contact with unseen forces. I find that all these traditions work with the core elements of shamanism. The shaman's role, moreover, crosses into other areas associated with seers and healers. My own practice of magick and witchcraft is intimately tied to the roots of what we now call core shamanism. Some traditions rely more upon the psychic medium, rituals, or otherworldly journeys, but they all create change on the physical level of reality by working in another layer of the reality spectrum.

All of these other levels of reality have rules and customs, but, since they are not physical, the dynamics working there seem very fluid and insubstantial to the normal linear mind. Travel there is often not physical, leaving the traveler with a dreamlike impression of the realm. Everybody can perceive these levels, and probably has at one time or another. We touch upon other realities during our dreams. Intuition and other natural, psychic gifts are senses that may not work in our physical definition of reality, but they are real and point the way to new levels of existence. Perception is the key. Perception is nine-tenths of reality. The other portion of reality is affecting us, but we are unaware of it. If we do not acknowledge it, then, for our personal reality, it is not there. We are multidimensional by nature, existing in this world and many others. Remember our relationship to our shadow. We will never realize the scope of our being if we choose to close off and block out these other realities. An openness to a new view of reality is the hallmark of the magician.

Although mystics often have a calling or strong gifts opening the way to other worlds, everybody can work with them on one level. If you've picked up this book and want to be a part of the magick around you, you probably already have what you need. Anyone can open to it if they really want to experience new realities. I've seen some of my students who were completely unconvinced of other magical realities have very moving experiences. I don't know if they changed their beliefs, but the experiences did affect them for the better on some level.

Hallucinogens have been used as tools for opening the doorways of perception by people who follow magical traditions and pop cultural trends. Unfortunately, many people who do so recreationally write off their experience as a good or bad "trip," not realizing that the world they saw exists beyond the effects of whatever drug they took. The door is open. It's your choice whether to keep it open, or even to remember where it is. These are tools. They shouldn't become crutches. They may help you achieve your goal, but you should never grow dependent upon them.

In most Native American cultures, the shaman of the tribe had the most spirit helpers and traveled to the other worlds more frequently than any other. Each member of the tribe, however, had some helping spirits. Each could partake in a form of vision quest or initiation, working with the spirit world. It was not an exclusive right of the shaman, but the shaman was considered the expert in these realms. The entire tribe was empowered. For those of us living in the Americas, living on the land of the Native Americans for better or worse, I see us adopting these principles as more and more people come to pagan and New Age circles seeking to connect with the magick. I think this is the best hope we have for the future survival and success of all.

Once you understand that there is more to reality than meets the eye, or any of our sensory organs, then you can start experiencing the other realms through meditation, magick, and journeying. Your perceptions and abilities will open up to fit your new model of reality. When working with the forces of the city, you will learn to walk the streets of the hidden cities, those realms existing side by side with normal reality, like any other nonphysical realm. Now you'll know where to look for the magick there.

◎ Rapture ◎

Everybody has a different key to open the magical realms. Everybody walks a different path and has different intentions. Some traditions share similar techniques, but their practices can be as varied as the number of practitioners.

Different forms of trance work have been the key to my personal magical work. Light meditative trances lower your brain waves from beta level, your normal waking consciousness, to between seven and fourteen cycles per second, or alpha level. While in this altered state, you can activate your psychic senses, perceive energy as color, light, or sound, and make changes in the physical world by shifting these newly perceived energies. You enter a new relationship with reality by altering your perception. "Gnosis" is another term for this phenomenon.

Start by meditating. Meditation is a simple and effective way to alter your perception of reality. It is a quieting of the conscious mind, the ego, to transcend normal reality and make a connection or union with the divine forces. It sounds much harder than it is. There are many techniques for doing this. Some focus on an object, breathing, or a mantra, a repeated word or phrase. We will start simply with an object, a candle flame. Many notice that time passes much faster or slower when meditating, as if they were in a different world. They are, or at least part of them is.

If you have never meditated or done any visualization exercises before, find a quiet place where you will not be interrupted. Turn out the lights, turn the ringer off on the phone, and light a candle. Feel free to light an incense that is relaxing and meditative for you.

E$_X$ERCI$_S$E 1 – SIMPLE MEDITATION

❶ Connecting to the Flame: Start by staring into the flame. Sit a comfortable distance away from it. For some people, the light may be too intense. If that is the case, stare past the flame. Look at the light and the shadows behind it. Let you eyes go in and out of focus. Turn all your attention to the fire before you. Feel the flame giving off white light, all the colors of the spectrum. The light fills the room you are in and protects you from all harm. Some people say a short prayer or invocation to any personal deities.

❷ Relaxation: As you stare at the candle, stray thoughts will come into your mind. You may have difficulty focusing solely on the candle. This is normal. Coach yourself through a relaxation of your entire body, starting at the top of your head and moving down. Relax the muscles in your head, face, neck, and shoulders. Feel your jaw relax. It is as if gentle waves of water are flowing down your body. Pay attention to the sensations of release and then let them go, moving on to the next part of your body. Relax your shoulders and arms, hands and fingers. Feel all tension leave you chest and torso. Work through your trunk, until all tension has been released. Work down through your legs to your toes. You entire body relaxes.

❸ Going Deeper: Count backward from 12 to 1, counting each breath, still looking at the candle flame. With each number, you go deeper into your meditative state. Let all extraneous thoughts go as you count. As they arise, acknowledge and release them. Thank your conscious mind for sharing, but now let it take a break for a while. Tell your ego that it does not have to be "in the driver's seat" for this. All outside noises only serve to deepen the experience. You will react to them only for your safety and highest good. Feel a gentle soothing sensation fill your body. You are comfortable and relaxed. It feels much like a lazy afternoon of daydreaming. The feeling of daydreaming is the alpha state. You have reached your meditative state with ease.

❹ Being Open: Be open to whatever feelings, sensations, or experiences you are having, without judgment. You are only looking for a period of relaxation by quieting the internal dialogue. This can be difficult. If you slip out of this state, gently coax yourself back in by relaxing your body and counting down. Just *be*. You do not have to do anything. Feel yourself simply at the center of your own universe, your own perspective.

❺ Grounding: When this experience feels complete, consciously count yourself up from 1 to 12 and open your eyes. As you return, you may feel light-headed and not quite all together. This is a normal response. You need to ground yourself back in this reality. Such flightiness is often caused by deep meditation or energy work. That is why so many New Agers have a reputation for being a little "out there." Most are just a bit ungrounded. To ground yourself, get on the floor and visualize any remaining energy flowing down into the earth. If you feel as if you are floating, imagine a ray of light passing from the base of your spine down into the earth, like a string tying a balloon down. Some people do something physical, like standing up, moving around, holding on to a piece of furniture, or hugging a tree. Eating is another excellent way to ground. That is why so many rituals use bread or cakes as part of the ceremony, to ground you afterward. Experiment and find a technique that works for you.

Even though you can eventually feel and perceive more than usual, you may not do so at first. That is perfectly normal. Right now, concentrate on achieving a daydreamlike state. Keep your expectations simple. Some people have very moving experiences and cry afterward, but that is quite rare. Most people think "no big deal" and cannot figure out what meditation has to do with magick. They are looking for action. The link between the two will become more apparent as we go along.

Practice this exercise. The more often you do it, the easier it will be. This is the first building block, one that may already be familiar to you. Soon, you will no longer need the candle and will be able to achieve this sensation in a matter of moments. It is a great trick when you are stressed out at work or with your family.

Achieving your trance state is the first step. By visualizing in this state, you affect reality. Magick consists of making a change with your will. All its forms have many practical applications. For instance, you are running late for work. You may be fired if you are late again. Don't panic, relax. Relaxation is the key. You don't even have to get into a deep trance state while driving to work. Just get a moment of relaxation. Imagine yourself getting to work on time, safely and easily. Imagine yourself walking in and looking at the clock. You are exactly on time. No one is angry. Then keep on driving, safely, confident that your magick is working. Reality will conform to your expectations. If you don't think you will be late, then you will not be. This is a great way to get parking spaces by the door. Visualize a spot near the door about ten minutes before you reach your destination. Visualization is co-creation in action. I did not think you could use magick or spiritual discipline for such things, but my teachers encouraged me. This little trick kept me sane during college, trying to find the ever-elusive parking space on a crowded city campus. Magick lets you flow with the universe and makes life easier. Things become less of a struggle. They flow easily when you are in the right place at the right time, doing what you need to be doing. Visualization is one way to tell the universe what you need.

Color and light are ways to manipulate energy in physical reality. By visualizing different colored light, you can change reality in situations that may be too complex to visualize in detail. If family gatherings are particularly argumentative, try this before going to the next one. Get into your trance state and picture everybody at the gathering surrounded by blue light or blue mist. Blue brings peace. It heals the spirit. At least, that is my interpretation of it. What do the colors mean to you? Each one has a different energy and has a different effect when used in a trance, changing with the practitioner's beliefs.

EXERCISE 2 – COLOR ASSOCIATIONS

Before starting this exercise, it can help to have a box of colored crayons or some colored paper. If you have strong visualization skills, these may are not be necessary, but they can help.

❶ Make a list of colors using the entire spectrum, or get out your crayons and paper. You can stick to the traditional colors of the rainbow—red, orange, yellow, green, blue, indigo, and violet—or mix in other hues, like gold, silver, brown, black, white, magenta, pink, and turquoise.

❷ Do Exercise 1 to get into a trance state (see page 17). Find a place of relaxation and awareness. You do not have to go too deep.

❸ Open your eyes to look at the crayon or paper. If you are not using such tools, keep your eyes closed and visualize the color. Think of something to spark your imagination, like a fire engine for red.

❹ Reflect on the color. How does the color make you feel? Do you notice any changes in your body, thoughts, or feelings? Some notice a temperature associated with a color, or perhaps a memory or a person. Write all these interpretations down without censoring yourself.

❺ Go through all the colors you plan to use that day. You can always go back and do more. When you are ready, count yourself up from 1 to 12 and ground yourself.

Hopefully, the colors will inspire a broad range of responses. The spectrum can be a useful magical palette, a simple tool for your magical toolbox. Colors can be used for healing, love, peace, self-esteem, good communication, success, prosperity, protection, and almost anything else. Simply visualize the color around yourself or any person or place you wish to affect. Many of these areas in life are too complex to visualize all their variables successfully, but colored lights and other constructs of intention work to give the energy a general intent. Instead of visualizing the actual physical healing, particularly if you are not sure what is wrong, apply the healing energy of light where it is needed. Colored lights can be used in conjunction with other shapes and intentions. Visualizing a shield around someone will give him or her general protection from harm without visualizing all the possible sources of harm.

Color and the Chakras

Part of trance work is becoming more aware of energy. All magick is a manipulation of energy to cause change. When you experiment with color, as you did in the previous exercise, you experiment with different frequencies of energy. Color is intimately related to the quality, the personality, of many forms of psychic energy. The first step in understanding and mastering such energies is to be aware of the energy within your own body. Altering your consciousness brings your awareness to the realm of unseen forces. There, you can perceive energy in yourself, in others, and across the world, but first, start with your own body. The human body has energy centers, vortices of energy, much like smaller versions of the energy vortices around cities and sacred sites. These energy centers have different names, but most commonly they are called chakras.

For those not familiar with the chakra system, it derives from Hindu metaphysics, but is now used widely in many other systems. Each chakra is a swirling energy center, a vortex of spinning light. Chakras are aligned, more or less, along the spine. Each one has a particular function, not only in our physical existence, but in our multidimensional existence as well (see figure 1, page 23).

The crown chakra is at the top of the head and is usually white or violet. Divine energy works through the crown. The third-eye chakra is at the forehead. It is purple or indigo. The third eye sees the space between space. Our psychic, clairvoyant powers operate through the third eye. The chakra at the throat is blue. Not only does it rule speaking and communication like telepathy, it also takes in sound, such as messages from spirit guides, gods, and totems. The gift of clairaudience works through the throat. The heart chakra is in the chest, colored green. Emotions work through the heart chakra. Through it, you seek a loving connection to others. You give and receive love through the heart, eventually moving toward an unconditional love of all. Below the heart is the solar plexus, in yellow, right below the diaphragm. The solar plexus works with personal power

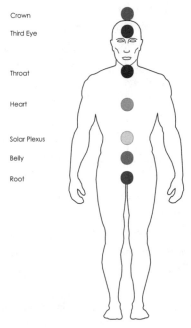

Figure 1. The seven chakras.

or lack thereof. Lessons of self-control and desires to control others work through this energy center. The solar plexus also helps you conquer fear. Near the navel is the belly, or sacral, chakra. This chakra relates to connection and sex. It is sometimes associated with the spleen and looks like an orange sphere. Through the belly chakra, you, as a spirit in a body, seek to connect to others like yourself. That intimate connection often occurs through sex. The belly is also related to your instincts, your primal reactions. Here, you listen to your "gut reactions" on matters. At the perineum, below the tailbone, is the root chakra, usually red. The root chakra works with life energy and, through it, survival. The root chakra works with the physical body and physical satisfaction. It is usually the first chakra to activate in the upward progression to the crown. One of my favorite books on the chakras, focusing on a lot of the traditional Vedic material, is *Wheels of Life* by Anodea Judith (Llewellyn).

Most likely, other chakras exist, but these are the generally accepted ones. There may be chakras that lie between these seven, and other smaller ones throughout the body, including the palms of the hands, soles of the feet, and major joint areas. Working with the energy in the chakras is a way to bolster personal power. We become more aware of the chakras while in the trance state. Some people feel them, while others see them, when doing magical work. By perceiving the chakras and the field of energy around them that some call the aura, you can tell when someone is healthy, sick, unbalanced, or unhappy. If you are more tactile, you can run your hands across the aura or over the chakras and feel "warm spots," "cold spots," and holes. Sometimes, the sensation is fluid and free for health, and thick, dense, and murky for illness. Those with clairvoyant gifts will perceive this information in terms of color and light.

Care of your own chakras and aura is an important part of magical practice. Most magical traditions use some ritual or visualization to open, clear, and balance these energy centers. They are particularly important to urban practitioners, since we expose ourselves to many other potential dangers. The city can be more hostile to us energetically than, for instance, a remote farm. In cities, we contend with concentrated pollution, electromagnetic fields from many power lines, and the sheer volume of psychic garbage strewn about by our fellow city dwellers. This garbage is created by stress, crime, and often simple unhappiness and disconnection from life. The thoughts of unhappy, unhealthy people actually pollute our astral mindscape. I personally believe that is why cities are often centers of violence. People are unaware of this psychic pollution, but it affects them, along with the physical contaminants in large urban dwellings. Those who are aware of it sometimes suffer more, but, once you are aware, you can protect yourself.

The Golden Dawn, a quite successful urban magical group that fostered many offshoots, has an exercise called the Middle Pillar. The Middle Pillar brings divine energy down through four energy centers in the body, corresponding with four major chakras. Our exercise here will focus on the traditional seven chakras, drawing energy up from the earth and down from the sky. This, or a similar exercise, is important to help you learn to control your personal energy, as well as all the energy around you.

EXERCISE 3 – ENERGIZING THE CHAKRAS

❶ Start Exercise 1 to get into a more meditative state and become aware of yourself and your energy (see page 17).

❷ Visualize a beam of light, like a rope or string, from the base of your spine, your root chakra, down to the center of Earth, much like the grounding cord discussed previously. This connects you to Earth. Ask to connect to the heart of Earth, and not to any intervening impurities. The energy of Earth is pure, clearing energy.

❸ Visualize energy coming up from Earth through this cord and through your legs, up to your spine. Feel your root chakra open, swirling around like a ball of red light. Feel the color red at the base of your spine. Some people see it, others feel it. Simply know this is happening. If your psychic senses are more developed, you may get more information. As you do this exercise, your psychic senses will increase.

❹ The energy moves up to your belly chakra, opening it up in a swirl of orange energy. Feel the color orange in your belly. Know it is there.

❺ The energy moves up to your solar plexus chakra, opening it up in a swirl of yellow energy. Feel the color yellow in your solar plexus, right below your diaphragm. Feel the power of this chakra.

6 The energy moves up to your heart. Feel your heart and chest open wide as the swirling green chakra opens up. Feel your heart open and know the color green is in your chest.

7 The energy rises up to your throat. Feel the chakra open up in a swirl of blue energy. Feel the color blue in your throat. Know the power of communication at your throat chakra.

8 The energy rises to your brow, or third eye. Feel the psychic chakra open up in a swirl of indigo energy. Feel the color in your head, opening up your psychic abilities. Know they are opening up.

9 The energy reaches the top of your head, your crown. Feel the chakra open up in a swirl of lavender or dazzling white energy. Feel the colors of your crown chakra. Know you are opening up to your own divinity.

10 The energy rises out of your crown up into the air, like a fountain, connecting you to the sky. Ask to be connected to the heart of the sky.

11 Feel the energy from the sky descend like a lightning bolt, entering your crown, and quickly moving through your brow, throat, heart, solar plexus, belly, and root chakras, descending through the grounding cord and into the earth. All your chakras are cleared, energized, and opened.

12 Continue any other magical work you desire. Once the experience is complete, feel any remaining energy that is not correct for you return to the earth and sky. You are left refreshed and realigned. Count yourself up from your meditative state.

You should do the chakra exercise before any magical work to prepare yourself for the shift in energies. Also do it whenever you feel
mired in day-to-day life or weighed down by the people around you.
It balances and aligns you to a higher power.

The next meditation can be done with the chakra work, since they
are very complementary. Part of our need to cleanse and rebalance
our energy systems is simply that we do not have strong boundaries
in this society. Most do not have the strength of self to be centered,
grounded, and protected from all the psychic pollutants and dangers.
We either take on other people's "stuff," or we project our own onto
others. Most involved in the magical arts are very empathic and are
often potential healers, usually taking on other people's problems
unknowingly. This never really helps anyone in the end. It is a bad
enough habit in day-to-day life, but in magical life, protection
becomes a necessity. There are many energies out in the magical
worlds that a practitioner would not want to take on and carry.

EXERCISE 4 – SPIRITUAL PROTECTION

❶ Do Exercise 1 to attain a meditative state (see page 17). The first
time you do this exercise, I recommend starting with Exercise 3
and remaining in a meditative state (see page 25).

❷ Visualize yourself inside a bubble. This is your energy field. It
may look like a giant egg or a sphere that extends at arm's length
around your body and a few feet above your head and below
your feet. If you do not see it, feel it, simply know it is there.

❸ Imagine and allow yourself to feel the holes in this field, any
place where you are "leaking" energy or allowing it to come in.
Usually, these places feel like cold spots. Imagine that you are
like a maintenance person, with psychic tools to the fix holes in
your "wall." Visualize yourself "spackling" over the holes with

colored light. Use whatever colored light from your psychic "tool-box" feels correct for you.

4 Once your repairs are complete, you will be inside a shield of pro-tection. Imagine it as a force field from a science fiction movie, or an unbreakable glass ball. Light can get in and out, but no harm can pass through. Now, program the shield, holding this intention in your mind for a minute or longer: "This shield pro-tects me from all harm on any level." Exhale strongly and release the intention into the shield. Feel your thoughts program the shield.

5 Once you feel confident that the shield is in place, count up from your meditative state. Reaffirm this shield before all magical undertakings.

Going Deeper

Deeper trance work brings you deeper in other realities. By entering a light trance, you can understand and work with other levels of the reality spectrum. You can affect the energy to make magick, to make change in your life. By going deeper, you open up the doors and peer directly into a strange new world, making all the connections. Some trances even let your consciousness pass the boundary between realms and travel there unencumbered by physical laws.

Ecstatic trance opens the doors to perception. The exercises above work by simply quieting and slowing down the mind. They are more inhibitory. Ecstatic trances are exhibitory, usually requiring more physical movement and action. They create rapture, a joy or harmony with the universe, allowing you to see the connections between all things. The layers of reality are exposed and the ladder, or tree, can be climbed into new worlds. Climbing the World Tree is a very shamanic practice, but all magick workers can function in this way. We all can work in a realm of multidimensional choice.

Raptures can lead to deep journeys in which you "undo" yourself. You undergo a journey in which you cease to identify with your physical body and personality. The undoing journey is a prime initiation. Sometimes, the traveler will have visions of being torn apart, only to rise from the dead in other realms. Often, the resurrection process results in a new piece being added to the body–a new bone, a stone, or a crystal. For the modern traveler, it may be a microchip. On the other hand, the process can leave the traveler with an injury that never fully heals. Lame legs are very common in Western mystery traditions, as with the wounded teacher, Chiron, of Greek myth. The father shaman of the Norse, Odin (or Wotan) is missing an eye from his travels of power. The reintegration process downloads a new, magical insight into the true nature of reality. Rapture is one key to this new reality.

Through the initiation, you understand your ego for what it is. The ego holds your fear of death. Your personality and your body may cease to be at some point, but your spirit self will live on beyond death. Through initiation, you cultivate a new relationship with your own mortality and death. That is why death is considered an ally of the sorcerer, because it brings change. Magick is the force of change.

By identifying with the spirit self, you transcend the ego limitations and the body limitations. You transcend limitations of the physical universe. Transcendence is the rapture, since you see that reality is larger in scope than you ever thought. This brings true, deep pleasure–a connection to everything. Other truths emerge, like divine inspirations, about your interconnection and unity, not only on this level, but in all dimensions. The experience can unhinge some people, because they are still physical beings. The job of the magick worker is to function well in all of these worlds. The undoing journey should give you strength, not end your ability to relate to your community, friends, and family. You must walk between the worlds, with one foot planted firmly in each.

Only the initiations of those deeply walking the shamanistic path can lead to such difficulties. Most who do so are ready for the experience and are guided by the higher powers. Often, the process is instigated by a shamanic sickness, such as a fever, forcing the individual into altered states in order to travel. Once the initiation is complete, the original physical illness is usually cured. Other traditions work with deep trance states through music, dancing, chanting, sex, prayer, or ritual. Their deep trance experiences usually focus on enacting a spell through visualization or intent, without the other-worldly journeying, even though the two are intimately related.

Achieving an ecstatic state is like reaching the daydream sensations of a light alpha trance. With practice, it will get easier and easier. The word "ecstatic" can be misleading, because it does not mean that the whole trance will feel like a continuous two-hour body-wide orgasm. There will be moments of pure pleasure, bliss, or enlightenment. Every part of your being will be in union. All internal conflicts will cease. For some, it is like an epiphany in which everything makes sense. Others feel a clear, but mindless, exhilaration. The ego is suspended. Some get a sense of tranquillity. These can all be forms of a deep trance connecting you to other realities.

This next exercise uses a more traditional form of trance-inducing techniques. It is more exhibitory than simple meditation techniques, but falls slightly short of being ecstatic. Sound, particularly rhythm, alters consciousness and brings a rapture all its own. Think about how your favorite song seems to spirit you away to some special place when you hear it.

With sound, your mind has something constant occupying its conscious, ego side. Repetition is expected, and no new thoughts or analyses are needed by the mind. You flow with it. This frees your spirit self, the other aspects of consciousness, to perceive a different reality and journey there. Some call this astral projection, others shamanic journeying. For now, we are simply focusing on what sound does to the mind and what other realities are opened.

To start, you will need some audio accompaniment. Sound is

sacred and can bring us to new worlds. Shamans are said to "ride the drumbeats" into the other worlds. If you have someone who can drum or rattle for you, that's great. Most of us don't and the noise often leads to complaints from neighbors. The stereo and walkman are the 20th-century shaman's best friends. When the goal is to work with city spirits, you have to become a techno-shaman and make friends with all your potential tools. Tapes of drums, rattles, tones, chants, and white noise are available in many music and New Age shops. The music should be something fairly rhythmic and atonal, since melody and chord progressions may distract you. Lyrics make things difficult. You don't want to end up singing along instead of journeying. Michael Harner, author of *Way of the Shaman* (HarperCollins), has a series of recordings with shamanic drumming that are quite good (see Bibliography). I've also had successful results with Mickey Hart's *Planet Drum* (Rykodisc) and Peter Gabriel's *Passion* (Geffen Records). You can even record your own music if you feel so inclined. Tape recorders, keyboards, and drum machines are musical helpers. Many inexpensive drum machines have preprogrammed beats and styles whose tempo you can adjust to suit your needs. Dance music that is low on melody and high on beat is also ideal for those suited to those styles. Using machines and prerecorded music may seem to run contrary to the magical idea that everything needs to be natural. As you delve into the urban magical world, remember that everything is natural. Technology is not inherently bad. We must only be vigilant against its misuse at the expense of others.

This exercise is facilitated by wearing comfortable clothing and a blindfold such as a scarf or even a flaxseed eye pillow. For deep trance work, lying down is recommended, as long as you don't think you will fall asleep. Falling asleep during spirit work is not always bad. Sometimes spirits cannot work with us on a conscious level, so we fall asleep to contact them. Lying down relaxes your body and improves the blood flow to ease you into a deep trance. Wear comfortable clothing and use a pillow under your head or legs.

E_XERCI_SE 5 – TRANCE WORK WITH SOUND

❶ Get into a meditative state using Exercise 1 (see page 17) and reaffirm your protective shield (see page 27).

❷ Start your musical accompaniment. Lie down, get comfortable, and tie the blindfold around your eyes. Physical light can distract you from a journey. Simply listen to the music and let it take you wherever it does.

❸ Feel the pulse of the music as if it were the rhythm of the world. Feel it move you, guide you. Feel yourself ride the drum, as if it were a great locomotive taking you on a mysterious journey.

❹ Feel, see, and know that you are traveling through the dark, through the beat, through a tunnel. Feel the sensation of traveling quickly through a tunnel.

❺ At the end of the tunnel, there is a light. You are simply traveling to the end of the tunnel and looking out without exiting it. Look around and be open to any images you see.

❻ Return from the tunnel. Travel back, again using the pulse of the music. Feel yourself return. When the experience is complete, return your awareness to the waking world and take off your blindfold. Ground yourself and turn off your music.

This simple experience can grant you new insight into yourself through important images and messages at the end of the tunnel. It can also serve simply as an introductory experience. We will be using these techniques to traverse the shamanic landscape of the urban jungle.

Sacred sound can lead you to another avenue of trance work: dance. Dancing–around the tribal fire or around your living room table–can bring you to a state of trance. Ecstatic movement is an age-old tradition. Tribal magicians do it. Voodoo practitioners, before being "ridden" by the loa (their gods) do it. The whirling Dervishes are famous for it. And now, the "club kids" and trendsetters do it. I have a student who has combined traditional belly dancing with witchcraft to move energy and invoke spirits.

Hopefully, everyone has had some experience with dance before, whether it be formal steps or the simple freedom of moving your body where it wants to go. By really going into the dance, you lose yourself to it. You feel the dance and experience a synchronization with the world for a brief time. You may not be completely graceful, but that doesn't matter. You are somewhere else.

Dance is a wonderful medium not only to open up your perceptions to other worlds, but to synchronize your physical body with your own subtle bodies of emotions, mind, and spirit. It raises energy for your magick. I do some dancelike movements in my tiny altar room to balance my body with my magical intentions and to raise energy. I can feel and see the energy swirling around my body as I move. The energy trails from my fingertips, often weaving into an image of my needed goal.

One sure way to destroy this trance state is to be self-conscious about your movements. If you are not comfortable dancing, make sure you are alone and in a place where you can practice this exercise without feeling self-conscious. Most of my practices are solitary, so that's not a problem for me. Judging yourself during this trance dance, however, can be counterproductive. You should simply thank your conscious mind for the critique and then ask it to sit quietly in the corner.

You will need a an audio support for this, as well. This time, though the beat is important, you can be more particular with the music you choose. If the music has words, sing along. Flow with whatever music you have, on the stereo or in your head. Make sure the music is something that resonates with you, from New Age world music, to tribal or ethnic pieces, to rock and roll or disco. It doesn't matter, as long as you can move to it.

Exercise 6 is not as regimented as others. These are simple guidelines to help you experiment with a technique in the privacy of your own home. As you explore the basic building blocks of magick, altering reality, and opening your senses, some will work better than others, but you should have experience in many different techniques. When teaching in a classroom setting, anything that requires movement or speaking is most difficult, simply because people are afraid of making fools of themselves. In tarot, the Fool is usually the one having the most fun and good luck. You now have the luxury of playing the Fool in the privacy of your own home. Do not skip this exercise. Play with it. Experiment with different music. Enjoy it.

EXERCISE 6 – TRANCE THROUGH MOVEMENT

❶ Prepare your space by making sure you are comfortable. Move furniture out of the way to give you more room if you need it.

❷ Ground and center yourself. Feel comfortable, calm, and relaxed.

❸ Start your music. Make it loud enough to dance to, but not so loud as to make you or others uncomfortable. Or wear headphones.

❹ Move in whatever way your body leans. You can start by simply swaying. Move only your arms and hands to the music, or only your feet. Do not try to do everything at once, but let the song build up within you. Feel the beats and do not think about it at all. Let it come with ease. If you are self-conscious, close your eyes, but make sure that you will not run into anything.

❺ When the process feels complete, stop the music. It may go on for one song, or for a whole album. Ground and center yourself.

Think about how the dance made you feel. If you were very self-conscious and based in the ego, repeat the exercise until you can let go a bit. This is a great exercise to do at a dance club if you like, since no one will be able to tell what you are doing, and you will be feeding off the energy in such a charged environment, instead of in a room alone.

In more complex rituals, you may see or hear the spirits whose attention you've attracted. You may see more light and color, as your second sight is opened by the trance. You may see with your third eye, or your brow chakra, above and between your two physical eyes. You may hear through your throat chakra, which transmits and receives all spirit communication. By entering an altered state, you become aware of your other chakras and the gifts they give.

For now, you are simply becoming aware of the many ways to enter an altered state. Later, we will build on these techniques to explore city magick.

◎ RITUAL ◎

City magick, country magick, or any other magick consists of making something happen. By making a change on the subtle levels, these other levels of reality, you make changes here in the physical world. Ritual is a tool to accomplish change. Some rituals are pretty powerful in themselves, but in essence, any ritual is simply a way for you to contact and raise energy. You then program this energy with an intention and the energy fulfills the intention you give it. Casting a spell is programmimg energy with an intent and releasing it. Spells are a lot like computer programs. You build them privately, with a general intent. Let's say the intent is money: *I want more money.* You then program in the specifics: *I want seven hundred dollars to pay my rent.* Then add certain restrictions: *I need the money before the first of next month.* I usually add a safety net: *This spell won't work if it hurts anyone in the process, including me.* I could get hit by a bus and collect the money from the insurance company, but I don't want to end up in the hospital. Magick is not moral in and of itself. It is neither good nor evil. Any energy is neither good nor evil. Energy and magick are potential. Like a computer program, they work within the parameters you give them—no more, no less. Just because some company's computer platform may have a lot of bugs in it doesn't mean it's evil. Well, some might argue it, but ultimately, the program is only working with the codes it is given. Blame the creator, or the spell, or the program, not the construct itself.

While the analogy of the computer code is all fine and good, I don't have a magical computer. So how do I use this? The vehicle to implement a magical program is ritual. A ritual starts with the practitioner in a trance state. It can be a light alpha state or a deep trance state, depending on what needs to be done in the ritual. Anything that requires attention to detail, like burning incense, reading words, drawing symbols, or lighting candles, may require a light meditative state, like the daydream, because you still have physical control over your body. You do not want to be deep in a sleeplike trance or on out-of-body state for this. Once in an altered state, you can, through ritual, perform actions to raise, program, and release energy.

Raising energy requires knowledge of what energy is needed. Energy comes in many forms. You can use the energy of Earth. You can call upon the four elements of land, air, fire, and water. Astrological magick is popular, beckoning the powers of the planets and signs. Specific symbols, spirits, totems, gods, and goddesses have specialties. Some may be able to help you in ways that others can't. Your intention rules everything. Research the powers you need if you are not already familiar with them. If you continue to seek power in the cityscape, you will find the spirits and powers there. Develop a relationship with them.

In the basic neopagan traditions I use, the magick circle gives you a great basis for ritual. The circle ritual can be modified to fit any tradition with a little creative engineering. In this ritual, you will visualize a circle around you. The circle is for protection. It is a place between reality levels where you can gather different energies, program them, and release them to work for your goal.

Magick Circle Ritual

The circle is a prominent symbol, signifying the neverending cycles of life and death, the very egg of life, the portal to other worlds, the shape of the planets, and the orbit around the Sun. Each culture has modified the circle, adapting its meaning to their changing needs. Many tribal cultures start their ritual and story times with the group sitting in a circle. In the Western world, we mimic ritual stories at our weekend nature retreats, gathering in a circle around a campfire. Witches gather in a circle, under the light of the Moon. They dance in the circle to raise their power. Modern witches, like ritual magicians, call upon the four elements to balance the circle and to guard and protect them. The guardians in each quarter may change with the tradition. Names vary—Witch's Circle, Magick Circle, Moon Circle, or Magician's Circle. Native American traditions honor the four directions in the Medicine Wheel.

Those who practice magick have long known the power of the circle. The circle holds energy during a ritual. Here, as you raise energy, it will build to a crescendo. Energy can be raised through ritual, dance, visualization, concentration, masturbation, or sex. Once released, the energy from the circle will fulfill the spells cast. The circle, when made correctly, protects the user from harm during the ritual. I actually visualize the circle becoming a sphere once it is cast. This globe of light and energy blocks out all unwanted forces. Only the spirits and energies called upon can enter the circle. I call only for those coming in perfect love and perfect trust, in complete harmony with my magical intentions. You qualify the energy you want in your space by charging the circle with those intentions. By calling on the four elements of earth, air, fire, and water, and the guardians of the four elements, you invoke added protection and balance.

The circle gives you a direct audience with the creative force, the mother/father spirit and grand architect of the universe. You don't have to go through many middlemen. Even when you are calling upon other forces, gods, spirits, or elements to fulfill your spell, the magick circle communicates your intention to the grand architect of the universe, assuring approval of your new project. From that approval, your desires will be worked into the plan of the universe. Sometimes, I am just as thankful to have a spell rejected when it's not for my highest good. I usually ask that each spell be for "the good of all involved, harming none including myself." That way, if it doesn't work, its very faliure may be in my best interest. I usually don't dwell on spells that don't work, because the majority of them do.

Start by cleansing the space where you will be working. Just as you protect yourself from harmful energy and psychic pollutants, you must similarly cleanse your workspace. This can be done by burning a cleansing and purifying incense like sage, lavender, frankincense, or myrrh. A simple way to cleanse it is to visualize a cleansing light in the space. What color felt most pure to you? Most people use white, violet, or purple light and ask that all harmful energies be removed.

To create the circle, visualize a ring of white light being drawn around you, filling your space. Traditional measurements are usually seven, nine, or twelve feet in diameter, but in the confines of an apartment, use what space you have. The boundary of the circle passes through walls, floors, and ceilings, but that's okay. Just visualize it wherever it has to go to be a perfect circle of light surrounding you. Even if you can't draw a perfectly round circle, just visualize it as perfect.

Start drawing in the north, and make three complete circles with the intention of creating sacred space. Sacred space is simply a temple, created etherically in this case. In the temple, your connection to the powers of the universe are emphasized. I strengthen my circle by casting it three times. I come from a Celtic witchcraft background in which most things are done in threes. It helps to make the circle more stable in my mind and others who practice with me can feel this circle, this energy field, more distinctly when it's done three times. I use three intentions, one with each pass. The first is for protection.

> *I create this circle to protect us from all forces coming to do harm.*

The second is to qualify the energy.

> *I ask for only those energies coming in perfect love
> and perfect trust, in complete harmony with my magical
> intentions, to enter this circle.*

The last is manifestation.

> *I create a sacred temple beyond time and space, between the
> worlds, where my magical intentions will manifest. So mote it be.[1]*

Many traditionalists use a magick wand, blade, or staff to trace the perimeter of the clockwise circle, but you can use your finger, the movement of your eyes, or pure visualization to accomplish the task. The clockwise motion is for those in the Northern Hemisphere. The circle is an energy field, and its magnetic aspect plays a role. I usually start in the north or east when casting. For those in the Southern Hemisphere, you may want to start in the south and cast the circle counterclockwise. The mechanics are much like the corollas effect, where water in the Northern Hemisphere empties from a drain in a counterclockwise direction, while in the Southern Hemisphere, it spirals clockwise as it flows from the drain.

Once in the circle, you can gather your power. Many practitioners take this opportunity to call upon the god and goddess in a gen-

---

1. "So mote it be" means let it be or so it is. I explain this phrase to my friends as the pagan Amen.

eral sense, or any gods, goddesses, elementals, or spirits that may help specifically with the spell. To balance the circle, I call upon the four quarters, marked by the four elements. Each tradition has a different way of assigning the elements to the directions. It doesn't matter, as long as you use all four and do so with respect and honor. In each quarter, you can call upon a guardian in harmony with the direction or element. A guardian is a spiritual helper who will aid the process and, if asked, protect you from any harm. I call on at least four of them per circle. A guardian can take the form of a spirit guide, totem animal, god, goddess, angel, saint, or alien. You don't have to meet them in your meditations first. I've called on the four archangels without working with them much in my meditations. If you use respect and ask them to come only in love and trust, you can ask anyone who is right for your spell to join you.

Table 1. Traditional Correspondences.

Element	Usual Direction	Archangel	Totems	god Archetypes
Earth	North	Uriel	Stag, Bear, Snake	Mother, Father Underworld, Nature, Land, and Animal deities
Air	East	Raphael	Birds of all kinds	Sky, Storm, Air Moon, and Sorcery deities
Fire	South	Michael	Salamander and Fox Totems	Fire, Forge, Light, Art, and Music Deities
Water	West	Gabriel	Fish, Aquatic Mammals, and Amphibians	Sea, Lake, River, Death, Healing, and Medicine deities

Start in the north and, moving clockwise, invite these beings to your space.

> *To the [direction], I ask the element of [name the element] and*
> *[name the archangel/totem/deity] to be with me, to guard, guide,*
> *and witness this magick.*

If you are not familiar with any of these beings, simply start at the north and ask the powers of the north to join you for aid and protection. Continue to the east, south, and west. As we delve deeper into city magick, we will talk about specific beings upon whom you can call, beings drawn directly from the cityscape.

Once all the powers have gathered, I then see the circle turn into a sphere, a bubble containing energy. To psychically "stoke" the flames I have called into being, I visualize the ball getting brighter and more intense as the energy grows. You can use movement, song, or intention to build the energy, then program it with your will. You can write out your intention and read it in the circle. Burn the paper in a flameproof cauldron, tear it up, or bury it. My previous intention might be worded like this:

> *I ask the goddess and god that I receive seven hundred dollars to*
> *pay my rent before the first of next month. I ask this harm no one*
> *in the process, including me.*

Your intention should be simple, direct, and clear. Once the energy is programmed with your intent, you are ready to release it. Through the ritual, you raise the cone of power, directing the beam of energy infused with intent through reality like a shot, a signal flare petitioning your needs to the universe. You raise it by raising your hands to the sky and visualizing the energy being released. Then let go of your intention with your conscious mind. Do not hold on to it, or your thoughts will sap its energy, bringing it back to you, and undermining

City Magick

your spell. As with the computer program, if the designer continually tinkers with the program, it will never run. You may lose momentum in your project, leaving it unfinished. If you let it run, however, regardless of the little glitches and worries, you will probably get the results you want. Be at peace and confident that your spells are at work.

After raising the cone of power, make sure to ground yourself and release whatever energy remains into the earth. Return the energy with the intention of healing for Earth and all who are a part of her. Then release the circle and close the sacred space.

To release, start in the north and thank and release all the powers that have joined you, moving counterclockwise. Thank each quarter's element and guardian and release them from the circle, with respect, honor, and gratitude. These are guests in your space and should be treated as such.

Once the four quarters have been released, retrace your circle in the direction opposite to how you cast it. Visualize the energy dissipating, fading away, going back into your wand, or expanding infinitely across the cosmos, working your magick. A good magick worker is one who can not only call up powerful energy, but one who also knows how to release it.

Other rituals have the same basic elements. The act of focusing on the circle is not mandatory. The circle is only a useful tool. Other ritual techniques, including candle burning, drawing symbols, crystals, herbs, or other tools, can be used in conjunction with, or in place of, the simple petition and circle ritual. I have gotten great results using them together.

In an act of sympathetic magick, by making the smaller action in accordance or in sympathy with what you desire, you create change. To program energy with intent, you can use a voodoo doll. By sticking a pin where there is illness, you program the energy to destroy the illness. You can use two candles to represent two people coming together in love magick. You can drop a dirt-covered stone in a bowl of water to purify your energy and spirit while in ritual. You can put your intent into a small bag of herbs and carry them with you as a talisman. All these acts program energy.

Using these ritual techniques with an urban slant will be explored later. For now, get a feel for the way magick works. Each ritual gathers energy, programs it with an intent through any combination of words, visualization, or action, and then releases that energy to do its work, like the computer running a new program. The tools and techniques are helpful, but, in the end, your intent is what matters.

The three Rs—reality, rapture, and ritual—are the basic building blocks of most magical work. They are the core from which your traditions can be built. You can modify the exercises given here to fit your personal needs, or throw them out completely and work with a method that resonates with you. If you are already practicing magick, these concepts are probably familiar to you, and you can modify your own meditations and rituals to fit your work with the city spirits.

Chapter 3
Metropolitan Spirits

THE GOD IS DEAD. ALL HAIL THE GOD.
gods come and gods go, but there is always one around inspiring some form of spirituality, or even a lack thereof, as with the god of science. As things change, they ever stay the same. Polytheistic cultures believe in the existence of many gods and goddesses, all coexisting. Each of the deities has a specific function to perform, or a tribe under its care. As needs change, the old gods change, die, and transform into new ones. The war gods of one tribe become the vegetation gods of their grandchildren's tribe, as the culture moves from conquering to farming.

Monotheistic cultures come along and deny the presence of any other god. They kill off all the old gods through propaganda. Those they can't kill become the devils of the new order. Minor gods become the little spirits, haunting old worship sights. These beings are never truly forgotten, never completely obliterated. They survive in our legends. They go under the hills and mounds, become the wee people and faery folk. If you continue to honor their old ways, even if you worship the new gods outwardly, they bring prosperity. They are the good people, the kindly ones. If you fail in your service to them, they make the land, harvest, and weather rise up against you. They still have power, it's only our perception of them that has changed. They are still the natural forces. They only change shape.

The monotheism of the West gave rise to the god of science. This deity is formless, shapeless, and with no true doctrine, but much literature that is often contradictory in nature. Some even deny it is a god at all. The new religion of logic, with the ritual worship of the five physical senses, has crept in everywhere. They even teach it in all the schools, regardless of the separation between church and state.

New religions always bring a backlash. Reaction to science has sent the world searching for its former spiritual heritage. The monotheists turned to their individual gods. Those dissatisfied with current monotheism looked to the old gods, who are not dead, but sleeping, changed. New philosophies arose from old practices. Neopagan movements began. What do you do, however, when the new god's temples of glass and steel surround you, leaving you far from an open field or forest? The answer is obvious. You don't have to go to your gods. They are always with you, hiding in the building, the machines, and the vermin. The spirit world hides in plain sight. It adapts. Its spirits are living and breathing in everything around you. They have always been there, waiting for you to find them again.

◎ City Totems ◎

Everybody has at least one guide in the spirit world—including you. Some have an entire entourage, or one for every day of the week. Spiritual guidance is a tough job. Spirits have to relate to us physically incarnate humans and we often do silly things. They may work in shifts, or one single entity may change forms as needed. They can appear as your deceased grandmother one day, your witch ancestor from pagan Europe another, a master from Atlantis when you are in an Edgar Cayce phase, or an alien when you start reading channeled space-brother-and-sister books. These are all valid representations, taking the form you need to help you along your spiritual path.

Many times, the guide may be a totem, an animal figure. The totem comes to you through a dream, meditation, or preponderance of encounters with its physical animal representatives. The meetings will grow increasingly intense, until you acknowledge the animal as your power animal, with lessons to teach and guidance to give. Some speak. Others are animal silent, or speak in animal language as they guide you on your vision quests through the unexplored realms of reality.

My own experience with my first totem was at 4 or 5 years old. A spider bit me, and I had an allergic reaction, and was rushed to the emergency room by my parents for a frightening visit with a doctor. I was fine after a few hours, but, looking back on it, I consider it my first initiation. I had a fascination for the comic character Spider-Man as a kid, but oddly as I was getting into magick, I became deathly afraid of spiders. I tried not to be, but I was. I didn't understand why. Bugs in general had never bothered me before. I was fascinated by them as a child. The more I thought about spiders, the more I saw them. I found spiders everywhere—in my home and in the homes of all my friends. They were only there, however, when I was around. Then it got really weird. If there was a spider in the house, it would make its way to my bedroom, get above me on the ceiling, or in the corner behind me, and jump down on me. I had no logical reason why they did this; they just did it. I felt that this onslaught of kamikaze spiders clearly had some message, but I had no idea how to unravel it at the time.

This pattern climaxed with a vision. While watching TV (not while mediating), I "felt" something and thought I saw it out of the corner of my eye. No spiders were about. What I sensed was big and dark—my first glimpse of what I now call my astral spider guide. It was a good five feet from back to front legs. I knew it wasn't physical, so I chalked it up to my imagination. That's not really there, I thought. I imagined it. Paranoia was starting to take its toll.

Before I knew it, I felt it on top of me. As I lay pinned to the bed, the spider told me in a strange, metallic voice to "get over it." Spiders wouldn't hurt me it said. And even if they did, it wouldn't amount to much. Afterall, if I could get through this, a little spider would be no threat. The worst that could happen is that I would be poisoned, die, and come into a new life. This experience told me that I knew death did not mean stopping life. Now I had to start living that truth. Then the spider guide vanished. For the first time, I seriously wondered if I had started to crack. Things got better from then on, however, and I had a wonderful conversation with a friend who explained the difference between shamanic and schizophrenic experiences. A shamanic experience is not physical. You can "turn it off" if you want to. I think I could have turned my spider experience off, but I'm glad I did not. I am guided now by many astral spiders who spin webs and leave trails for me in my travels. They teach patience, industry, and artistry. Now, watching physical spiders make their webs is an endless source of fascination and appreciation for me. I often feel them around me a lot. Even now, as I write this, I can feel spiders crawling on me, but it does not bother me—much. I'm still processing the spider wisdom. They give me great lessons on how to conquer fear and access my creativity.

I am sure your home or apartment has spiders, even if you don't see them. They are good at not being seen and they control other insects. Your home has many little creatures of which you are unaware. Perhaps this is for the best, unless one of them is a power animal for you.

The city often seems lifeless and barren, but there are so many creatures living under its skin. Most of the wild things are forms of vermin, strays, or insects. Any animal surviving and thriving in a city is a testament to the powers of adaptability. You need adaptability as well in order to survive and prosper in the urban jungle. You should ask to make contact with your totem. If you have a totem not normally found in the city, particularly if you practiced magick before you moved to the urban Mecca, you may ask for a new guide for your new environment and work with both. If your totem is the wild moose, for instance, you may have difficulty working with him as your explore the power spots in the city. The moose will always be there, but, for some experiences, a guide native to the cityscape is best.

Here are a few potential city totems you can encounter in your magical journeys. Watch their habits and their own body wisdom. Each animal has its own lessons, its own "medicine," as said in Native American practices. Medicine is not simply one lesson, but a lifetime of learning, refining the lesson, and living it. The meanings here for each animal are general. You will discover the specific lessons your totem has for you as you work with it.

Cats

Cats are the great urban settlers, coming from the wild to be domesticated by humans and led to the new temples. Cats have lived quite comfortably in the company of humans, from the cat cults of Bast in Egypt, to the posh penthouse cats shown in cat food commercials. They are survivors. Abandoned felines become alley cats and survive on their diets of garbage scraps and the occasional rodent. In fact, they were probably urbanized to control rodent populations. Cats are hunters. They have acute hearing and night vision that let them pounce on their prey. They teach self-preservation and attaining your own comfort. Mystically, the cat is associated with the Moon and magick. They are so skilled at survival because they are aware of their multidimensionality. They walk between worlds, often seeing things we can't see. They work strongly through the collective unseen realms, working through dreams and the astral plane. Cats are harbingers of mystery and hidden secrets. They are the perfect pets for the practitioner—self-sufficient, and having their own power. Black cats are said to bring bad luck if they cross your path. I think of them as good luck myself, but then, I am a witch and most superstitious people see witches as bad luck, too.

Dogs

Dogs are man's best friend, and woman's too. They love their service to humanity. They only ask to be loved in return. Dogs embody loyalty and love for their masters on one hand, and fierce and wild protection, a trait from their genetic ancestors, on the other. Dogs are often employed for security and safety. My family always kept a German shepherd to guard the house. And we did feel very safe. Once, when a neighbor came into the house uninvited to deliver something, and no one in the family was around, our dog bit him. In the dog's mind, the neighbor was trespassing. Dogs are great guardians. The gateway to Hades, the Greek underworld, is guarded by a three-headed dog. The Norse Hel is guarded by a wolf creature named Garm. Anubis, the jackal dog-headed god worked both as a soul guide to and a guard for the Egyptian underworld. Each works with this totem animal's key lessons—service, loyalty, and protection. When working with this animal spirit, you have a kind and loving totem to guide you on your journey, a friend and companion, and a fierce protector of your safety. A dog totem is a wonderful spirit to find. Unfortunately, in the city, many physical dogs are strays or abandoned. They do not have the same independence as cats. Dogs want to be with people. Be sensitive to the pet population in the shelters in your area, particularly if your totem is dog. If you can adopt a kind companion and take care of it, you will not regret the friend you make.

Rodents

Rodents include all manner of critters, squirrels, ground hogs, and beavers, but, in the city, we are dealing primarily with rats and mice. They are the underbelly of the city, the great garbage disposal system we don't like to acknowledge. Rats are the larger of the two and the more intimidating, but they are similar. Rats eat almost anything with their sharp, chisel-like teeth. They live in the shadows, in the hidden worlds, the wall spaces, cellars, sewers, and subway tunnels, but they can climb to the rooftops. They make their nests in secret hiding places. They find comfort in the dark. They move through the night, being nocturnal creatures. The eyes of the rodent often seem other-worldly and unreal. Mice, in particular, scrutinize everything in their environment. They move by feeling everything with their whiskers, paying attention to the tiniest detail. If the mouse is your totem, you can be very particular, or be working on your organizational skills. Do not get mired in the details and fail to see the larger picture.

Rodents are often blamed for disease. Rats were responsible for spreading the bubonic plague throughout Europe. For that reason, they have a bad reputation with humans, but they also destroy many insects and weeds in farm settings. They naturally recycle a lot of our food waste as well. Rats often travel in packs and lead a very clan-like existence. People are surprised to hear that rat spirit medicine teaches family skills and strong relationships with loved ones. If a nursing mother rat is killed, another nursing mother will raise the orphaned rodents without hesitation. Perhaps we have more to learn from our rodent friends than we think.

Squirrels

Although the squirrel is a rodent, it deserves separate treatment from mice and rats. Squirrels usually make their homes in the remaining city trees, mostly in parks. They build their nests in the trees and surrounding areas, preparing for the winter. Most of their time is spent gathering nuts, seeds, and berries. "Be prepared" is their motto, and I am surprised that the Boy Scouts do not have a "squirrel badge," since they work with the squirrel totem intuitively. When you can see impending changes on the horizon, you can take care of them more easily by planning ahead. You are given warning signals for a reason. Save money if you need it. Have a safe place to go if you need that. Do whatever you need to prepare for future changes. And be aggressive about it. City squirrels are daring. They look all fuzzy and cuddly, but there is a survivor living under their fur. They come right up to you to take your leftover food. They dig through trash cans and picnic scraps. Do what you need to do to survive.

Ants

Ants are another infestation in the life of the city dweller. If you find your apartment filled with ants, watch out. These little insects are tenacious. The virtue in working with an ant spirit is patience. Ants will travel far and wide to bring food back to their anthill. And the anthill leads to the other lesson of ant medicine–communal living. In this nest, they serve their leader, mother, and queen. The good of the entire community is put over the good of the individual. Each exists in a communal melding of the minds. There is one spirit running through all and they honor it. They remind me of more communal modes of living, to which I think our society may return. I hope, however, that we do not sacrifice our own individuality in the process. Sacrifice of the self is a strong watchword for the ant spirit. Individual needs are put behind community needs. Long-term goals are placed over immediate gratification. You may find yourself struggling with these themes if this totem comes to visit you. If physical ants themselves come to visit, it may be a message from the spirits to honor your community and think about the greater good. Once you get the message, go into a meditative state and politely ask the ants to leave your home. If they are persistent, which they often are, try speaking to the queen through your own totem spirits. Cinnamon or powdered garlic sprinkled where ants enter your home is often a deterrent, and much safer than a chemical pesticide. I always watch for messages, not only from spirits, but from physical animals too. Animals are messengers when they need to be. They come when you close your spiritual ears and eyes to the message. You cannot ignore an ant colony feasting in your kitchen.

Cockroaches

The great survivor lives in this nasty little critter. Considered vermin by most, cockroaches normally live in the wild and have nothing to do with humans. Those living with us are scavengers, however, eating our food and garbage, and contaminating it with their waste. Just the sight of them can be quite disturbing. The first time I saw a cockroach was in Mexico. It came crawling out of a hole in a broken streetlight, and was much bigger than I ever thought roaches could get. I had a teacher who had me meditate with various animals and pets. I'm glad I never got her hissing cockroach. They teach us the greatest lesson—survival. The cockroach has lived virtually unchanged for 300 million years. They are the planet's greatest survivors. As we poison them with chemical pesticides, they build up immunities. I have heard jokes that claim humanity could be destroyed by nuclear war, pollution, or a chemical accident, but cockroaches would still survive, roaming the planet unhindered. Cockroach totems may be working with your fear of the ugly and unloved, the outcasts of society. Their alien visage inspires an almost primal revolt in the modern psyche. Like many insect and arachnid totems, they work on our own fear issues. Many of us fear what is different. We can relate to animals, since many share similar traits, skeletons, muscles, and hair. Insect totems, on the other hand, wear their bones on the outside, making them alien to us. That's why so many horror movies rely on the insect motif, to frighten us with something different. This animal medicine also works with issues of change and adaptability. The simplicity of their "design" teaches us that change isn't always the answer. You can persevere and build immunities to the toxins in your life without remaking yourself. Consistency can be an asset.

Spiders

Spiders are a particular favorite of mine, as you may have guessed. If you do not have a cellar in which they can dwell, they often take up residence in the shower. Both are cool and damp. A friend of mine had a "grandfather" spider watch her shower every morning, until she had a little chat with it and learned his message. He left after that. There are many types of spiders, so spider totems vary in power and function. Most spiders have eight eyes, fangs, and the ability to spin webs. Some are poisonous to humans, most are not. All are carnivorous, and usually feed on other insects. Never kill a spider in your home, even if they are not your totem. If they are staying alive, then there is something to eat. If you kill it, then whatever the spider was eating will infest your home. Many of my eight-legged friends spin webs and then wait there for their prey. Once the insect is caught in the web, the spider retrieves its meal. Spiders are not evil, but merely fulfilling their role in the cycle of life. Spiders teach industry, home building, creation, and patience. They are the artisans of the animal world. Their webs are like the webs of space and time connecting us. Spiders weave the story of creation in detailed form. Many weaving gods work with spider imagery. Those who weave thread often weave fates from the past, present, and future. Spider Grandmother is a Native American goddess giving us spider wisdom. This conceptual force is often seen as feminine, although, personally, my spider totems seem to be either male or female at different times. Those working with spider energy are very creative with visual art and writing. The lines of the spiderwebs are like the lines of the first alphabets, seeming very much like the Norse runes in some ways. Spider energy also holds the center of anything, and you may find yourself as the linchpin of any group or organization. You hold the center and others work around you, in the web.

Crows

Crows are indicative of magick and mystery. Their black color is the dark womb of the goddess. Crows and their cousins, the ravens, are associated with gods, goddesses, and the act of creation in many mythologies. Crows are seen as patrons of modern witches and magicians. The crow is another of my personal totems. I work with Macha, a Celtic crow goddess, and Odin, whose messengers are two ravens. Crows are the keepers of magick and sacred law. Invoking crow medicine and working with this totem aligns you with your magical purpose and often rekindles psychic powers and past-life connections. Crows know the natural order of the world. In the city, they are survivors in the sky kingdom, omnivorous and adaptable. They are sentinels, perched high in their nests, warning of danger. Many harkening to folk tales count crows to tell the future, but some say all crows are good luck, even a dead one. They speak the sacred law in their very complex language of caws, and encourage others to speak their divine truth.

Doves

The dove is a cousin to the more familiar pigeon. Both are ground feeders, keeping contact with the earth, even when the land is coated with asphalt. The dove is traditionally considered a feminine bird and is associated with many goddesses. Both birds are known for their distinctive voices, but the dove is truly the keeper of song. The song of the dove has a distinctive, soft, feminine nature, heard best at dawn and dusk, the transition points of the day. Doves are associated with the travel of the spirit into the realms of death. The dove's cry is also said to indicate water, and water is associated with the realms of the dead. Doves are also linked to prophecy, love, and spiritual connections.

Ducks

Cities near the water may be home to the duck totem. Most ducks are freshwater birds, and prefer marshes and wetlands, but some are saltwater fowl. Generally, these birds have webbed feet and are proficient swimmers and flyers. They are social and vocal animals, making the familiar quacking noise, among others, to communicate with their brethren. Some calls indicate flight as they move in specific patterns with others in their group. Once a year, for a period of three to four weeks, they molt their flight feathers, robbing them of their ability to fly. Hunters take advantage of this helplessness. Duck totems may work with social skills or feelings of powerlessness. We all lose power at times, in order to adapt, change, and grow. These growing pains may leave us vulnerable to others around us. Ducks, in general, are less graceful on land, indicating a lack of desire to meet

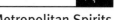
others halfway, or even leave their comfort zones. The duck's down feathers are also excellent insulation from the cold, used in their nests, and often used by people for pillows, blankets, and padded clothing. The spirit medicine of the duck is much like the shaman's own lesson, that of working between worlds. Ducks adapt to the water, sky, and land. Each home has advantages and disadvantages. Ducks shift between all three. Ducks deal with losing access to the air, and the totem's energy helps us work with temporary power loss.

Finches

The finch comes in many forms and guises. These little birds can be seen in parks and sidewalk cafés, coming right up to the fair citizens of the city. Most become acclimated to people if they hope to survive in the city, and they are abundant in the surrounding suburbs. The sheer number of species of finches indicates diversity in this animal's lessons. Those working with the finch are working with diversity within and diversity in their lives. Look for more intense and new experiences when the finch comes into your life.

Pigeons

These creatures are often described as rats with wings. Some think they are like vermin, living anywhere, eating anything, and leaving their droppings behind them to get underfoot. They are quite common in city parks, flocking together. Kind souls, the special guardians of the pigeon, often feed them seeds or bread while in the park. Pigeons have a richer history than most people think. They were used as food in Egypt and Rome, and protected for religious reasons in Islamic realms. Both males and females feed the young by regurgitating high-protein "pigeon milk." These social creatures make beautiful "cooing" sounds of courtship during mating season. All bird totems teach song. They tell tribal stories through the songs they sing. The most remarkable thing about these animals is the homing instinct of some breeds. Pigeons have carried messages since biblical times up to the present day. Scientists now believe that they may perceive the geomagnetic fields of the earth to find their way. They, and perhaps other birds, have a special kinship with Mother Earth, and use her energy to guide them. Pigeons may work with trust issues. Trust your self, and trust your own guidance systems. Pigeon wisdom helps bring us home, wherever that may be. Working with this totem will lead you to where you need to be, both spiritually and physically.

Seagulls

Another form of waterfowl for coastal cities is the seagull. Most of these totems are scavengers, and the gull is an aggressive one. Gulls start their search in the coastal realms, swooping in and snatching things from the shallow waters. They drop hard-shelled mollusks to smash them open and feast on the meat inside. Some will bully other birds and take their food. When food is scarce, many will fly inland to garbage dumps for their next meal. I remember finding a seagull skull on the beach with my father as a child. It looked a bit otherworldly and scary to me as I hunted for seashells. Seagull spirits work with aggression, perseverance, and desperation. They make noise to get attention, or to scare off other predators who would take their food. Gulls use speed, diving in, getting what they need, and then leaving. In many ways, they remind me of the Hermes/Mercury figure, traveling far and wide, going to the heavens and reaching far below. Sometimes their moral character can be dubious, but gulls fulfill their function, doing what they must—doing what comes naturally.

City Zoos

The city is filled with many other animals, both seen and unseen. Your totem may not be on this list. Your personal totem may not even be in the city. If you need to make contact with a more exotic physical animal and you can't easily find it, remember your city zoo. Zoos are not my favorite place. I dislike seeing animals in cages, but humane zoos with natural habitats are becoming more popular. Seek one out. Take a walk through your city zoo and connect with the animals there, whether they are your totem or not. If the conditions are not the best, take the time to speak to the animals, physically or psychically. Connect and commune with them. Comfort them. Honor them. Volunteer at the zoo, animal shelter, or a wildlife preserve near you. These places are a part of your cityscape habitat now.

◎ JOURNEYING ◎

A primary method of communicating with unseen spirits and energies is to "meet" on a spiritual plane. Astral travel is a technique in which you send out your consciousness, your perceptions–what many call the astral body–to a common ground between you and the spirits, a place some call the astral plane. Your spirit feels as if it is rising out of your body and entering a new reality.

In our efforts to walk the magical path of the urban shaman, we explored shamanic journeying techniques that employ sound and movement in the previous chapter. The shamanic journey is a form of projection, the path and tunnel a type of astral plane. Discussion of the shamanic worlds, or views of the astral and many other planes of existence, will be forthcoming as we explore the urban mythos. Shamanistic techniques, whether traditional or modern, are a great place to start such spirit work. The following exercise builds upon earlier material to aid you in your quest for a city totem.

EXERCISE 7 – TOTEM JOURNEY

❶ Start with an intention to meet your city totem animal. Do not think about what it could be, or what you hope it will be. Just affirm out loud or to yourself that you intend to know your city totem.

❷ Start Exercise 5 (see page 32). Before you feel yourself enter a tunnel or step on a long and winding road, ask and intend that your city totem be at the end of the pathway.

❸ When you reach the end, your totem will appear in your inner vision. Let it come easily. The animal may speak to you, or may be silent, communicating through actions, intuition, or by leading you to something you need to see. The meeting is often simple and brief, or it may lead to a journey. Follow the spirit vision quest and let your unconscious mind take over. You will go from a point of visualizing your creature to letting go of preconceived notions. Go with the flow. Let the adventure lead you where it may.

❹ When the journey feels complete, ask your totem to guide you back through the path or tunnel and return your perceptions to the physical. If you feel light-headed upon return, make sure to ground yourself.

Through your intent and this exercise, you will, hopefully, connect to your totem. Success comes at many levels. Those with shamanic experience or good visualization skills can have vivid breathtaking experiences. Others get a glimpse of the totem, or "hear" its name in their minds. Once ending the meditation, you may have psychically seen nothing, but the next animal you encounter may be the totem you asked to meet. You will know. At the core of magick is intuition and instinct. You could even have a strange event or a problem with an animal immediately after your meditation, to tell you, without a doubt, it is your power animal. Please listen to such messages, because nothing is coincidence.

Repeat this exercise many times, working with a single guide, until a new one shows its head. If you have not experienced some form of journey with your totem, hold off on exploring other shamanic exercises in this book until you do. As you continue your adventures

with your totem, it acts as guide and protector on your journey, possibly the first of many such spirit helpers to come your way.

◎ SUMMONING AND BANISHING SPIRITS ◎

Totem animals and spirit guides have a distinct role to play in our magical development. Many feel they are cosmically "assigned" to us, or have some past-life association with us. These entities have a special bond and vested interest in our higher good. As such, practitioners often feel their presence even when not doing magical work. They are guardians and counselors, often that little voice we so often ignore, pointing us toward our best potential.

Other spirits can be as helpful and useful, but do not have such an immediate, intimate link with us, unless we develop it over time. Often, chance encounters lead to such relationships and pacts. Sometimes, you may be required to aid the spirit in some physical way. Most shamanic traditions talk about making bargains with higher beings for shamanic power and protection. If this smacks of the old myths of European witches signing pacts with the devil, such tales are simply corruptions of the European shamanic practices performed by wise women and cunning men.

These spirits need to be summoned or invoked to be empowered to work with you. You need to seek them out through journey work, or invite them into your space. When you are done your work, they need to be released, allowed to continue on their own journey. For unhelpful spirits, it is necessary to banish them from your space.

Your first option for obtaining the services of such spirits is to embark on a journey similar to your totem animal journey. In fact, ask your totem to lead you to the most appropriate being. Your second option is to bring the spirit to you. Cast a magick circle for protection, as described at the end of chapter 2. While in the circle, declare your intent. Ask the spirit you want to contact to join you in the circle. I usually add "for the highest good, harming none." There, you can meditate and open yourself to the information or experiences this being has for you. Knowing the name of the being or its area of expertise is helpful. When you are done, thank the being and release it from the circle.

On rare occasions, you may run into an unhelpful spirit, one who makes mischief or leaves a disruptive energy in your home. Sometimes you have summoned it, and other times it shows up without any act on your part. Telling the spirit to leave is the first step, not taking it seriously. Most spirits of this nature like to play games and want to feel important. They soon tire of you and leave. Other forms of banishment include using substances that raise the vibration level of a space. Incense like sage, lavender, cinnamon, copal, and a combination of frankincense and myrrh are tried and true. You can also use salt and water or rose water to clear a space. It is a good idea to use these occasionally in your ritual space and before most major rituals.

Another effective technique that doesn't rely on external tools is a variation of the Golden Dawn's Lesser Banishing Ritual of the Pentagram. Many versions are used by ritual magicians all over the world. This example does not use the Hebrew prayer and names of god, but is very simple and effective for clearing a space and protecting you. The pentagram, the five-pointed star, is a strong symbol of protection (see figure 2, page 61). It is a symbol of incarnation, of opening the spiritual doorways and invoking something, or closing the doorway and banishing an unwanted presence. This exercise focuses on the banishment aspect.

EXERCISE 8 – BANISHING

❶ Start Exercise 1, getting in touch with your inner strength (see page 17).

❷ Face the direction in which you feel the presence or unwanted spirit. If you are unable to sense a direction, face north or east.

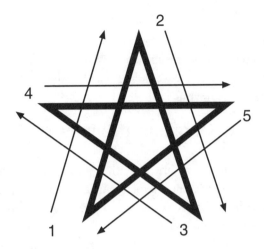

Figure 2. Banishing pentagram. Draw the pentagram starting in the lower left corner, then complete the star pattern.

❸ Draw a pentagram, a five-pointed star, starting in the bottom left-hand corner as you face it, and move up to the top point. Complete the star and visualize it with glowing fire, usually white, gold, or blue. Feel its energy project outward in the direction you are facing and cleanse that area.

❹ Turn clockwise and repeat step 3.

❺ Turn clockwise again and repeat step 3.

❻ Turn clockwise again and repeat step 3. At this point, you have made a pentagram in all four directions. Continue the process by drawing one on the ceiling and another on the floor.

❼ Say forcefully, "I banish all energy that is not correct and for the highest good." Feel it as you say it, and know your entity has either been transformed or fled because of the change in vibration.

This is a good exercise to do whenever setting up residence in a new home, or when traveling and staying in an unfamiliar room. It cleanses the room of unwanted psychic pests and keeps harmful past psychic imprints from affecting you.

◎ MECHANICAL SPIRITS ◎

Scavenger animal spirits are not the only ones to be found. Everything has a subtle energy force animating it. Everything has a form of spirit. Some believe only the living, organic life-forms have spirit and power. Animals and plants are some of the strongest spirit energies with which humans can work, because we have a similar life force, growth patterns, and cell structure. Some concede these to mineral life as well, the natural crystals grown in the living Earth. Natural crystals are powerful, but do crystals grown in a laboratory have less spirit? Do test-tube babies have less of a soul than a naturally conceived child? I do not think so. I view the entire planet as an experiment, a laboratory of diversity engineered by the higher powers. Regardless of the method of creation, the great creator spirit works through all acts of creation and imbues them with spirit energy. We are creators too, and we give our creations the same powers. My experience has shown me that all things have this subtle energy, including man-made devices. Strong mechanical spirits live in the city, taking the form of trains, subways, cars, planes, and streetlights. Go to them, if you are drawn, or let them come to you, like any other spirit.

Your astral allies and spirit helpers may not even come from the organic world. They may be drawn from the piles of steel and chrome. If that is the case, by all means go with it. Working with mechanical spirits is an exciting frontier in modern magick. Accepting mechanical spirit work is difficult for most traditional mages. The idea of personifying a car seems almost blasphemous to the devout nature magician. In the end, however, is it different from personifying a tree, rock, mountain, river, or rainstorm? The personality traits of all spirits and energies, be they guides, animal totems, goddesses, or other "nature spirits," are simply vehicles for communication. All spirits are beyond our simple linear understanding. To communicate with us, they must use techniques we can understand. In essence, we are "downloading" information and wisdom from the spiritual realm. The form the spirit wears is an interface we use, like a computer program. It doesn't matter what the interface is, as long as we get the information. People who are comfortable using IBM computers use them. More intuitive people may prefer Apple computers. Both do the same thing, but if you are not comfortable with one, you will not get the information easily. Some magical seekers prefer traditional techniques and paradigms. Others fail to resonate with them, since they are not living in an ancient culture. Modern viewpoints, like mechanical spirits, give modern practitioners a chance to find what interface is comfortable for them.

You can do variations of the previous two exercises to connect with a mechanical spirit. Here are some potential mechanical spirits manifesting physically in most cities.

Subways

Subways are great electric serpents running through the city. They are akin to underworld gods, like the great king worm burrowing under us. They already work with us, taking us to destinations all over the city, but their subtle power is not often recognized. On subway cars, I often feel my psychic perceptions elevated. I am not sure if it's the electrical energy from the third rail, or the close proximity of people inside my energy field, my aura. I only know that I become more open to receive information. Perhaps I am more defensive and open all my senses. Chakras on other people appear, and I can sometimes see if there is sickness in the body, indicated by abnormally dark or light spots of energy on the body. Strong images may appear near or above the heads–little aura movies, as I call them. Random thoughts come my way, and I am sure they are not mine. I try not to focus on anything in particular, not to invade anyone's privacy, but I remain open to any information that may warn me of harm. Spirit guides also talk to me a lot in a subway car. I am not certain if it is because I have some quiet free time, or because of the nature of the transit system. I am certain most homeless people wandering, particularly in the subway stations, are having actual conversations with spirits and not muttering to themselves, as most people think. Look closely with your second sight and perhaps you will see or feel their conversational partner.

Train

Similar in spirit, but larger, is the train. The train is bigger and more comfortable for travel, but often lacks the underworld associations of the subway car. The passage of a train in your area, usually marked by some substantial noise, is a great timekeeper for ritual and daily living. Trains run almost like clockwork, and they can set our schedules, both mundane and mystical. I think the train spirit's future lies in the super-speed "bullet" trains, like the Japanese Shinkansen and experimental magnetic trains. These train spirits will work with even more powerful natural forces. Magnetic technology will play a great role in all areas of life, including health. I wonder if future civilizations will think of the train tracks as a mystery, marking power spots, as we see ancient monuments and standing stones today. I must admit to rarely traveling by train, so I have little in the way of practical experience working with its spirit energy.

Automobiles

Cars are a dual-edged sword. On one side, they bring us freedom to go wherever we want, whenever we want, and to be in control the entire time. Car spirit is freedom and independence. They are the steel-age chariots for knights in shining armor, now that horses are no longer appropriate. From another viewpoint, however, they are the demons of industry, filled with fire, brimstone, and the internal combustion engine. They devour some of our natural resources and poison the rest with their noxious chemicals. A city filled with them is a difficult place to breathe, and breath is life. Are we trading our life force for our freedom and independence? Judge for yourself when working with the automotive spirits. I have found healing magick, crystals, and Reiki work well on machines, and on cars in particular. If your car has trouble starting in the morning, do not simply visualize it working. Help heal the car spirit. It may tell you what's going wrong and give you insight into its care and maintenance for the future.

Airplanes

A discussion of trains and automobiles would not be complete without mentioning planes. Airplanes fly overhead, like majestic metal creatures. Some are heralded by sonic booms, others by a dull roar. They may paint trails in the sky, unknowingly creating new symbols of power when crossing the clouds. Look for these symbolic markers. Write down their shape and meditate on the new symbol to discover its magical purposes. Their "nests" are usually located somewhere on the outskirts of the city, although they often fly overhead. They are clearly instruments of waste and pollution, but your first flight on one does have a magical quality. To fly through the air is an amazing feat, no matter how you do it. When an airplane's life is tragically cut short, however, it is a horrible spectacle. My father and I once saw a small plane crash and were able to help the surviving pilot, but the old bird, itself, was done. If you live near an airport, or travel frequently, you may have better opportunities to take advantage of airplane spirit.

Streetlights

Streetlights are silent sentries around the city. They see everything. They bring illumination to the darkness of the night. Unfortunately, as protectors, they can be rather impotent, since they cannot go far. Many, however, use their beacon for protection. Light spirits warn us of danger. Parking under a streetlight for safety has become a new folk remedy for protection against attackers. They are also good spirits to question, since they stay and watch all.

◎ Devas of the City and City Nature Spirits ◎

Recently, I have started working with the devic world, the universe's architects in the vast landscape of Earth. I guess I have always worked with them, but never acknowledged it. Devas are energies, or spirit forms, who create the patterns of reality on higher levels of existence. The word is originally from Hindu myth, meaning something akin to angel, but the New Age has adopted it to mean creators, or angels, of nature.

Nature spirits, sometimes identified with the faeries, plant life, and elementals, come in and fulfill the deva's patterns, making them a physical reality. Sometimes, the two terms are used synonymously, but nature spirits and devas are not the same. They work as partners and want to include us in the partnership.

The idea of "city nature spirits" may seem contradictory. Would a nature spirit not be in nature, in the wild? That very sentiment is the antithesis of the magick we are working here. The prevailing belief is that cities are unnatural, while the country is natural. You must break that existing belief structure to acknowledge that all is real, all is sacred, and, ultimately, all is natural.

Everything on Earth has a deva. All species, places, concepts, and organizations have a deva. There is a deva of strawberry fields, both the location, in England, and the Beatles' song. There is a deva of healing and of grasshoppers. General Electric has a deva helping the company, as do the Boston Red Sox and Greenpeace. One does not have to be all-natural, or doing only charitable, humane, or healing work. All things with structure and organization, which is pretty much everything, have some sort of devic spirit working with them. Anything created, naturally or by humans, has a deva. They move the right things into place. When you are not aware of these forces, some projects are more difficult, because you may be fighting against the natural structure the deva wants to use. Construction projects may take years longer than planned because of unseen delays. The city deva in that area is trying to tell you to do something different. Devas want to work with humans, as they do with nature spirits, in partnership, but most humans do not listen to them. I think if they did, our communities would be much more beautiful and harmonious. Cities would not be seen as evil or dirty. They would be in a stronger balance with the whole, and not based on the arbitrary judgments of power-hungry men in control. They would be based in a co-creative partnership with the land below and around them.

Some devas are called "overlighting," because they organize their peers into subcategories around them. The main deva of healing is the overlighting deva of healing, because it works with all the devas specializing in heart healing, brain healing, or muscle healing. Each deva works with the appropriate nature spirits to make the new patterns take hold in physical reality. Although never called overlighting, Pan, the Greek god, is considered a global nature spirit capable of guiding other nature energies to the right positions. Other gods have similar roles, like the Celtic and Sufi Green Man.

As I came to realize this, I gained a profound insight. All cities have a devic spirit in control of them. In many ways, this is the spirit of the city itself. The overlighting deva of the city organizes the other spirits. The deva of New York City works with the deva of the Empire State Building, the deva of the Statue of Liberty, the deva of Central Park, and the devas of the East and West Villages. I am sure there are some pretty fabulous divas in the village who would be disappointed to know they were not the "Deva" of the village.

Call upon these forces in ritual. They want to make contact with you. They want to work together. Doing magick on their territory is going to affect them. The energy you send out for your spells will be working through these city architects. They do more than guide the physical structure of the city. Meditate to make contact with them.

Call upon the city spirit if you are not comfortable with the more "New Agey" paradigm of devas and nature spirits, but do work with them directly, regardless of the label you give them or the form they take. Devas, nature spirits, faeries, or elementals are just labels for energies, to make the discussion easier. Call upon the spirits of your apartment building or house. Call on the spirit of the land around you, the neighborhood, your company, or your own intuition. These things all have their own energy, their own metabolism and life force. By living in them, they transfer attributes of their own life force to you, and vice versa. Apartments, homes, and neighborhoods take on the characteristics of the people who live there, and people often take on the characteristics of the neighborhood spirits. The exchange is symbiotic, but mostly unconscious. These spirit forms want to be in partnership with us. They want to be acknowledged by the mystics living with them. They are all waiting to be asked.

Do another variation of the totem exercise, asking to speak directly with these city spirits and devas around you. Request to feel and commune with the deva of your home, block, building, or city. Ask how you can enter into partnership with it, and how it can work in partnership with you.

◎ ELECTRIC GODS ◎

We have finally come to the gods of the hidden city, those with electric eyes and engine hearts–the electric, mechanical, and concrete gods of the city, never seen by the waking eye. Like so many other gods, they live in the shadows, working from a distance. While there may be one spirit overseeing the development of the city, a whole new pantheon of gods may be lurking in the cities of North America alone. Some may be gods from other times, taking on new guises for modern practitioners. Others may be renegade spirits growing in the power from our collective unconscious.

The images of these gods enter our dreams if they want to work with us. The gods of this new frontier are strange indeed, taking unusual forms. Often, they are not human or animal at all, but something else entirely. Some may be local deities, of a particular province, like tribal gods guiding one people, and others may be working in many places at once. They move beyond space and time. Their voices bleed through the cityscape's noise. By listening carefully, you may discover their secrets. The traffic sounds hide their messages from others. Record the noise and, when you play it back, you may hear the message, like a subliminal recording etched in the back of a heavy-metal record. Playing the tape backward may help. The voice of the godhead is hidden in the static of your television, when the last program ends and you have fallen asleep in front of it. The voice speaks to your dream self. Other messages are hidden in the whirls of machinery, in the tones of the Fax machine, and in on-line signals from an Internet phone connection.

If you ask to receive your messages in this way, you will. Let the new gods approach you first. Such sounds and recordings are great substitutes for the traditional shamanic drum. White noise can be very inspiring. Be open to the modern mythology, and you will see themes repeating. The archetypes have only chosen new clothes in these fashion-conscious times. Cuthulu draws upon the same forces as Tiamat. He is only more frightening to our modern minds because someone entering this age introduced the gruesome package. H. P. Lovecraft, the potential psychic turned horror writer, filtered the energies through the perspective of one who was fearfully uncertain of his abilities and of the forces coming to him while his society was rushing headlong into the maddening world we call the 20th century. Is it no wonder that his creatures are fearsome and his mythology grim, lacking in hope. We come from a framework similar to Lovecraft's, particularly when compared to the ancient Sumerians. The Cuthulu pantheon is scary to us because we believe it may be true. Tiamat seems a more distant deity from an ancient culture, and so has less relevance for us now.

Here are some potential new archetypes and classic images revis-
ited. Always let the image come to you in your meditations and
shamanic journeys. Do not judge it against your expectations. These
are some possibilities from my own experiences.

City Archetype

This archetype is the patron spirit of the city, the deva or vortex of
the city personified. Many cities still retain their ancient pagan
patrons. Venus, the goddess of love who rose from the foamy waters
of the ocean, is the patron of Venice, Italy. Venice is filled with water
pathways connecting the island buildings. Sicily is named for the
mother goddess Ceres and renowned for its home-cooked food and
family customs. Ceres is the goddess of the grain. Paris takes its name
from the mythic hero Paris, who was forced to choose between the
gifts of Aphrodite, Hera, and Athena. He chose Aphrodite and true
love. Paris is the city of lovers. New patrons for the cities in the new
world will reflect the character, customs, and terrain of the city.

Building Archetype

As each city or town may have a patron, so are there spirits within our
homes, apartments, and entire buildings. They manifest in the same
way as city spirits do, often holding allegiance to the city deity, as if a
minor player in the pantheon. You may find them to be particularly
powerful spiritual allies, especially the spirit of your home or office.
You experience and respect this spirit's power daily. The honor you
give it will be reflected back to you as ease and grace within your natural environment. These places will be places of power and comfort for
you, regardless of the circumstances. You must be sure to bid farewell
to these spirits in an appropriate parting ritual when moving away from
these places. Spirit energies need closure as much as people do.

Construction Archetype

This godform is busy at work in the modern world. I cannot take a drive without seeing cement mixers, cranes, and bulldozers. The spirit commanding the forces of progress–construction, in the modern mind–is hard at work. Although we may have enough buildings, homes, and offices, we are unsettled and seek more. Newer and bigger office buildings are constructed, even though there are two other buildings completely unused. We do not want what we have. We want more. I hope this archetype takes a backseat to the nature deities coming to reclaim their space and power. I am sure it will involve a struggle.

Transportation Archetype

This is not just one deity, but may be several, with one archetype for each form of transportation. There is a spirit for cars, trains, planes, and boats, each the overlord of its respective mechanical totem. Some gods held different animals sacred. These gods hold different mechanical creatures of transport sacred.

Music and Art Archetypes

The old gods wear new masks. No longer do we write Orphic poems about lands of the dead and lost loves, or motets of about mythic events. We follow similar themes, but have created movies and television. We listen to jazz, rock, country, and broadway. We tell stories, but in different styles and traditions, forging ahead, as any good artist would. The artistic gods–the gods of music, wine, theater, song, and changing form–are embodied in our rock-opera gods, our movie stars, and our aging pop icons. They embody the old gods and quite a few new ones as well. Who's to say that John Lennon or Miles Davis are not the spiritual patrons and saints for the few new rising stars of their genres, sequestered past the veil, in an eternal afterlife of good music? In many ways, after their passing, they both contain the mythic attributes of a saint or a god, as do Jim Morrison, Marilyn

Monroe, Kurt Cobain, Bette Davis, and Eva Peron. Who inspires you from the past? Think about the qualities they have and how they pertain to your life. Only you will know if they are worth seeking out as patrons and personal interfaces with higher wisdom.

Electricity Archetype

Thunder and lightning are always awe-inspiring. Ancient people credited them to storm gods like Thor and Zeus. These gods brought the needed rain, but their will struck out as lightning. No less impressive in modern times, lightning strikes less fear in those living in warm, dry, safe buildings. At most, we lose electricity, which can create problems for us. In some ways, our reverence for natural forces has been transferred to the powers we generate, like electricity. Unconsciously, we must be in awe of it, since it holds so much power for so many. Even though we harness it, we are still subservient to it in so many ways. The ancient gods of lightning may now be wrapped in copper wire and conductors, mastering the electrons running through our house.

Television Archetype

As different spirits animate and hold sacred other technological devices, the television god keeps us all linked through world news and reports. We can see things across the world, as in a crystal ball, only we have our choice of many pictures. Most fortune-tellers only give you one. This energy, however, and those working with it—broadcasters, network executives, and public-access talk-show hosts—control what we see. I am always wary of the manifestations of this form. They are like the psychopomp, the great trickster gods, tricking us into a new world through a tiny screen, making us think that we are there, that these people are real, and that their lives matter to us when they really do not. They are just entertainment. The trick is to remember that. The static of the defunct television channel or the sign-off signal noise can be a sacred hymn to these powers, and another substitute for the traditional shamanic drums and rattles.

Computer Archetype

The technology nets continue to grow around us. We have alluded to a spirit presence in wires, electrical lines, phone lines, and television waves. The Internet is the best example of a living presence in the world communication system. Many science fiction writers have already come up with AIs–artificial intelligences–getting loose on the Internet and trying to exterminate humans to make way for better computers. These plot lines are going to be very popular in the movies for the next few years.

I think silicon life-forms, beyond crystal and rock devas, will eventually be a reality. We had better make friends with our creations quickly, and hope that they do not do to us what we have done to our own mother, Earth. The great fear we have when we watch not-too-distant science fiction like *Blade Runner* is that the android will rise up and supplant the human.

Some spirits in the Web or on the Internet are akin to spider totems, weaving and walking the strands of information, decoding endless series of zeroes and ones. Like the spider, they are creative and intelligent, and may hold the center, the universal *axis mundi,* linking us together. We have to be careful not to get caught in the web, because computer archetypes, like spiders, can be carnivorous and may mercilessly suck you in. On-line and chat-room addictions may be the first step.

Medicine Archetype

The old gods of medicine were skilled in more natural forms of healing. Herbs and home remedies were used. Surely these god-forms either adapted to the changes in modern medicine or new archetypes arose to fit these needs. There are new beings who are patrons of aleopathy, of surgery, and of medical equipment. Hospitals are often named for patron saints, and perhaps those forms have adapted and adopted these potentially life-saving techniques, strangely mutating from their Christian originals into something more reminiscent of Voodoo or Santeria.

◎　◎　◎

A new age is dawning and the old gods are resurfacing. Some are taking on new identities and others are being born. Through our attitude to and perception of the world, we help shape the new mythology. Don't be surprised to see celebrities and other world figures, alive and deceased, creep into your personal cosmology. You may be conversing with Einstein in your meditation, as he explains to you the newest trends in quantum physics. Could he not be the modern archetype of Merlin in this age of technology, one who knows all? Through movies and musicals, Eva Peron has become a Black Madonna figure, revered as a saint by some and deplored as a monster by others, showing the duel role of the goddess energy in our culture. While teaching guided meditation classes, I found that someone saw Sonny and Cher as celestial father and mother figures. If you have read a lot of ancient mythology and expect to meet the gods of old, then you probably will. If not, they will come and find you, wearing whatever new faces the world has provided for them. Although it may be frightening to grasp the secrets of the shamanic mysteries, we can enter a time of partnership with these forces. Through shaping the mythology, we can shape the world.

Chapter 4
Meeting the Makers

REALITY IS MUTABLE. That is one of the basic facts of magick. Magick makers have this unique view of reality. This particular viewpoint is what makes them extraordinary in what others perceive as a mundane world. Shamans and witches see the world for what it really is–an illusion. The Hindu myths call the illusion the Maya. Breaking through the Maya to find oneness is the goal of the spiritual seeker. Other paths and traditions understand the many worlds and dimensions interacting with ours. By understanding the cosmology of reality, you understand where the different powers reside.

Many reality maps exist. You can use systems like the Norse World Tree, Yggdrasil, the Kabalah, the seven rays, or the twelve dimensions. They all work well if you resonate with them. Systems of mythology, runes, tarot, sounds, and colors relate to them, and are used as a system of correspondence in magick. The basic shamanistic concept of reality has a middle world in which we reside, an upper world, and a lower, or underworld. The World Tree, a cosmic axis, is the connecting force between them. Trees are traditional in European groups. Mountain and butte imagery is more familiar in the Native American and Australian aboriginal faiths–a stone reaching up to the sky and rooted deep within the earth. Or, if you live in a city, the three worlds are connected by the most obvious image of a skyscraper.

City Magick

The skyscraper is the perfect vehicle for connecting the realms (see figure 3, page 77). As a tall, multistoried building, the structure exists in the middle world. The main entrance is on the ground floor. You start any journey from the middle world. The tower itself reaches toward the sky, to the starry realms of the sky gods. The foundation of the building is deep in the earth, and connects the building to the city's tunnel and maintenance systems. Some see the construct as a world engine or world machine, keeping the universe moving in the right place and time. For our uses, I think the tower image, like the tarot card, reaching high to the heavens, is more conducive to shamanic work.

The image of the skyscraper is so evocative. Each has a steel skeleton, with beams and bars holding it together like a cross between the human skeleton and the exoskeleton of some giant insect. The structure is so powerful, practically defying the laws of gravity. In their own way skyscrapers can be as impressive as many ancient wonders. They have their own modern magick.

Even though American skyscrapers originated in Chicago, I cannot think of them without evoking images of the New York City skyline, where each building is taller and grander than the next. The Empire State Building, the Chrysler Building, and the twin towers of the World Trade Center immediately form in the movie of my mind. Now tall buildings exist all over the world. Each is unique, with different characteristics and quirks. The styles, from neogothic to the more modern, bring a certain response from us. Some may be scary, evoking primal feelings. Those are the best images for your shamanistic travels.

Through the skyscraper, you can travel to these other worlds by a shamanistic elevator, counting the floors you pass, as in a meditative countdown. This technique is used in hypnosis to regress someone into the past, or into past lives. Each floor represents a different time period. Some adventurous practitioners choose to climb the astral elevator cables through the shaft that runs up the building. Others journey in the stairwells, the dangerous caverns and tunnels

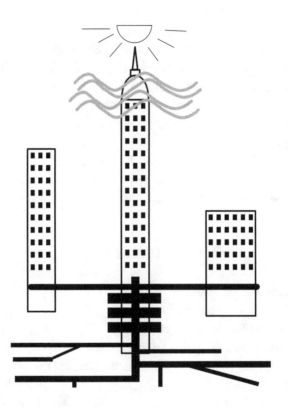

Figure 3. The Worldscraper.

connecting the levels. The traditionalist can try climbing the outside of the building, like climbing the branches of the World Tree. I see my favorite childhood superhero, the Marvel Comics character Spider-Man, as a shaman when I picture someone climbing up a building.

Imagine, in your own worldview, your own image of a skyscraper running through the three worlds. What would it look like? The Worldscraper may be shiny and new, glass and steel reflecting the dimensions upon itself like living liquid silver. The building may look archaic and abandoned, with broken windows and elevators that fail to go all the way to the top. This may be an aspect of your beliefs about the universe, your unconscious bleeding through into the images you see. One reality flows effortlessly through the others. Incorporate the image into your personal mythology and use it as your vehicle for dimensional travel. Then learn the three realms. It is here that you will find the city's power and helping spirits. Here reside the unseen makers and masters of the worlds upon worlds. Spirits, the etheric and astral worlds, form a template for the physical world. Its actions affect us as we affect them. Each one has power over different areas in our lives. As you travel on your power quests, your totem will often guide you.

◎ THE VISIBLE CITY ◎

- ◎ **WORLD:** Middle World
- ◎ **COLORS:** Gray, green, yellow, brown
- ◎ **ELEMENTS:** Earth, but all elements
- ◎ **TOTEMS:** Cat, dog, spider, and all household pets
- ◎ **ARCHETYPES:** Mortals, mythic heroes, physical man, nature spirits, elementals
- ◎ **POWERS:** Physical change, career, home, money, divination, physical healing, past, present, and future lives, time travel

The middle world is the world of the here and now. It is the visible city, the physical world. The things everybody else can see are a part of the visible city. You live in the middle world. You work in the middle world. Time goes forward there, and you are bound by the laws of space and physics. The territory of this world has been mapped well by the scientists and philosophers of the world. This land can be measured by the physical senses, at least up to a point. Once you start stretching your sights to the levels below the subatomic, you reach the boundaries between the worlds. When you look deeply into the entire spectrum of energy, you reach another boundary of this dimension. Science is discovering this even now, but there are lots of places to play in the middle world. Our perception of reality, as always, is the key.

All time is the realm of the visible city. All time has far-reaching implications. All diviners, whether looking to the future or watching the past, work with the ethers of the middle world. Our perception of time is linear. Part of our perception is biological, but it need not be completely linear if we choose not to look at it in that way. We generally look at events as beads on a string. In reality, we are all in a big bowl of loose beads. The string exists only in our perception. Everybody's string is different. Without the string, you can pick and choose any event in the bowl.

The physical world clouds our perception as well. There are many layers of it. Even within the bounds of the visible city, there is something hidden. Everything has a physical energy to it, but we can not always see it. Radio waves, electrons, and oxygen molecules all have a physical nature, but we do not see them with our physical eyes unless we amplify our senses with physical equipment, without which we can not see the more subtle aspects of physical reality. The same can be said for auras, chakras, and spirits. We can see such phenomena with our psychic eyes, amplifying our physical senses with psychic abilities. By opening our perceptions, we can see the invisible. By looking deeply, we can see the worlds within worlds and feel the unseen energy coursing around us.

EXERCISE 9 – SIDEWALKING

Take a middle-world journey in the visible city. This is a walking meditation. Yes, that's right. Disregard incense, candles, tools, or anything else. It is just you and your favorite boots, or whatever you use to decorate your feet. Pick something comfortable. Start your experience walking down the streets where you live. You may be walking on the sidewalks, but, by the end, you will be walking between the sides of reality, or walking between worlds.

We have all taken walks to think about our lives. The walk clears our heads, a great prescription for the troubled mind. Here we are free from distractions, can find solutions, and come to decisions. Perhaps such journeys make us feel better by distracting us from the problems we have. This journey is a little different. Instead of thinking, or marching mindlessly, you are going to walk mindfully. You are going to peel the layers of the middle world, just to see what is beneath.

Begin your journey with a prayer to your gods and guardians to watch over you. You are not going to be doing anything dangerous, but you will be out in the city, and you never know what is lurking. Always be careful in the jungle. Reaffirm your protective shield in your mind, or perform the shield meditation (see Exercise 4, page 27).

Call upon your totem to build a strong relationship with it. Ask for the totem's guidance. You feel or see it psychically on your walk, going before you, or alongside you. If you have difficulty perceiving it, don't worry. As long as you ask it to be there, your totem will be present.

Before starting, pick a general path or direction—a destination and a general way to get there. You do not need to know specifics. It can be on streets with which you are intimately familiar, or on more unknown streets. Just make sure not to get lost. Keep a map in your back pocket if you feel the need. Preparation is a sign of a good sorcerer, but so is trust, so, first, follow your instincts, and carry cab fare. Then start your journey.

You can alter your appearance by dressing differently than you normally would. Wear your magical street garb—a special jacket, coat, or shirt. These garments can become your magical armor, your own ritual robes. Magicians wear robes to put themselves in a magical mind set, reserving special clothes for magical adventures. Such special sidewalking clothes can serve the same purpose. Wear them only when out walking like this. Soon, you will notice your perceptions wake up on all your walks.

As silly as it seems, entering a magical state is like playing pretend. Children enter these magical states all the time. Do you really think there is no one there when so many children talk to imaginary friends? I know that someone is talking back to most of them. You can play pretend even more by changing your energy appearance, much like an actor taking on a new role or guise. By pretending, you take on elements and images that are not physical, but that change your self-perception and other people's perception of you. Such etheric masks are called glamours in Celtic traditions. They are usually used by the fairy folk to make the unattractive seem beautiful. Create a glamour to suit this new adventure and adopt it mentally. Imagine yourself in the role, and your energy will conform to your intent, as an actor does. You may start out feeling foolish, but as the journey progresses let go of your self-consciousness and really get into the new role.

Be mindful of your environment, and put yourself in a light trance state to make everything more interesting. Open up your psychic senses. Visualize your third eye opening up, letting you see the worlds between worlds, while still fully conscious and open in the physical world. You will see people and places in ways you have never imagined, but you will stay focused in the physical, not delving too deeply in the trance work. You will not have a shamanic journey, and will still be able to see cars and other pedestrians. You will, however, be seeing the things that cross into the middle world, now into your own personal visible city.

As you walk around, your psychic senses may make you more mindful of other people's thoughts and intentions. By looking at them, you may get "good" or "bad" vibes from them, perhaps more strongly than ever. My empathy gets stronger in the city, especially in subways. You can see auras, and know if someone is happy, sad, healthy, or sick. As you walk, you won't be able to look at any one person for long, so keep going and look at many different people. Some will be closed off and others will remain quite open. Take a break from your journey, sit down somewhere discreet, and people-watch. Let the world pass you, as you soak it up with magical eyes.

Buildings will speak out to you. Each home has a spirit. By walking by or touching something, you can activate your psychometric powers. You can "read" the past, present, or future of an object. Touch is not always necessary to get this information, but it often helps. By walking by an object, you breathe its energy. You read the vibrations of the objects around you. City gods are speaking through the statues and sculptures. Be prepared for anything.

Go to various shops and look around, remembering that nothing is as it seems. Everything has a hidden story. Get a feel for each place you go. Make it a quest. You have to retrieve something from each place. Find simple tools to use in later ceremonies, like matches from a bar to light your candles, a magazine with the picture of whatever you desire to use in a ritual, and some good bread from a bakery to leave on your altar as an offering to your gods. Make it a small-scale adventure.

Look up at times, into the sky and between buildings. Look for the lines of power that cover the earth. These Earth grid lines, ley lines, or dragon lines (which may or may not all denote the same thing) flow in and around the cities. The vortex upon which the city is built is probably connecting to a lot of energy lines. You can feel them in your hands as you walk, or in your gut or solar plexus if you pass through them. Energy lines feel warm, tingly, hot, or cold. As you do several of these sidewalking trips, see if you can start to map out the lines of power. Mark them on a special magical map of your city. Mark special places that feel particularly powerful to you magically. These places make you feel good. Also, note places that lack power or feel malevolent to you. You will want to avoid these energies in ritual. This magical map will come in handy for later spell work.

Most energy lines go right through buildings, while other lines are disrupted by the concrete and steel. In some cases, steel beams can act as lightning rods for magical energy, grounding it into the earth. The city street grid may flow with some of the natural lines, since old roads often follow natural paths of power. Later, these paths are paved over, becoming the random lines in what is otherwise an ordered grid. Physical power lines from electric and telephone companies also disrupt the grid. They have their own brand of not-so-subtle power, making a second grid across the city. I think energy-line disruption is one of the reasons why cities have grown unhealthy for many, when they could have turned out differently. The next time you charge your protective shield, ask it specifically to protect you from electromagnetic and energy pollution. This harmful energy comes from power lines, television screens, computers, and most other electrical devices.

Besides energy lines and power centers, other hot spots include haunted areas and time loops. In some areas, you may feel a presence, especially if there is a strong historic element to a tragedy or death. If the public continues to visit, it can be difficult for the spirits to move on. Boston has a lot of historic spots connected to the Revolutionary War. Their energy is still highly charged. Ellis Island is another such place. You may have an eerie feeling, or get chills up and down your spine, when visiting such places. My father, who is not particularly psychic, feels this presence on Ellis Island and the Arizona Memorial in Pearl Harbor. Astral sight reveals the spirits of those who have walked Earth, or other beings not in a human shape. Some hauntings are not even occupied by independent spirits. They are like time loops, in which an event was so strong that it was recorded into the energy patterns of the area. Every so often, like a bad record, the event gets played again. Visions of ghosts walking down the same stairs, again and again, and making no other contact, are an example of this. Ghost battles at historic sights, where people can swear they hear cannons or catch glimpses of that long-ago battle are another example.

Animal totems besides your own can appear to you in the physical or astral realm, with other messages and warnings. Certain messages or signs jump out at you as important. They may come in the form of street signs and billboards, where some words stick out as more important than the others. Take note of all significant events. Use you intuitive skills.

Spirit guides, or the guides and higher selves of other people out walking with you get your attention when you are in this state. When you are in a trance, even a light walking trance, you are "open" to these things and must be careful. Confirm that the influence is for your highest good before heeding these voices. If you do not feel love emanating from these beings as they give you a message, be careful. Remember that the difference between schizophrenia and shamanism is control. If you are uncomfortable, bring yourself to normal consciousness. If you have a hard time doing that, get something to eat. This will ground you, snapping you out of the altered state. Get a chocolate bar, a cup of coffee or tea, or a soft drink. Believe it or not, caffeine is grounding. It brings you back to the body, even if it leaves you a little strung-out.

If you reached your destination with no problem, you may be up for walking back the same way, retracing your steps, or walking back a new way. Or you may want to call it quits for the night and take a cab or bus home. If you are tired, you can walk back anyway, but return from your meditative state. Once you get home, sit quietly and think about your experience. Write it down in a magical journal. How did this open your perceptions? You may have to do this several times before you get over the feeling of being foolish or entering your normal walking mode, particularly if you already do a lot of walking in the city.

◎ The Sky City ◎

- ◎ **World:** Upper World
- ◎ **Colors:** White, blue, gold, orange
- ◎ **Elements:** Air and fire
- ◎ **Totems:** Pigeon, duck, seagull, and all other birds
- ◎ **Archetypes:** Divine father, sky kings and queens, celestial beings, angels, ascended masters, aliens
- ◎ **Powers:** Mind, clarity, perception, memory, weather, knowledge, direct communication, direct information, channeling, higher self, spirituality, enlightenment, power

The sky city is the home of the gods, the upper world in the shamanic traditions. This is the celestial realm, a fabled city of gold where nothing goes wrong and everything is in harmony. The sky heroes and masters live here, drinking the ambrosia of immortality and enlightenment, which I imagine looks like drinking liquid light from crystal goblets. Their very presence is illuminating. It is hard to believe that this world of light and love so far above the waking city exists. This is the mythic heaven, or one version of it.

Some shamanic traditions have abandoned the celestial city in favor of the denser, earthy underworld. They find the sky gods too remote and impersonal, uncaring about the everyday needs of the people. Darker gods know better how to feed your hungers. I think the sky city helps feed the extraordinary hungers, not the commonplace ones. Perhaps humanity stopped reaching for the sky at one point, for the higher ideals, but we are starting to reach up again. The upper world is the realm of the spiritual seeker contemplating the eternal question of existence, the nature of the universe and one's role in it. These answers can be found in any or all of the three worlds, depending on what you seek. Those who need to understand, not just know or feel, the answers seek the upper world. These practitioners seek enlightenment, not just a simple remedy to their problems. The airy realm is the domain of the mind, as well as of the spiritual fires. With modern culture's new fascination for winged cherubs, guardian angels, and alien saviors, we are reaching yet again to the realm of the sky gods. Hopefully, we will ask the right questions and get the answers we seek.

To get to this sky city, you must fly. The Worldscraper pokes its head through the cloud barrier that veils the upper realm from our view. Even on a clear day, the astral clouds form a protective shield between the realms. There are many ways to master the air. In your meditative journey, as you climb the tower, you must reach the roof. Once there, you can see and feel the shining city. You may have a totem capable of carrying you. Even if you have a winged totem, like a bird, how can it carry a person? You are not bound by the rules of physics on this journey. On the spiritual journey, thought and intention are the laws of reality. Will yourself to be smaller and carried easily, or will your spirit totem to be bigger and able to carry you. Merge with your totem, as it carries only your essence. Winged totems and all kinds of sky creatures—birds, planes, clouds, and shooting stars—are messengers from the celestial realm.

If you do not have a winged totem, there are other means available, again through thought and intention. You can fly, float, or cloud-jump. Magical ladders or ropes can materialize to assist you. The means is not important, but the journey is. Anything you can imagine, you can do on the shamanic journey. Think about how you will fly or climb to the sky city.

EXERCISE 10 – TRAVEL TO THE SKY CITY

❶ Prepare your ritual space. If you choose to use a sound accompaniment, prepare your material. Dim the light. Light candles and incense if you like. Get comfortable.

❷ Start with the intention to travel to the sky city. Think about the qualities of that city. If you have a specific reason to journey there, such as to find higher guidance, think about your reasons. If you don't, this can be an introductory journey to acquaint you with a new magical realm. Even if you have been to other upper-world realms in other traditions, working in an urban environment and intention can yield different results.

❸ Repeat Exercise 3, the chakra meditation (see page 25), and start it with the simple meditation technique found in Exercise 1 (see page 17). Visualize each chakra as a floor in a cosmic skyscraper. The elevator shaft carrying this energy is your spine. Continue on to Exercise 4 and affirm your protective shield (see page 27).

❹ Before you, visualize the Worldscraper, a building of immense power connecting the hidden world to the sky city and to the visible city in which you live. It towers above any building you have ever seen, cutting through to the hearts of the three realms. You stand before the entrance. Reaffirm your intention and ask your animal spirit to guide you. Then step inside.

❺ Wander around this first-floor lobby. Search for your path to the top floors. Let your guide lead the way. The terrain may be completely different from a typical office building. You may be in a swamp, forest, or desert. They may be mixed with the terrain of the office, as if nature had reclaimed part of the building. Imagine a lobby filled with water, plants and reeds, trees, soil, or sand. Will you take a path through the elevator, or up the stairs? Are there other options for you? Explore and climb upward.

❻ You reach the top floor, possibly an observation deck of some sort. Looking down at the street below, everything looks completely different. Colors and shapes are strange. The light above you is blinding, coming through the cloud covering of the sky cities. You must determine how you will cross this airy abyss to the next world. Can your totem fly and will it carry you? Can you fly? Does a rope greet you? Or perhaps a god of the upper world lends a helping hand. You are so close, yet a bit too far away. Use your ingenuity to get there. Everyone has his or her own personal solution to this riddle.

❼ Once in the land of the sky city, explore. Is it a city at all? The images may be traditional, heavenly, or futuristic—a technological wonder built above the old world of the visible city, as in so many science fiction movies. Seek out the powers you want to contact. They may be in the form of gods, angels, aliens, or other beings who have the information or power you seek. Things in the upper world tend to be much more direct and straightforward. There are few games or riddles. If you are worthy, you will receive knowledge or be pointed in the right direction for the next stop in your quest. Thank any beings who help you.

❽ When you feel the experience is complete, return to the World-scraper and climb down to the lobby. You can retrace your steps, or follow an entirely new path. Exit the building and bid farewell to your guide. Let the image of the building fade from your mind's eye.

❾ Reaffirm your protective shield, using light to clear and release any unwanted energies that may have crossed back into this realm with you. Make your shield burn bright, vaporizing and transmuting any harmful energies or thoughtforms. Use whatever color is for purification and transmutation, as described in Exercise 2 (see page 20). If in doubt, violet is a good transmuting color to use in your shield at this time. Ground and balance yourself after the experience, and write down any insights you gained from the adventure.

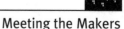
My own experiences in the sky city have been mixed with past expectations. Coming from a Celtic witchcraft background, this realm started to look more like the rolling fields of milk and honey, a paradise realm, when I first journeyed there. As I continued on my path, influenced by the urban culture around me, the sky kingdom morphed into something akin to the ancient city-states imagined in places like mythic Atlantis. The artistry and technology was almost magical, with flying chariots, floating lights, magical fountains, healing temples, and power supplied from magnificent crystal pyramids. All of the instant comforts of the 20th century, without the overpopulation, pollution, crime, and disease, were contained in the heavenly kingdom. Later, my images depicted a more futuristic Utopian society, not relying on the past, but on a mythic future, in which disease and social inequalities were conquered and everyone loved truly and deeply. People flew as easily as walking, tapping their natural psychic abilities as part and parcel of this new enlightenment. The sky city was the bright shining city of Utopia, where living beings reached a balance with nature and incorporated nature's designs into the landscape.

Your first experience in the sky city may be very different. What do you envision as a modern heavenly realm? What is the new mask of heaven? Many people anticipate that space brothers and sisters will carry them off in the final hour, whisking them away to another planetary heaven. And that is just as likely as pearly gates and saints greeting you at the door. All of these images are simply interfaces to something indescribable. Which mask works for you? No matter what you think about now, your actual experience may be quite different than your expectations.

◎ THE HIDDEN CITY ◎

- ◎ **WORLD:** Lower World
- ◎ **COLORS:** Black, red
- ◎ **ELEMENTS:** Earth and water

City Magick

- ◎ **TOTEMS:** Rat, cockroach, ant, and all burrowing creatures
- ◎ **ARCHETYPES:** Earth Mother, dark gods and goddesses, deceased spirits, guides
- ◎ **POWERS:** Transformation, rebirth, symbolic knowledge, life guidance, initiations, emotional healing and balance, knowledge of family or clan, prosperity, power

The hidden city is the vast underworld found in every mythology. The world's myths range from picturesque landscapes and happy hunting grounds to realms of hellish fire and brimstone. Even though I was raised as a Catholic, my personal images of the underworld are more of a primal forest lit by an unseen luminous underground Sun. Aztec mythology tells us that the underworld Sun is made of iron. When working in the city vortex, the underworld becomes the catacombs beneath the city. The tunnels are really sewers and subway systems. The caverns are hidden rooms and bomb shelters. There is a whole world beneath the city, both physically and spiritually. We barely dream of it, but it exists.

The underground realm is the home of the dead landlords, the kings and queens of passed spirits, like Hades and Persephone of Greek myth. The dark king and queen come in many forms. Their subjects consist not only of spirits of deceased humans who, from the waking of Earth, have made this unusual pit stop before relinquishing themselves to the great hereafter, but all manner of spirits and totems that may never have had a physical body. Since the hidden city is a realm of emotional healing and guidance, many spirit guides make their home there, communicating with their charges though underworld dreams and symbols, hopefully giving the guidance needed. We often cross the barrier and travel to the underworld as we sleep. Some of our more lucid dreams occur here, wrapped in our own subconscious symbolism.

When making direct, conscious contact with the hidden subterranean city, we experience trials, initiations, and rebirths. The death and rebirth journeys are common among shamans undergoing a shamanic sickness to awaken them. Usually, the journey occurs during fevered dreams or seizures. As they are being reborn in the underworld, a new element, a new bone, stone, or crystal, is added to them, marking this change and new power. City shamans may get a microchip implanted or computer-program-like wisdom downloaded directly into their nervous system.

All underworld journeys need not be so traumatic. You can go there anytime, visiting the dark tunnels for rejuvenation. You can seek out knowledge from relatives who have passed to the other side. Many find an underground spring flowing water through a tunnel, or special edible mold or mushrooms growing on a wall. By partaking of these spiritual sacraments on your vision quest, you transform yourself on all levels.

EXERCISE 11 – TRAVEL TO THE HIDDEN CITY

❶ Prepare your ritual space. If you choose to use a sound accompaniment, prepare your material. Dim the light. Light candles and incense if you like. Get comfortable.

❷ Start with the intention to travel to the hidden city. Think about its qualities. If you have a specific reason to journey there, such as healing, knowledge, guidance, or power, think about your reasons. If not, this can be an introductory journey to acquaint you with a new magical realm. Even if you have been to other underworld realms in other traditions, working with an urban environment and intention can yield different results.

❸ Repeat Exercise 3, the chakra meditation (see page 25), and start it with the simple meditation technique found in Exercise 1 (see page 17). Visualize each chakra as a floor in a cosmic skyscraper.

The elevator shaft carrying this energy is your spine. Continue on
to Exercise 4 and affirm your protective shield (see page 27).

❹ Before you, visualize the Worldscraper, a building of immense
power connecting the sky city to the hidden world, and to the
visible city in which you live. It towers above any building you
have ever seen, cutting through to the hearts of the three realms.
You stand before the entrance. Reaffirm your intention and ask
your animal spirit to guide you. Then step inside.

❺ Wander around this first-floor lobby. Search for your path to the
lower levels. Let your guide lead the way. Will you take a path
through the elevator, or down the stairs? You can count the steps
or floors, leading to a deeper trance state. Are there other
options for you? Explore and climb downward.

❻ At the end of your descent, you reach the hidden city. The typical shamanic primordial forest is replaced by the concrete-jungle
darkness of underground tunnels and caverns made from stone
and concrete. You step into the concrete catacombs beneath the
building. They seem to stretch forever into the darkness, mapped
by water pipes and electrical cables. Your totem guide will lead
you to the main hall, from which many other tunnels and rooms
branch out. In this immense alley, you look around. What do you
see in the darkness? The pipes and wires guide you, if no totem
is available. Follow the trail that calls to you, for it is obviously
leading you somewhere you need to be.

❼ Explore your trail. In this adventure, you will meet spirits and
deities to help you with your intent, if you have one, or you may
simply acquire powers that allow you to introduce yourself to
potential allies. Stay on the paths that feel comfortable and good
for you.

❽ Once the journey is concluded, follow your trail back to the elevator or stairwell and return to the first floor or lobby of the

Worldscraper. Exit the building and bid farewell to your guide. Let the image of the building fade from your mind's eye.

 Reaffirm your protective shield, using light to clear and release any unwanted energies that may have crossed back into this realm with you. Make your shield burn bright, neutralizing and transmuting any harmful energies or thoughtforms. Again, violet is a good transmuting color. Ground and balance yourself after the experience, and write down any insights you gained from the adventure.

◎

The underground realm is frightening for most people. I know I was scared to enter it the first time. I have no love for enclosed spaces or of the dark. The image of the cityscape underworld can be as frightening as a primal forest, if not more so, since daylight never touches the underground. We associate the sewers below us with disease, dirtiness, and death. Life, in its own form, does thrive down there. We send all the problems we want to avoid down the drains, along with our waste, our garbage, and our dead goldfish and baby alligators. The sewers and tunnels are not places we visit, except when taking the subway or crawling down in the basement to look for things we have almost forgotten. The underground is an image of our unconscious in many ways, spiritually and literally.

Overcoming my fear was pivotal for navigating the paths of city magick. When I started to work with these images, I tried to change the underworld back into a primal forest, when it was really the concrete tunnels that I needed to address. I was working and living in the city, not the forest. I was living in the modern world and had to deal with what I had a hand in creating. I didn't like the images. They revolted me. And I felt ashamed for not being made of sterner stuff. On one of my first adventures in this realm, I met a being, a god, who showed me I had nothing to fear. Yes, it was dark and scary, and it's okay to feel scared, but as long as I stayed true to my path, there was nothing to fear. That was a tremendous revelation. No one ever told me it was okay to be afraid. Being told it was okay to feel fear actually stopped me from feeling it.

◎ Helping Spirits ◎

Helping spirits are the guides and guardians you find along your travels. Everybody has some form of spirit help in this world, like totems, but those who work in the magical worlds between worlds tend to have, or at least to be aware of, more helping spirits.

Helping spirits come in many forms—and form is the correct word. The form we perceive is not necessarily the shape of the spirit. These helpers can come in a form that is comfortable for you. They are energy and essence, not flesh and blood. Our concepts of form should not be applied to them. They are spirits, after all.

Helping spirits can be distinguished by their function. We have already identified some spirits. You have already met your totem. Totems embody natural animal wisdom from the spirit worlds. Sometimes, thinking is not the right path. Humanity is focused on the mind and brain. Sometimes, however, natural laws and instinctual wisdom are needed. Totems help us with those lessons. They are also great spirit helpers, often guiding us on our meditative journey.

Another spirit helper is our spirit guide. I believe everybody has at least one spirit guide, if not a whole spirit group working together. Acting on the suggestion of a friend, I started calling mine "the entourage" in fun. This friend has an entourage, too. I think many people do. These spirits have agreed to help you in this life as they can. Some are very distinct in function. I have one working with emotional and healing issues, while another is more analytical and full of knowledge. They work together, but approach things from different angles. Sometimes, it takes them awhile to reach a consensus when working together. My psychic flower-essence practitioner wishes my guides would reach a conclusion before talking to him. He often asks advice of his clients' guides before giving a new essence for emotional healing and balance. With me, his initial answers are often contradictory, until my guides work it out.

Other spirits are more diverse, working with a full range of concepts and characters. gods and goddesses from old mythology appear in journeys. New gods and goddesses of whom you have never heard before may appear, particularly gods of technology and modern living. Some will be in accord with the foundations of life, others will not. It is the same in all pantheons, and in the human race itself. We have discussed some of the possible archetypes. Other paradigms include angels, spiritual aliens, and ascended masters who were once human, but became something more than human when they reached the heavens. Some spirits may appear as demons or beasts, and others may have no real form. The last are probably closer to the form of the spirit world than any other. Because we perceive things in color, shape, form, and sound, the spirits comply, to aid us on our journey.

Those seeking favor from the unseen world enter into compacts with the spirits. An agreement is struck between the journeyer and spirit. The unseen ally will help you do something, if, in return, you do something for it. The task can be as simple as leaving them an offering on your altar. Or they may ask you to build an altar in their honor. Some ask for specific offerings of food or incense. The task is often spiritual in nature, helping them succeed in their own quest. I have been asked to give messages for those not psychically open to their own guides and gods, or to teach simple techniques to get them in touch.

Some seek to bind spirits for all time, making them servitors to the sorcerer. I think such a ploy is foolish. It can anger a spirit, even if you succeed in binding it as your familiar. There are many more spirits out there willing to help you for the highest good. Some minor constructs and servitor spirits can be created by the practitioner for a specific function through willpower and ceremony. This technique is the foundation of spell work. These semiconscious thoughtforms are quite useful as protector spirits. Why get a spirit that does not wish to help, when you can create a helpful temporary thought form? I think compacts and bindings are more trouble than they are worth. In my experience, if I need a specific spirit guide, teacher, or totem for a quest, the Great Spirit provides what I need. No force or coercion is needed.

Discernment is the key to working with new spirits. When asking for a guide, ask for one who is correct and for your highest good. Ask them three times if they come for your highest good, and wait for an affirmative response. Ask them for their names and to send you unconditional love at the same time. Follow your instincts. If a spirit feels harmful or dark, ignore it. Or better yet, laugh at it. Spirits hate to be mocked, while those of a lighter nature will laugh with you and send out love and joy. These are all factors to get a discernment reading. If you have a negative feeling toward a spirit, or feel it is being deceptive in any way, do not work with it. If other guides with whom you have traditionally and successfully worked do not cooperate with this guide, do not work with it. Wait until you can discern the true motives of the spirit. You may simply be unsure or not ready to work with that particular energy. Or it may be a spirit you should avoid. If so, use the banishment techniques found in Exercise 8 (see page 60). In either case, follow your inner wisdom. Let your intuition and your own body be your guides. If you have a bad feeling, honor it, but don't let it control you. Ignored spirits will leave in boredom. Or you can light a clearing incense like sage and use a banishing pentagram. Each of these will remove unwanted energies from your area.

◎ FURTHER SHAMANIC JOURNEYING ◎

These are simple introductions to the three worlds. From this point, explore on your own. Now you have your road map, or, more likely, your building plan, to move between the visible and invisible cities.

Hopefully, you have a native guide in your animal spirit. Your guide may come from a more mechanical kingdom as well.

If you use the elevator in your journeys, you can push any buttons to reach a different dimensional realm between the under and upper worlds. You are not limited to the descriptions given here. There are many more worlds for you to explore, and each comes with its own unique landscape. Sometimes, even though you desire to go to one realm, the elevator will take you to another, if it is for your highest good. You may feel pulled in another direction, regardless of your conscious mind's desire. I was often pulled down to the hidden city before I got the chance to fly into the sky realms.

Once you are familiar with the techniques, you can explore the dimensional frontiers to your heart's content and, through it, explore the nature of your partnership to the city.

Chapter 5
Urban Magick

THE SPIRITS AROUND US ARE ABUNDANTLY clear now. They are in everything, all around us. Totems are making themselves apparent. The new gods are showing their faces, and the old ones are wearing new clothes. The shaman's worlds come into view. The magician's secrets are revealed–partially. The practice of the witches is clearer now. Through ritual, they all gather the energies around them. They enter their ecstatic trances and deep meditations to infuse a desire into the ceremonial energy. They release the intention to do its work.

For the woodland witches, natural representatives from the four elements are probably near. The powers of the land and sky are with them, inspired by their setting. The green living land is beneath their feet. The clear sky covers them like a canopy. Ponds and streams are fairly common. Fire from the candle flame or bonfire guides many workings. These magick workers use the forces already present with them. They work in partnership with their setting. Urban spell casters may not relate as easily. The green land is not always beneath their feet. Instead, there is concrete, but other powers are at work. Their magical partners are all around the city. They need only to be recognized.

◎ The Elements ◎

So much importance is given to these four forms: earth, air, fire, and water. Some practitioners have difficulty understanding them. Everything is made out of a combination of the four elements. Alchemists told us so in their quest for gold. It sounds silly to the modern mind. I may have water in my body, but I certainly don't have soil or rocks there. My desk is made of wood. If it had fire in it, it would burn. Water would make it a bit soggy as a writing surface. Logically, it is only dry wood, nails, and some paint; and, logically, wood and paint are its physical makeup. This view fails to recognize that there are many realities co-existing. Nothing is what is appears to be.

The elements are not always physical forms, but sometimes concepts represented by these physical materials. Through these concepts, we have a greater understanding of how all things exist on many levels. Although everything is a combination of elements, not all combinations have all elements visible. I may not have rocks and soil in my body, but I have a physical representation of the earth element in my bones, and in the minerals and trace metals throughout my body.

Earth embodies the physical aspect of existence. Everything on this common playground we have co-created and called the third dimension is represented by earth. Earth is physical structure, affected by rules of space and time. The planet's surface, along with all soil, rock, crystals, minerals, and metals represents this simple, resilient physical structure. Earth is physical form.

Water is the first step away from the physical. Water is elusive and nebulous, flowing wherever there is room for it to move. Water has structure, but it is not as solid in its framework as earth. Water represents the emotions. All the elusive emotional aspects obviously have some sort of order and structure to them, but our responses to them can be unpredictable. Their structure is less stable and more intuitive. Logic from the earth gives sway to feeling, the realm of water.

Water is intimately connected to the astral. You can effectively argue that only human beings have an emotional component to their being, but everything with physical form has an astral component. The astral dimension is the energetic blueprint for the physical. It provides some of the framework for the physical body. Everything has some form of astral body. Living beings with some training or talent have more control over their astral forms, and can move freely along the astral plane, beyond space and time, leaving the perceptions of their physical bodies for a time. There are beings with an astral form who do not have or want a physical body.

Feelings often take form in the astral realms and then manifest in our physical form, particularly as disease. If you are upset about something and hold it in, the emotional energy creates tension in your astral body or somewhere around you. This tension manifests as a physical malady, depending on how strongly and how often you feel it. It may start as a headache or a weakening of your immune system, precipitating a cold, or eventually manifesting as a tumor or some other serious disease.

As in the physical world, air is above water, but the two are bonded, mixing and mingling in clouds and bubbles. Air is the realm of the mind. All thoughts move like currents of air. One moment they are here, then, like a breeze, they move on, to be replaced by another thought. Through thought, all form comes into being. The mental aspect brings the geometry of reality together. Understanding how things fit together can make them a reality. You need a concept before you can start a project. Reality consists of the thoughts of the divine mind, god, goddess, or however you may view a higher power. Thought manifests into reality, first creating a template in the astral realm, the realm of water. Thoughts often trigger emotions. As bonded as the two are, emotions can likewise travel upward and inspire new thoughts. After an astral form is created, the physical world can react, bringing it about in the realm of earth.

Farthest from the physical world is fire. Fire itself isn't even a physical representation of this concept. Fire is the transition state between matter and energy, which embodies this concept very well. Fire is the unseen energy animating all things. Fire is the life force, the will and spirit permeating all things on all levels. Fire is the passion and energy of creation, and of destruction. Reality starts as a spirit and the desire to change. From that energy, a thought is created on the mental level. The thought trickles down to the astral and emotional realms, taking form. The creation can then condense and manifest in the physical. Fire is the key to this chain of events. Without the connection and infusion of spirit and will, none of this occurs.

◎ THE ELEMENTS IN THE CITY ◎

The traditional elements are omnipresent, and have been with us since the start of life. We have recognized their physical representatives in the most basic of ways, hearkening back to earlier, simpler times. For those of us living in the hustle and bustle of the technological world, however, the elements are still ever-present. Their forms are hiding in the unfamiliar, but their power is with us all the time. Though the forest, jungles, and mountains are far away, the actual elements are all around us, always. You just need to know where to look for them. By recognizing this, you can reconnect with the elements and honor the sacred in all your life. The more we connect to the sacred, the more we will simplify our lives and create more balance with our world.

Earth now comes in the body of the city. Structure and form come from the buildings, the homes of people. Like the Neolithic cave dwellers, the element of earth, although redistributed, provides shelter from the outside world. It gives us homes, places to do our daily work, centers for storytelling, and areas for games. All these things are well-loved by the people, then and now. Our structures are a bit more specific than the all-purpose tribal caves, but each brings a fond memory. Remember the house where you grew up, the local theater where you saw your favorite movie or play, and the arena where you first went to a game or concert. They are not unliving structures, but places of happiness. Each has character. Love of the earth element comes to us now in the form of cut stone, brick, concrete, and steel. I'm not saying our structures shouldn't be built in harmony with the environment and use ecologically sound principles. They should, and I feel we are moving toward a partnership, rather than a war, with the environment. Older houses seem more in harmony, because they were more of an artistic endeavor rather than strictly a money-making proposition. Old houses tend to have more character, but once any house is occupied, it takes on a character. Spirit energy from the inhabitants animates it, interacting with the natural ambient energies of the structure. In many ways, it comes to life. It acquires its own personality. The spirit of your home is a great ally in magick work, much as the spirits of the forest and grove have traditionally been. It is only a small step from recognizing the spirit of your home to acknowledging the spirit of everyone's home, and, eventually, of the entire city.

A miracle of modern cities and towns is their ability to provide water wherever you are. Most civil districts are formed near a supply of fresh water, such as a lake or river, but technology can bring life-giving waters to those who would not normally have easy access to them. With running water and plumbing, towns can materialize in desert regions. The city is a network of waterways, connecting remote places. The water system links the wealthiest man in the financial district to the poorest family in the projects. Plumbing is a nice metaphor for life, both good and bad. We are all connected, even if we do not know it or recognize it. We are connected by water. We are connected by the common bonds of emotion and feeling. The two may never physically meet, but if the water supply is polluted or disconnected, it affects both the rich businessman and the poor family.

The presence of water can also be felt in the mist rising from the harbors of seacoast towns. Water vapor eventually collects to form rain clouds. The rain falls down upon everyone, city and country folk alike. Water is all around. I find the spirit of water in the glass buildings around us. Believe it or not, glass is a liquid. It is an incredibly slow-moving liquid, but a liquid nonetheless. Glass relates to the emotional aspect of water. Sometimes it is crystal clear, and other times, clouded. In the right light, glass is reflective, like a contemplative nature. It can be rounded and smoothed, easy to handle, or broken, jagged, and sharp, like an argument.

Air is the breath of life, and highly valued in a city potentially filled with pollutants like car exhaust. Air is another way in which we are all connected in the urban Mecca. We all breathe the same air, just as we all use the same water. Air is a very direct connection. A portion of the air you breathe out in a crowded subway train, I breathe in.

This element contains the very life-force energy in the material plane–prana, mana, or shakti. Whatever you choose to call this energy, we draw it in with each breath. Our energy bodies metabolize it as our physical bodies extract oxygen and release carbon dioxide. Cities have a different, and somewhat lower, level of prana than other places. The higher the prana, the easier it may be to feel healthy and make magick happen. City dwellers go to the country to recharge their psychic batteries, relax, unwind, and feel refreshed because they absorb more life force there.

Prana does exist abundantly in the city, if you know where to look. City prana is not as obvious as in other places. It flows in and out of the streets, but is often blocked by buildings and doorways. In an effort to improve the energy balance of our homes, Feng Shui is making a comeback. Feng Shui is an Asian art of placement for the interior and exterior of a dwelling, placing it in harmony with the beneficial forces. Feng Shui is a complicated art that goes beyond the scope of this book. If you would like to discover more about it, particularly in a more Western vein, I suggest *Earth Design: The Added Dimension,* by Jami Lyn (Earth Design Inc.), and *Gaiamancy,* by Maureen L. Belle (White Doe Productions).

We must learn to align our bodies to the beneficial forces and be more connected to pranic energy. Meditation to quiet the mind, the realm of air, is a start. Slowing yourself down allows you to see the patterns you are in, to relax, and to move toward balance. Breath-control exercises and meditation are very helpful. Much like Exercise 3 that runs energy up and down the chakras, pranic breathing exercises create a flow of energy with the intent of love and healing. Energy is drawn in through the top of the head and the bottom of the spine, joining the energy stream in the heart and spreading the energy out through the body. The effect, if not the technique, is akin to combining the Middle Pillar ritual mentioned previously, with the Circulation of the Body of Light exercise. Both are techniques practiced in ceremonial magick traditions. For easily accessible instructions on these rituals in their traditional forms, consult *Modern Magick*, by Donald Michael Kraig (Llewellyn).

E_XE_RCI_SE 12 – PRANIC BREATHING

❶ Start with the simple meditation technique of Exercise 1 (see page 17). If you like, continue on to Exercise 2 (see page 20), opening the chakras, and Exercise 3 (see page 25), spiritual protection. These are not mandatory for this exercise, but they are helpful. Once you feel the flow of energy from pranic breathing, you can easily reproduce the effect without being in a meditative state. You remain calm, but alert, and simultaneously connect to the life force of your environment. I have often practiced it while driving to work.

❷ Breathe deeply and pay attention to your breath. Pay attention to the sensations in your body as you breathe. Feel the rush of air down your windpipe. Feel your lungs expand and contract.

❸ Visualize the cord or tube running out from your spine, grounding you to the earth. As you inhale, imagine that this tube is a straw, sucking up pranic energy from the earth and the environment around you. As you inhale, you draw it up through the tube and into your spine. A physical sensation, warmth, or tingling usually accompanies it.

❹ Continue paying attention to this sensation. The deeper you breathe, the higher the prana will rise along your spine, through the chakras. Your goal is to reach the heart chakra with a full breath.

❺ Once you feel comfortable drawing prana from below, visualize the tube extending up from your crown, in alignment with your spine, and reaching up to the sky. With each breath, you draw prana from above. Again, the goal is to reach your heart with one full breath.

❻ Once you feel secure drawing prana from above, alternate the breath. First draw prana from below to your heart. In the next breath, draw prana from above. Repeat. Feel comfortable with both areas.

❼ Now draw prana simultaneously from above and below, making it join in your heart. It fills the heart chakra with life force. Do this for a few moments to get comfortable with both the sensations and the visualizations.

❽ Continue as above, but on exhalation, visualize the prana from your heart expanding to fill your body. You are saturating your cells and energy body, your auric field, with life force. Feel your temperature rise slightly, your body come to life, and your metabolism quicken. You are healing and cleansing your own body.

❾ When this process feels complete, simply stop paying attention to the sensations and images.

Your body may continue to breathe prana without your direction. This is good. A yoga teacher of mine said that the yogis told her, "a wise man breathes through his feet." This is a variation of that phenomenon.

Since pranic breathing is not an ingrained response, we usually need to jump-start it frequently, just as we correct other breathing patterns. If you notice your deep breathing in meditation, you know your normal breathing is pretty shallow. It gets deeper the more you meditate and breathe deeply, but, in times of stress, we go back to our ingrained behaviors. It is the same process when drawing in the fires of life.

Fire is the energy of life, and cities are busting with energy. Energy and excitement are all around, but the energy is literally surrounding the buildings and streets. Power lines, electrical wires, streetlamps, neon signs, and household lights bring the illumination of the day. Theirs is the light of inspiration and spirit, shining into the dark. Darkness is no longer binding. Light as bright as daylight is available at all hours. Readers, writers, and workers are no longer confined to the daystar's hours. As a trade-off, however, from these urban outlets, we can no longer see the stars of the night sky. They are obscured by our own earthly illumination. New cycles and seasons are found by those not bowing to the daylight god.

Wire is the new conductor, bringing volts of power to every structure. Electricity is power. From the lightning bolt to the electric blanket, the flow of electrons is most similar to the burning flame. In my own mind, I see this force as its own separate element. The power is so primal, it's amazing that we have ever learned to harness it. Like the wood fires of other places and times, electricity and gas are used to cook meals, heat homes, bring illumination, and dispel fear of the unknown. The representatives of fire are all around you in your home. Electric light fills your dwelling, reconnecting you to the source of your astral light, spirit itself. Please don't shy away from natural sunlight, however. Like firelight, electric light does not contain the full spectrum. I think it's healthy to walk in natural light each day.

◎ ALTARS AND SHRINES ◎

To prepare for your journey through the crossroads, the place to claim your power, you should set up a home base. Your base of operations is your altar, a place of power in your home, office, or other sanctum. Rituals are done at the altar. The more you use it, the more it grows as a base of power. Altars can be out in the open, set up permanently and in active use, or more discreet, hidden in your home. Your tools can be hidden casually among the knickknacks on your bookcase, mixing the magical and the mundane on the shelves. You can hide your altar in a closet, or have a special room only for your magical workings. Finding a room to dedicate to an altar can be difficult, however, for the space-conscious apartment renter.

The altar is not only a space to work your spells and meditations, but a temple to honor the powers who work with you. Traditional altars honor patron gods and goddesses, spirits, totem animals, spirits of deceased family members, and the four elements. If your working altar is not set up permanently, you can create small shrines to your powers discreetly in your home to honor them and to ask for help. Special shelves can be reserved for them. Make one corner of a room only for items honoring your totem. No one else needs to know your intentions, as long as your totem does.

Urban magick often necessitates change from tradition–from seeking out the divine in the city, to experimentation with new techniques, totems, and rituals. Necessity is the mother of invention, and urban altars, shrines, and offerings should reflect these creative changes. Don't follow an altar setup you read about in a book, including this one, unless you want to. Take the ideas and make them yours. There is no right or wrong to building an altar. There is nothing you can put on the altar that will be disrepectful if you do not use it with disrespect. As a modern practitioner, use the tools available to you in the city.

Traditional principles are revered because they work. They have to work, or they would not continue to be used. There are many mag-

ical traditions and cultures out there from which to draw. Many practitioners have success with them in the urban environment, because
that is all they desire to use. They may have had successful practices
and training before embracing the urban environment. These traditions are their anchor and safety zone in a somewhat hostile atmosphere. Traditions that focus less on the spirit manifesting through the
land and nature, and more on the actual practice and development of
magical techniques, thrive in urban environments. Magical societies
such as the Golden Dawn and lodge organizations such as the
Masons work well here.

Before we delve into experimentation and design, let's look at the
basics. While earning my degree in music, a wonderful composition
teacher of mine always told me, "You have to know the rules before
you break them. Once you know them, you can do anything you like."
Little did he dream his words would sing true about ritual magick.

Most altars have representations of the four elements (see figure
4, page 109). A chunk of concrete works nicely to represent the element of earth on an urban altar. Candles are a staple on most altars
as the element of fire. If you dislike candles, try electric lights. A
friend of mine from college lived in a dorm where no candles were
allowed. She used Christmas lights on her altar. They work quite
well. Around Yule, I have Christmas lights on my office altar. People
just thought I was being festive. Little did they know that it was a
shrine to the powers to keep the business afloat! Air is traditionally
represented by incense, but you may be tempted to use air freshen-
ers, oils, or other aromatherapy products. Be creative in your scent.
Many quest for the perfect chalice for the element of water. An
upscale urban practitioner may use a cut-crystal goblet, wine glass, or
brandy snifter. The bottles left over from these delectable spirits can
even be used as candleholders, if you choose (see figure 5, page 109).

Voodoo is an excellent example of urban magick. The basic tenets
of this faith come originally from Africa, but, as it has migrated across
the Caribbean and to America, it has changed, adapting from the

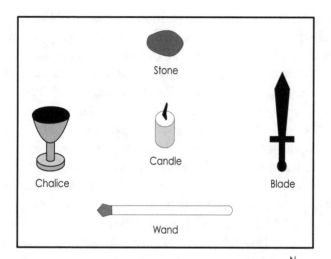

Figure 4. A traditional altar.

N

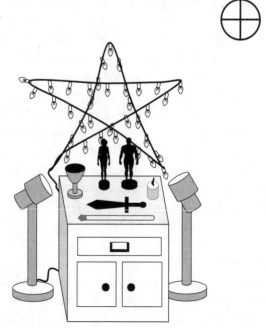

Figure 5. A modern altar.

culture of the mother continent to the streets of New Orleans. African deities are masked by Catholic saints. Magical tools are hidden as household items, much like the witches underground during the persecutions in Europe. Santeria, a spiritual sister to the practices of Voodoo, has a similar history. Voodoo practitioners' altars use all manner of modern magical items not available in their ancient African home, like votive candles and red brick dusts. These faiths are beautiful amalgams of the new and old worlds. In short, the tradition learned to adapt. Magick will always adapt to the current culture. City magick is one stage in that long process. For more information on Voodoo, particularly from the perspective of the city, *Urban Voodoo: A Beginner's Guide to Afro-Caribbean Magick*, by Jason S. Black and Christopher S. Hyatt (New Falcon), is an interesting resource.

Icons for your gods, goddesses, and totems should fit the character of the spirit with whom you are working. If you deal with a more mechanical god or subway totem, machine parts and tools are perfectly acceptable in this space. Cobble together your own statue with nuts and bolts, in honor of these powers. Use pictures cut out of magazines for icons. Frame them, create a collage, or create a cardboard stand for each, making two-dimensional statues.

A television makes an excellent surface for the modern practitioner. There is no better icon from the urban age than the magick of the TV (see figure 6, page 111). The workspace should be strategically placed somewhere in the room where you will have space to work. The altar surface provides a resting place for your tools and symbols. Entertainment centers can add shelf space to store your magical items. The static on the TV can be used as your ritual tones to enter gnosis, or videos and music can be added to your ritual. The TV's constant chatter can supply quick word association to clear your mind. Often, the steady rhythm of drums and rattles in traditional shamanism serve to distract the conscious mind, bringing it deeper. Other constant noises from the modern world can be used in the same way. Tune the TV to something about which you do not

Figure 6. A TV altar.

care or don't understand, like a foreign-language channel. The television background "chanting" is like a modern Tower of Babel, connecting us to the world both magically and visually.

I have found the TV to be a medium for magick traveling over a distance, much like a photograph or voodoo doll used in traditional magick. In some ways, the television screen can replace the crystal ball as a divining surface. On a mundane level, it brings such terrible information to us about the world. Although we need to be aware of these atrocities, they often convey a feeling of helplessness. News stations rarely report all the beautiful things people do. This feeling of powerlessness debilitates many. Many leading-edge health experts suggest a "news fast," in which the chronically sick or depressed abstain from newspapers or TV reports. When I see a tragedy, my immediate response is to help. Sometimes it is too late. Sometimes the most reasonable action is to get involved. At other times, my reasonable response is magick.

When sending healing energy to a war-torn area or disaster zone, I go right up to the TV and send my intent through the image to the actual people and place needing it. It can work with any spell. When you see a tragedy, send colored light for comfort through the screen to the grieving family, starving child, or accident zone.

These techniques can be applied to personal magick as well. When doing money magick, watch or tape the stock market report. Then send your intention for increased prosperity through the image. Send thoughts of peace, love, and acceptance of all when watching The 700 Club. It will not only help them, but will diminish your own prejudice against persecutors.

Others have used the television screen, both on and off, as a reflective surface for scrying, as they might use a crystal ball. Transform your TV from a tool of dis-information and hypnotism to a global healing device.

EXERCISE 13 – TV PROJECTION

This technique requires that you actually watch a television program. You should use a program that is fairly consistent, sticking to one location for a time. News specials focusing on a troubled part of the world are good. Documentaries on public television, science channels, and arts-and-entertainment networks can supply education on a particular place. The many documentaries on Egyptian or South American pyramids spring to mind. If you have a VCR, use it to record several programs, so you will have a choice when you desire to do this exercise. With a little experience, you will be able to re-create the exercise easily, using whatever programming is available.

1 Do Exercise 1 to enter a meditative state (see page 17). I also suggest doing Exercises 2 and 3 (see pages 20 and 25). Turn on your TV and watch the program depicting a particular place.

2 Watch the screen for a moment. Then close your eyes. Visualize yourself there, at this place. Open your eyes again. Repeat the process in little steps, spending more and more time visualizing and less watching.

3 Close your eyes and visualize the entire setting overlaying your own room, as if were a ghostlike hologram. In your living room or bedroom, you are simultaneously sitting in another part of the globe. The setting is complete. Feel the air change. Smell the different smells. See the images overlaying the physical reality. Hear different sounds. Use all your senses. Imagine that the TV is projecting the entire scene, like a three-dimensional movie. Imagine that the television screen is a gateway, and that your mind/astral body is projected through the gateway, to the new location.

4 Use this time to observe or interact. By becoming a part of the scene, you can psychically retrieve information that you wouldn't see on a flat TV screen. If it is a place of trouble, you can use intention, sending light or any other healing and calming techniques at your disposal.

5 When the process is complete, put out the intention you wish to close this link. Imagine wiping it away, dissolving into the light of the glowing screen. You can also draw a banishing pentagram over the screen, as in Exercise 8 (see page 60).

Once you have this experience, you can re-create it, using the local news or any other show. I think it is best to stick with "real" places, physical places on Earth. When you see the news and feel horrible about a crisis, you can lend your psychic support. If you simply want to experience a place in greater detail, let's say there's a show on Hawaii, use the screen, not only as your window on the world, but as your psychic door. It does not matter if the show is taped or old, the doorway is not encumbered by time. You can specify through your intention whether you will focus on the present, or on the time period when the film footage was taken. Later, you can experiment with fictional settings and let these settings be a mask through which the shamanic worlds speak to you.

E$_X$ERC^I$_S$E 14 – TV SCRYING

The following exercise can be a little unnerving for some, particularly those used to traditional scrying techniques. I suggest that you try the exercise as written, but if it simply does not work for you, substitute your favorite scrying device, like a crystal ball, bowl of water, rising smoke, or tea leaves. As always, the rule for adapting magick is to use what works. I was very comfortable with scrying through crystal, but have experienced success with this technique as well.

This exercise needs a channel with no intelligible programming, such as a station of static or a scrambled pay-cable station. Use something with a fairly steady random noise. If you like to watch scrambled channels to guess what the movie is or what the characters are doing, then stick to simple static.

❶ Do Exercise 1 to enter a meditative state (see page 17). I also suggest doing Exercises 2 and 3 (see pages 20 and 25). Turn on your TV and watch the unintelligible channel. Set the volume to a comfortable level. You may prefer a light reflecting off the television screen. If so, either point an electric light at it, or light a candle before the TV and watch its reflection. Experiment both with and without a light.

② Stare into the screen and let your mind wander. Stare past the screen. You are not so much looking at the static as gazing beyond or behind this veil of white snowy noise. Let your focus go in and out. Let the sound distract your conscious mind.

③ Ask whatever question you have. It can be a simple yes or no question, or a desire to see something or someone. You can ask for details about the future, past, or present, or to ascertain the wisdom and consequences of taking certain future action.

④ Let you mind wander, being open to the answers you receive. Scrying tends to work in one of two ways. You may get an image or series of images depicting real-life events. Imagine your mind's eye playing a personal movie that appears to be moving on the screen (or a crystal ball, if you are using that). Or you may see images that are symbolic in nature. You may ask if your new job will be successful. If you see a dollar sign, that is a yes. If you see a zero, then it is a no. When asking about love, you may see a star. For some, a star may be a "good" sign, like a lucky star. Others may first associate it with the dark star or the Dog Star, and make other interpretations. Let the symbols trigger a series of nonlogical thoughts to give you your answer.

⑤ Repeat the process with all the questions you have. When the experience is complete, turn off the screen and return to "normal" activities.

The techniques here can be adapted in many ways. Try closing your eyes and using the static sound as a method for triggering shamanic journeying. Combine it with other sounds and music. One of the most intense journeys I have ever taken was with a tape of white noise playing on one machine, a drumming CD in another, and someone doing live drumming and rattling over me. The random mixture

of these sounds was intense. The whole effect resulted in a very successful journey. My goal was to make peace with my grandmother
who had recently departed, and I did.

◎ OFFICE ALTARS ◎

What gods are petitioned more than the deities of career, prosperity,
abundance, and good fortune? Perhaps the gods of love and passion,
but, while some can do without romance, almost everybody has a job.
The career mind-set has been hammered into our collective psyche.
You have to work, get a nice place to live, and be near your job, so
you can get nice things. Then you have to work more to pay for it all.
The cycle is neverending, but the doctrine rarely asks you what you
want to do. Are you helping anyone but yourself? Is your job or
company moral and ethical, or making the world a better place? No,
the first question we ask is how much money are we making. I like to
have nice things and a comfortable home, but I also want to be happy
with my life and decisions. We all have stepping-stone jobs that,
hopefully, lead us where we want to go, but many of us get stuck on
the rock and completely forget the direction we are headed. We all
still pay homage to these deities, asking for more money, more vacation, and better benefits.

The office building has replaced the ancient temple site. Most people work outside the home, and those who do usually spend over
forty hours there, if not more. Religious fervor has been replaced by
career fervor–the desire to get ahead and meet your financial and
career goals. Here, many make their bargains with unseen powers,
asking for more and often offering something in return. Here is where
so many do magick, regardless of whether they use the word or not.
If you are going to put so much of your personal power into your
career, you should make space for it. You should honor it. Take some
space and create an office altar. Make your work sacred.

You may think you can't do this. You work at an uptight corporation, or deal with clients directly, and can't keep an altar. You can't even let your employer know you are involved in something as strange as magick. It's okay. I'm not asking to you to hang a sign over your desk saying "Sorcerer Here" with an arrow pointing to you. Coming out of the broom closet, so to speak, is a personal decision everyone must make for themselves. I can't imagine not being open about it, but we all have our own life path to follow. Follow your inner guidance, not your inner fears. If you have space on a desk, windowsill, or shelf, take some small personal items that mean something significant to you (see figure 7). You don't need any traditional tools, just some simple items that grant you a renewal of your personal power in times of stress. Pictures of loved ones are an excellent

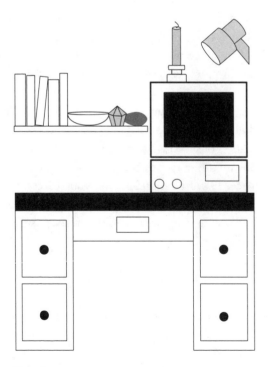

Figure 7. An office altar.

source of power on any altar. Particularly in an office, pictures can be a simple way to honor the balance between your office life and your home life. You can have a desert rock for the element of earth. When someone asks, say you picked it up while hiking on vacation. You can have a bottle of seawater, from another vacation. You can substitute a snow globe for the bottle. Both contain water. For air, aromathera- py products can again be used. I had a supervisor who had a bottle of stress-relieving eucalyptus lotion. You can rub it on your temples to relieve headaches. Charging such a lotion with the intention to relieve pain and bring mental clarity is very effective. Something like that can be used for the element of air, and still be easily explained. Everybody gets headaches at work. The element of fire may be a lit- tle more difficult, but you can keep a lighter or a book of matches vis- ible to represent fire in your mind. Plants bring in a real living quali- ty, and may even grow better in this sacred altar space. Depending on how liberal your office is, and how comfortable you feel there, you can put crystals or other small power objects on this impromptu office altar.

Whenever you are in a time of stress, look to your altar to remind you of the things that are important to you. When preparing yourself for a presentation or meeting, gather your power and keep your cen- ter by offering a little prayer to the powers with which you work at this altar space. It works wonders for your career and prosperity magick, and it makes you happier in your day-to-day job. This sacred space may lead you to happiness in your current position, or lead you to a new life change.

◎ RITUAL TOOLS ◎

The last items, and possibly the most important on the altar, are your ritual tools. The type of rituals you do decides what tools you will need. Standard tools include a wand, for directing energy. Wands are usually made out of a wood sacred to you, harvested from a special

place with the permission of the nature and tree spirits. A wand perfect for your environment could be "harvested" at your local hardware store. Go to the plumbing section and get yourself a copper
pipe. Copper tubing makes a very nice wand. Copper conducts energy.
Mechanically inclined individuals may use a screwdriver or wrench
to direct energy.

Traditionally, wands are the length from the tip of your middle finger to your elbow, but use whatever length is comfortable for you.
You can cap it with a crystal or cork, fill it with herbs, small crystals,
or other stones. You can keep and charge small vials of oil in the
wand. Make sure you don't glue in one of the ends so you can take
them out if you need to access them. Wrap the wand in cloth or
suede for a firm grip. Retractable TV and radio antenna, broken off
from their mountings, or business presentation pointers are conven-
ient wands too, since they are very portable. Wands are often used
to set boundaries, marking off the ritual space to contain the energy
raised, creating a magick circle.

Another ritual tools is a blade, which can also be used for directing energy and casting a circle. The blade cuts energy, and can be used
to break bindings. Like the wand, it represents the masculine force.
In witchcraft, the blade is used with the chalice to unite the masculine and feminine divine energies through the Great Rite. The blade
may also carve candles and harvest plants. Some reserve a special blade
for material-world cutting, and another for spiritual-world cutting. Use
a special knife, or even a letter opener, for your ritual tool.

If you are burning anything in your rituals, be sure to have a flameproof container. I use a cauldron to burn offerings and intentions I've
written down on paper. Mythologically, the cauldron has been used
to represent all four of the elements. I see it as the element of spirit,
like the womb and the grave, reaching beyond our realm. I use it in
the center of the altar, uniting all the powers I've called.

Other tools depend on personal tastes. Common ones include a
shield or peyton, a ritual pentacle used for invoking the four elements

and spirit, and incense burners and devices for scrying, like crystals, mirrors, and bowls of water. Some crystals are used with healings and intentions. A good supply of magical herbs is needed for some spells, but you can find many in your kitchen spice rack. They are used in homemade potions and remedies. Protection items adorn an altar to protect from harmful energies. Mixtures made with iron pow- der and salt are used, since these two substances attract and neutral- ize harmful energy. Iron powder can be hard to get, so fill a bowl with sea salt and iron nails. Consecrate it through a ritual for protection and keep it on your altar. You can add to it other protection items, like sage, or frankincense and myrrh. Drums, rattles, and bells can induce a meditative state, but many modern shamans turn to the mys- tical tool of the walkman and drum machine to provide their trance music. The tools are as varied as the practitioners. Those you make or discover yourself are always more powerful than someone else's. Work with the common tools you find around you, discovering their magical correspondence.

◎ CONSECRATION AND SPIRIT FOOD ◎

All magical tools should be consecrated, or charged. By charging them, you place a portion of your ever-renewable personal energy into the item. You program the energy and tool for the task at hand, like programming a VCR. You put specific information and a set of instructions into the device that it will carry out. You can charge your wand to direct energy. Even when you are not in your most magical state, a programmed wand will easily direct your personal energy in the manner you wish. Anything can be charged in this way.

Some substances hold a charge better than others. Metals, miner- als, and woods work nicely. Clothing or cording can take on an intent. Paper talismans can be used, but I find that their charge is not as permanent, just because paper seems so fragile and transitory to me. Pencils, in particular, fade fast. If you take good care of paper charms, they can last a very long time. Herbs hold a charge, but not as long, so charge them before you use them for best results. Some find plastics difficult to charge. I suspect that is, at least in part, because of the complex molecular chain that makes up plastic. It may also derive from fear or a personal bias toward "unnatural" materials. Nothing is really unnatural. Some things are more processed than others, but anything existing exists in nature, created from basic atomic components found, not only on this planet, but on many others. Most plastics are made out of petroleum products, which come directly from the earth. Most substances are ruled by a planet, meaning that they have many traits or energies in common with it. Neptune, the planet of illusions, rules petroleum and plastic. Sometimes, illusionary powers make spell casters uncomfortable. Use plastic in magick only if you are drawn to it. I am not particularly drawn to it, so I do not use it much, but I do not fear it. We, as a society, have created it. Now it is time to deal with it.

All items used on an altar or in a spell should be consecrated. When you first use your altar, hold a dedication ceremony, charging all your major tools. First, purify them, visualizing and requesting that all impurities and unwanted energies be removed. Specific items for individual spells can be charged right before you use them. Permanent tools can be fixed, so the charge always remains, unless you say otherwise. Fill the item with your intentions. Here is an example of charging a piece of concrete.

> *I ask all unwanted and harmful energies be removed from this concrete. [Blow on it to blow away these energies.] I charge this concrete to represent and hold the energy of earth on my altar. I charge it to bring me grounding, balance, and physical health when I touch it. I fix these intentions so that none may change them except me, unless it is for the highest good. So mote it be.*

"So mote it be" is a saying from my witchcraft training. It simply means "so be it," putting your intention into a positive, "present" statement. Items that are not permanently on your altar do not have to be fixed. Dried plants, candles, and incense all get used up, and their energy moves on to other realms. They should not be fixed, so they can complete their function and move on.

During this altar dedication, you can leave an offering of food or incense for the powers who aid you. This offering should be charged with your personal energy. You are not really offering physical food to these powers and expecting it to be consumed. You are offering energy. You are offering time and intent. You are offering respect. By charging these gifts and placing them on your altar, you are offering a portion of your energy. This gift is only fitting, since these powers always give you energy and intent for your magick. Certain totems, spirits, and gods like particular items. Some favor exotic perfume oils, incense, or food prepared in a special way. Research it and use your common sense. Seed is a great offering for a bird totem. Ask what would be the most appropriate offering.

Now you are ready or re-create your magical base of operations.

Chapter 6
Tools of the Trade

OTHERWORLDLY ALLIES HAVE JOINED YOU.
Your altar is set. You have learned some of the basics for this crazy little thing called magick. Now dim the lights and raise the curtain. It's spell time.

A spell is a specific act of magick. Through intention, ritual, and visualization, you set magical forces in motion to fulfill your desire. Many times, spells may not seem magical at all. Through seemingly natural occurrences and coincidences, your desired goal manifests. When many people first get involved in magick, they imagine their spells will be something out of the next blockbuster movie, complete with lights and special effects. They hope for lightning bolts from the sky and mists rising out of nowhere. Although a theatrical element and mood can aid a ritual, the actual manifestation of a spell is much more down to earth. You do a spell for a new job, and you soon hear about a new job, from a friend, the newspaper, or the Internet. The position conforms to what was asked for in the spell. Your interview goes smoothly and you soon have a new job. No smoke or lightning bolts involved. The desire manifests through quite ordinary channels, seemingly through a series of coincidences. The only factor that makes people believe in magick is that, prior to the spell, they had been searching for this new job for two years. After the spell, it manifested in as little as a few days. For people apprehensive about doing their first spell, I compare it to a traditional prayer asking for help. Mages simply have a different way of asking.

Spells are simpler than most people think. They do not require elaborate rituals or exotic ingredients, but sometimes such things make them more powerful and more fun. The quest for these magical items is as interesting and informative as the actual results of your spell work. By discovering your own tools and designing your own rituals, as exotic or simple as you desire, you are adding your personal power, your own magical touch, to the spell. Do not feel compelled to follow something written hundreds of years ago, particularly if you don't understand it. Never do magick you don't completely understand. You never have to follow a program written by the latest New Age guru. A true teacher in any field will give you the basic understanding and skills, the tools of the trade, and encourage you to go off and create on your own magick. Pursuing spiritual practices is like giving bread to a person who is hungry. You satisfy the momentary craving, but the hunger remains. On the other hand, you teach someone how to plant grain and bake, you empower them for a lifetime. Magick works in the same way. You are your own guru. Others only help you realize it. We all have our own paths to follow and we learn more by following our own road than by following someone else's.

◎ Designing Your Own Rituals ◎

The first tool for spell work is the magick circle. As you learned about reality, rapture, and ritual, you learned the basic structure of a circle. Mark off an area of sacred space and honor the four powers to aid in your work. Now it is time to meld this ritual with the powers of the city.

The circle is one of the most effective ways of making magick. It not only protects, it also puts the participants in touch with sacred space and the vibrations of creation. The energies and powers gathered in this bubbling cauldron work together to manifest your desires. You can do any spell outside the bounds of a circle. Personally, I have found that spells cast in a circle are much more effective.

Cast the circle as described in chapter 2. Visualize the ring of light in a perfect circle, marking the boundary of your space. If you live in a tiny apartment, imagine the ring going through the walls. Make it a comfortable size for you and your equipment. You can cast a circle anywhere, but most people cast it when standing in front of the altar, simply because all their tools are present there. The altar is a place of devotion, but it doubles as your magical workspace.

Next, invite in the powers you wish to aid you, including Gods and Goddesses, totems, guides, or angels. Most start by honoring the four directions and asking a being to anchor and embody the elemen-tal energy. Traditionally, you would ask one of the four archangels, a totem animal, or a deity to stand in the quarters, then ask other beings into the circle, depending on how appropriate they are to your intent. If you are doing a love spell, you might invite Aphrodite, the Greek Goddess of love. If you are doing a spell for healing, the Celtic Goddess Brid, a great healer who later was known as St. Bridget, may be appropriate.

With city magick, you can go beyond the traditional standards and invite the beings you have experienced into you sacred space. For those with previous experiences in magick, this does not exclude the right to call in traditional images and beings you have worked with, but it does open the door to city totems, mechanical spirits, and any archetypes you've met and worked with in your shamanic travels. You can do magick by calling strictly on only city totems, or only spir-its of transport. You can call on the spirits of different neighborhoods and districts in your city. If you are doing magick to help you travel without danger or delay out of the city to your family for the holi-days, you can call upon Mercury, the Roman God of travel, or on the archetype spirit form of airplanes. I would call on both, since I like and feel comfortable with both. Such quarter calls and invocations can seem strange at first, but the more intimately you work with the city, the more familiar it all becomes. By combining the modern and the traditional, you create rituals unique to your own experience.

Table 2. Elemental Correspondences for City Magick.

Element	Direction	Totems	Archetypes
Earth	North	Dog, Rodent, Squirrel, Ant, Spider	Subway, Automobile, Construction
Air	East	Spider, Crow, Dove, Duck, Finch, Pigeon, Seagull	Airplane, Building, Music and Art, Television, Computer, Medicine
Fire	South	Dog, Ant, Cockroach	Subway, Train, Automobile, Streetlight, Electricity
Water	West	Cat, Spider, Crow, Duck, Seagull	Boat, Music and Art, Medicine

The invitations into your circle can be as prosaic or as simple as you like. You can write out an elaborate ritual, with poetry and scripted verse, or do something completely off the cuff, following what is in your heart and mind at the moment. If you are a good speaker, you may prefer the latter. If you get nervous easily, you may want some type of script, or at least an outline. Modify the guidelines in chapter 2 to suit your own tastes and preferences.

Once the powers are invited into your sacred space, perform your spells. This ensures that you are in the right environment to do your work, your experimentation. Labs have their standard conditions and temperatures, and magick workers have their own standard conditions. Now you must decide on your goal. What do you want the spell do to? What do you want to manifest in your life? Your spell work can be as simple as asking for help and guidance, or reading a petition you've written. You can ask in the name of the Universe/God/Goddess/Great Spirit, to grant your desire. It is a good idea to ask that it be "correct and good for you," and that the spell "harm none," including yourself. Whatever you put out into the universe, you want to make sure that you are causing no harm, since you don't want that harm to return to you. For a long time, the majority of my spells were simply petitions that I burned in a cauldron during the ritual.

Another aspect to consider is the Moon phase. In the tradition in which I was trained, a form of witchcraft, the Moon played a very important part. During a waxing Moon, I did spells to bring things toward me. During a waning Moon, I did magick to remove, banish, and cure. You can easily find out the current phase of the Moon by looking at a calendar. To be even more accurate, get an astrological calendar that will tell you the exact time when the Moon becomes Full and New. Once the Moon becomes Full, it starts to wane, and once it becomes the New Moon, it starts to wax. Llewellyn's *Astrological Calendar* or *Daily Planetary Guide* will have all the information you need. Many other traditions pay no attention to the Moon and still have good results, so it all depends on how strongly this silver orb pulls on your own beliefs and abilities.

More complex spells, using ritual tools, plants, minerals, and household items, will be described later in this chapter. So many of them are right under your nose. You never suspected that everyday items could be used for magick, but they can. Everything is magical. Use these tools to inspire your own magical workings. If you desire, follow the instructions carefully while in a magick circle, and experiment. Once you are comfortable, you can mix and match and design your own completely unique spells and rituals. Each bit of information you acquire is like a new color crayon added to your box. Soon you'll have enough colors to make and do anything you want.

As we walk through the various urban environments surrounding us, our magical tools, our vehicles for intent, become more obvious as we open to the unspoken language all around us. Magick is inherent in everything, including everything in the city. Many tools of the urban mage are not traditional, but are just as powerful nonetheless. Always judge a tool by its results, and not necessarily what it looks like or where you found it.

◎ HOME TOOLS ◎

Anything can be a weapon if your intent is violent, and anything can be a magical tool if you look at it through magical eyes. If everything is connected and made from energy, as most mystics believe, then everything is magical. You can turn all sorts of mundane items found around your home into your magical allies if you desire. Masterfully handcrafted tools and talismans reflecting the tastes of ancient traditions are wonderful, but mystics of those ancient ages often used what was in their own culture, items made out of the materials available. They seem more romantically magical to us because they are steeped in the mysteries of an age-old past. Perhaps in a thousand years, the telephone will be viewed as a magical device by our progeny, although we consider it a mundane household item now. Everything has an inherent power, and as a practical spell caster, you can use whatever power is available, even if it means raiding your shelves and closets. The only limit is your own willingness and imagination.

The greatest arsenal an urban magician has is right in the kitchen. During the persecution of the European midwives and wise women, these witches hid their magical tools in their kitchens. Spoon, knives, brooms, and bowls became their ritual tools. Everyone had them, so one could not be accused of witchcraft just for possessing them. These wise women knew the herbs that would heal and hurt, and many of their magical remedies and charms came right from their spice racks. You can get many herbs from a holistic center or an organic herb farm. For students of medicinal herbalism, that is probably the best place to go. If you are making magical charms, however, try visiting your spice rack. Look in the refrigerator. Check the cabinets and medicine chest. You will be amazed at what is available. Each herb has a magical energy. Each has a vibration that can be harnessed by burning it as incense, ingesting it, or simply carrying it with you in a small charm.

Here are some kitchen ingredients, followed by some additional tools you can find in your home. For more extensive lists of both household herbs and more exotic varieties, refer to *Cunningham's Encyclopedia of Magical Herbs* (Llewellyn), or *The Master Book of Herbalism,* by Paul Beryl (Phoenix Publishing Inc.).

Allspice

Allspice is usually burned as an offering, or as incense to attract the forces of good luck. The energies drawn by allspice make things go your way, and align you with the natural flow of the universe. As things are flowing in harmony, money magick and healing work are most favorable.

Basil

This is the herb of love. Basil forms a bond between two people, increasing the chances of a harmonious relationship. It soothes people and can promote fidelity. It is used in love potions and incenses, and in many Italian foods. No wonder my Italian ancestors were noted as such good lovers. Since basil holds such a high level of love vibration, it is also used for purification, protection from evil, and drawing good fortune.

Bay

Bay leaves are an herb of the Sun. The Sun rules physical health and well-being, along with prosperity. Priestesses of the Sun God, Apollo, used bay in their prophetic works. It promotes psychic abilities and can also purify when used before a ritual. It clears your space and energy.

Black Pepper

Pepper is the partner of salt. In many ways, it has properties similar to salt. Its main function is protection. Due to its hot and spicy nature, pepper is a fire herb, and used to ward off evil, including curses and bad spirits. As salt absorbs and neutralizes, pepper banishes and wards off. When used together, they make a powerful protective one-two punch.

Chili Pepper

Like black pepper, red chili pepper embodies the power of fire. Protection is its nature. Red pepper not only protects, it also breaks any harmful energy. Fire is passion, energy, and life. It can be used in love magick to add spice and fire to your relationship.

Cinnamon

On the material level, cinnamon draws money, good luck, and prosperity. When using it, the doors of opportunity open to you. On a higher level, cinnamon raises vibrations in the room, particularly when burned. The first step seems like a grand opportunity, but it also leads to an awakening of consciousness. You open your worldview to encompass others. A sense of unity and unconditional love may follow. As the vibrations rise, harmful energy and spirits dissipate, granting the powers of protection. Cinnamon is a very spiritual herb, associated with both air and water.

Cloves

Cloves and clove incense have effects similar to cinnamon. In addition to raising spiritual vibrations, however, cloves increase psychic powers and tend to attract harmonious relationships, making them useful in love magick.

Coriander

Coriander brings strength to all love and healing magick. Its seeds have protective properties and promote peace. Coriander relieves tension, headaches, and nausea and is related to the elements of fire and water.

Cumin

Cumin seeds are used in lustful potions and magick to promote sexuality. They can be a spicy addition to a love charm. Cumin also promotes fidelity, strangely enough. Like many kitchen spices, due to its fire associations, cumin is an herb of protection.

Dill

Dill is a healing herb, relieving stomach pain and gas when taken as a tea. It is a primary herb of the kitchen, used to bless it and protect the entire home. Due to the numerous seeds each plant produces, dill is used to increase your own finances and fertility.

Food Coloring

Food coloring is an excellent way to add color and light to any potion or oil. Many magical supply shops have colored oils. While some of the expensive ones use natural herbs and minerals for their colors, they often tend to be a bit drab. Those that use bright vivid colors usually use a coloring additive or vegetable dye. You can use the food coloring in your pantry. Add a few drops to whatever you are making. Just remember that, if you are applying it to your skin, it may leave a little dye on it. Think back to Exercise 2 and your own color associations to personalize color magick (see page 20). Reflect on the chakra colors. Here are some traditional magical color correspondences. Love works with the colors red and pink. Green is for healing and money. Blue can be for money and prosperity, but it also invokes peace. Purple and violet are for spirituality and transformation. Yellow brings energy and strengthens the mind. Orange is another strong energy color, used for healing.

Flour

This ground grain, used for making breads, is the essence of the harvest. Most flour comes from wheat, but, depending on the bread being made, other grains may be used. In the ancient worlds, grains were held sacred to many Earth Goddesses, since they were the lifeblood of many societies. Akin to flour and grain are cornmeal and corn. In the Americas, corn is the sacred grain in native traditions, used in offering ceremonies at sacred sites. Both cornmeal and flour can be used in ritual offerings and spirit food. Offerings are particularly powerful if you take the time and energy to bake something yourself.

Garlic

No one can forget the tales of vampires and garlic. The legend comes from the reputation of garlic as an herb of protection, both magical and mundane. Garlic absorbs and neutralizes all harmful energy. Evil spirits, monsters, and disease are warded off. Bad weather is banished. Warriors eat it to dispel fear. On a physical level, garlic is used as a disinfectant and antiseptic. If you have something you want to get rid of, use garlic.

Ginger

In general, ginger is an herb of power. It can be used in any ritual to increase the power available to the spell caster. If you eat ginger, it increases your own personal energy by raising your metabolism. Added to any herbal charm or potion, it boosts all intentions in it. Ginger activates the immune system and wards off disease. Use this root with caution.

Grapes

Grapes, filled with water, resonate with the planet Neptune, the planet of the sea king. They are tools for both love and illusions. The waters of Neptune can bring escapist illusions or unconditional love.

Different-colored grapes mark different abilities, so, consult your personal associations with color magick.

Lemon

This citrus draws the power of the Moon, used in feminine, Goddess power, and with emotional healing and past-life magick. Lemon increases psychic powers, like the Moon. You can use the fruit, juice, or peel.

Mace

Mace is linked to the element of air. It can be used, like most spices, as an incense. When activated in ritual, mace will increase mental powers, clear thoughts, perception, memory, speaking ability, and psychic skills.

Marjoram

This herb eases the heaviness of existence, bringing new life to any situation or person. It resolves tension gently, bringing happiness and levity. Marjoram can aid in dispelling depression. Love spells may use it to bring freedom and happiness into a relationship.

Mustard

Mustard seeds have a variety of uses. They are used to aid psychic powers, particularly in astral projection. It is an herb of prosperity and protection. Mustard seeds are also used in fertility spells for women.

Nutmeg

Nutmeg is the herb of good luck. It brings an advantage to all spells using it. Money and prosperity spells often use nutmeg to "stack the odds" in the spell caster's favor.

Olive Oil

Olive oil can be another magical staple. Herbs steeped in olive oils will dispense their magical and often medicinal properties into it, along with their aroma. Leave the herbs in the oil, in either the sunlight, to use its energy, or in a dark cabinet away from the light, depending on the intent of your magick. Olive oil also makes an excellent base for essential oils. Use about half olive oil and half essential oils. Many magical oils are created using both of these techniques.

Onion

The onion is a plant of purification. The tears released when you smell an onion release emotional blocks within your entire body. Often, when you cry for no reason, the same process is occurring. Onions only help it along. Onions are very juicy, filled with water. They, therefore, relate to the emotional realms. The many layers of the onion indicate its protective powers. The many layers of armor in our own lives, however, can be a detriment to healing. To heal, we must peel back the layers. Onion and onion peel are used to treat illness by absorbing the disease, much like garlic. Although fresh onion is good for this, onion powder works well too.

Orange

As lemon is to Moon, orange is to the Sun. The bright citrus fruit invokes the life-giving power of the Sun and its warming rays. Orange is used in general healing and health magick because of its vitamin C content. Usually, such spells are for preventive magick, for warding off colds before they come. Orange can be used for success, wealth, and energy. It makes you shine brightly, like the Sun. You can use the fruit, juice, or peel in your magick, just as with its sister fruit.

Oregano

Oregano is another herb of love and passion. Sprinkled in food, it increases the powers of attraction between two people.

Parsley

Parsley is an herb of both the heart and mind, of air and water. It is used in love spells, but for also seeing clearly in a relationship. It can be used for fertility and protection.

Peppermint

Peppermint is similar in function to both parsley and cinnamon. It is a very spiritual herb, increasing the energy and vibration of an area, promoting mind-and-heart unity. Peppermint is also an herb of healing. When drunk as a tea, it acts as a general tonic and relieves stomach pain.

Rosemary

Rosemary is one of the first incenses. It has many powers similar to those of frankincense, and can be used for a variety of magical works, including protection, purification, love, peace, psychic powers, and increasing memory.

Sage

Sage does exactly what its name implies. Sage imparts wisdom. This herb can be added to any magical undertaking, bringing greater understanding to the work. Sagebrush is burned by the Native Americans to purify an area. Although slightly different from kitchen sage, both have protective properties. Sage fumes definitely raise the energy of an area to a higher level, driving out all harmful forces. It's used to smoke out unwanted spirits.

Salt

Salt is a mineral of protection, even though we use it to flavor food. Traditionally, salt absorbs discordant, harmful energy. In other words, it sucks up "bad vibes" and other energies that can cause harm or illness. Sea salt is best for magical purposes, but regular table salt has the same properties. A diet high in sodium chloride is not only physically unhealthy, but also spiritually unhealthy, because you become a magnet for unwanted forces. You can use salt in a protection charm by filling a bag with salt and other charged items. Some keep bowls of salt in the four corners of the basement or attic to absorb harm. When consecrating the salt, charge it with the intention to absorb harmful energy. Charge it to immediately neutralize this energy. Eventually, you will have to empty the charm and refill it with some fresh salt. You can similarly charge all your cooking salt to neutralize harmful energies, making the properties of salt work with the natural cleansing powers of your body. Make it a part of a general food blessing, activating all the healing properties of the food you eat, every time you sit down to a meal.

Sugar

The sweet taste of sugar, whether refined white sugar or brown, is a mark of its powers of love. Like milk and honey, sugar represents the loving paradise, euphoria, and cosmic bliss. Sugar and sweet foodstuffs like chocolate are natural aphrodisiacs, used in love magick the world over. Why else would sweets be so popular as Valentine's Day treats?

Thyme

Thyme increases your sense of peace and tranquillity by increasing your sense of connection to all. It works through the element of water, the conductive world of relationships and emotions. Through this peace, powerful healing or increases in psychic abilities can occur.

Tomato

Tomatoes invoke the fiery powers of the red planet, Mars. They are used to initiate things, to have the courage to face obstacles, to maintain health in adversity, and for protection. Mars is also used for passion and sexuality. The magical nature of the tomato can be called on for these attributes.

Vanilla

The vanilla bean is a powerful bean ruled by the planet Pluto. It is an innocent flavor, loved in ice cream and cookies, but the actual properties of the bean bring transformations and change reality. Pluto is the planet of life, death, and the underworld. Vanilla beans can be found in gourmet shops, but often their properties, in diluted form, are transferred to vanilla extract and vanilla oil. Add a few drops to an herbal charm when you need these strong transformative powers.

Vitamin E Oil

Although less likely to be found in the home, vitamin E oil is becoming more popular. Medical science is discovering the healing properties of the oil for skin irritations, rashes, warts, and burns. Like olive oil, it can be used as a base oil for other magical works.

Vitamin C

Vitamin C has become a common daily ritual sacrament for many. It can aid the immune system. As a preventive tonic, it wards off colds and flu. It's nontoxic and there is little chance you can overdose on it by taking too much. Try using vitamin C in healing spells, catalyzing its natural properties. You can either consume it, or add it to a charm.

Blender/Food Processor

Although I really love my mortar and pestle, I have to concede that, when grinding some of the really tough herbs and resins, the touch of a mechanical blade can ground more finely than my hand, and in a fraction of the time. If we are considering the efficacy of mechanical and city spirits, then we shouldn't turn down the helping hand our kitchen tools offer. Some say herbs that are processed mechanically will lack power because your personal energy isn't added in the grinding process. My solution is simple. While the blender is shredding away, I focus my energy and intention toward unlocking the power of the herbs. Intent without the elbow grease can work just as effectively.

Needle and Thread

A needle and thread are another set of invaluable tools. Not only do they come in handy when you lose a button, they can be used in binding and sympathetic magick. If you want to contain something, something causing you harm, you want to bind it. There are many ways to do this. An easy way is to write out the name of the person, place, or thing causing harm on a piece of paper. Then, during a ritual, roll it up and tie it with the thread. I find black thread works best for me, as a color of protection. Keep this talisman someplace where it will not get loose, or bury it. These tools can also be used to make poppets, or dolls, used to represent someone else. These images can then be used to heal. Needles or pins can be placed in the place where the illness occurs, to bind and banish it. The needle is an extension of your will, like a ritual blade or sword.

Newspapers, Magazines, and Catalogs

Periodicals are an endless supply of images. If you are doing magick to gain something, like a good deal on a new car, cut out an advertisement for the car you want. You can then cross out the price and write in your ideal price. Use this image as the focus of your spell. Anything you want, from new living quarters, to employment, to myriad consumer goods can be found here.

Pillows and Stuffed Animals

For those not ready to make their own voodoo dolls for healing sessions, a pillow or even a plush toy can be used as a surrogate. Reiki Masters encourage the use of surrogates when doing distant healing sessions. It gives the healer something on which to focus. This isn't just for Reiki, however. It can be used in most magical forms of healing, visualization, and intent. The image of the recipient, the thought form of the one in need, is placed within the pillow surrogate. The pillow is treated just like the recipient, only in miniature. Once the session or spell is complete, the thought form is released and sent to the recipient, bringing healing energy.

Stove, Pots, and Pans

The modern stainless-steel kitchen vessels now replace the bubbling iron cauldron of the witches of old. Mixtures can be created and heated using your own stove. Some find that electric stoves disrupt magical energy and only do magick on gas stoves. I think this is a personal prejudice. Find out if it makes a difference to you.

◎ MAGICAL FORMULAS ◎

Using the tools of your home, you can create magical charms. Use the information here as a guideline and follow your intuition to personalize these works of magick. *Incense, Oils and Brews* (Llewellyn), by Scott Cunningham, was one of the first resources that encouraged me to create my own formulas. It is an excellent book and I highly recommend it to those who like to get their hands dirty. Such creations are used in ritual as a focus for more specific spell work, carrying the intention and vibration you originally infused into it.

Ritual Oil

Many traditions use holy water or a protective potion used to bless items and the self before entering the temple. Now you can make your own and anoint yourself with it before and during the ritual to bring your focus back to the task at hand and to keep your mind from wandering with the daily distractions around you. The oil can also be used to anoint tools before you consecrate them. This ritual oil contains substances for protection, purity, and harmony, the ideal intentions for most rituals. Since I love making potions and getting messy, I usually make them in small quantities, so I can experiment again, and to prevent large quantities from spoiling in my altar cabinets. To lengthen the shelf life of any potion or oil, add a tablespoon or two of salt to each cup of base oil. Sea salt or kosher salt is the best to use. The salt prevents the mix from fermenting. I've had some potions last for years, while others didn't last nine months. The salt definitely extends their shelf life, however. For now, start with a base of 1 cup olive oil. Charge each of these ingredients and add them to the oil:

> 1 teaspoon basil
> 1 teaspoon bay
> 1 teaspoon rosemary
> 1 teaspoon sage

Some people like to warm this mixture gently over low heat on the stove as they make it, while others prefer to let it sit in a dark place for a few weeks and let the oil and herbs steep before using it. The advantage to heat is that you can use the oil as soon as it cools. Stir or shake it, as needed. Once you are ready to bottle the oil, strain the herbs from it with a cheesecloth. Keep it away from the light and use it in your ritual practices.

Sacred-Space Incense

This incense is used to raise the vibration level of your ritual area, bringing a sense of peace and spirituality, while simultaneously removing any unwanted energies. Most of us are used to buying incense in stick or cone form, already complete with charcoal inside the mixture. Simply light it and let it burn. Raw incense is a bit more demanding, but the rewards are worth it. I simply like to use tools I've crafted myself, including incense.

To use raw incense, get self-igniting charcoal discs. These are found in most metaphysical and New Age shops in silver rolls, like large coins. Hold the charcoal over a candle flame with flameproof tongs. Metal sugar cube tongs work nicely. Do not hold it with your fingers. (I know it sounds silly to warn you, but I've known many people who have done it.) Once the charcoal is ignited, the flame spreads throughout, so holding the part furthest from the flame does not help you. Place the charcoal in a heat-proof container, like a bowl filled with sand. Then sprinkle the raw incense on it and let it burn. Be warned, when making your own recipes, that burning herbs smell a lot different from their dried counterparts.

Mix and grind equal parts of the following three herbs, putting the intention of sacred space into them. Then burn them prior to or during your ritual.

cinnamon
cloves
rosemary

Prosperity Incense

Use this blend of incense to promote the powers of prosperity, abundance, good fortune, and luck when doing magick in harmony with those intentions. Incense can be like a battery or power cell. You've stored up the energy of prosperity in this incense, and you can release it when you need to do a specific money or career spell.

Mix and grind these herbs together, charging them with the intention of prosperity. Charge them again in your ritual circle prior to use.

1 part allspice
3 parts cinnamon
2 parts clove
1 part nutmeg

Love Oil

Although they are not part of your kitchen cabinet spice rack, roses are not too hard to find in the city. You can obtain rose petals in potpourri and flower shops. There is nothing more magically romantic than a rose when doing love magick. This love potion will attract love to you and promote the powers of love within you, which is the first and most important step. After your love oil is created, using a method similar to the one for creating ritual oil above, you can wear it like a perfume or use it to anoint other tools. If you are doing a specific love spell to attract someone correct for you, anoint a pink, green, or red candle with the oil, charge the candle with your intention, and let it burn. The flame will attract the person who is right for you.

Start again with 1 cup olive oil and 1 to 2 tablespoons of sea salt. Add and charge each of the following:

Petals of 1 red rose
1 teaspoon cloves
1 teaspoon rosemary
1 pinch sugar
1 whole vanilla bean, 1 teaspoon vanilla extract, or 12 drops vanilla essential oil

Stir or shake, charging the entire oil for love, for attracting and generating love that is correct for the user of the potion. Strain when done and use in your magick.

Psychic Oil

Since most of us were not raised from childhood believing in our psychic gifts and other powers, we've closed down part of that reality. These different incenses, oils, and charms can help make us aware of our own natural abilities. Many substances are reported to open the psychic pathways and increase awareness of our gifts. You can use this oil to bless your third-eye and throat chakras, and to open your psychic seeing and hearing. They are powerful when used with tarot cards, runes, I Ching, or any other divination device.

Make the oil in the same way as the ritual oil, either heating or steeping the herbs. Charge each one as you add it to the base oil.

2 teaspoons bay leaves

1 teaspoon cloves

3 teaspoons lemon peel

1 teaspoon thyme

If possible, keep this mixture on your windowsill or rooftop on the night of the Full Moon. Let the oil absorb the power of the moonlight, which increases intuition, magick, and psychic powers.

Speaking-Easy Charm

For those in any business where you must speak, the prospect of making presentations in front of large groups of people can be fearsome. Many are calm, cool, and detached under pressure, but for the majority of the world, public speaking is difficult. I give many lectures, classes, and workshops on magick, witchcraft, and healing, but it took me a long time to get comfortable speaking to large groups of people. Sometimes, smaller groups are even worse. If you teach, lecture, or present in a boardroom, you may face similar problems. This charm eases those anxieties, while promoting eloquence, peace, and harmony within.

Take a small blue bag or piece of blue cloth and tie it into a charm bag. Do not make it too big. You want to be able to carry it in your pocket when making your presentations. Blue is the color of the throat chakra. Charge and add these herbs:

1 part allspice

1 part mace

1 part marjoram

1 part rosemary

Tie the bag tightly and seal it with a vision of yourself being calm and detached, speaking eloquently in front of any crowd. The words simply flow off your lips. Charge this in a magick circle and carry it with you when you are speaking to the public.

◎ OFFICE TOOLS ◎

Urban practitioners can find tools at home, but the workplace can also be a resource for a little bit of magick. Some find these tools in their home office, where privacy lets them do magick anytime they like. Others have to be more discreet, completing their rituals in the privacy of their minds, setting their intents out gently and quietly. The magick can be disguised as something as simple as sending a letter.

Most of these tools are focus points for sympathetic magick. An act performed in ritual, with intent, will manifest in the physical world. When you create or destroy an object that magically stands for something else, something larger, you affect the larger item. The traditional image is the voodoo doll. The doll acts as a proxy for a person, often using something connected to them, like hair, clothing, or a fingernail. The word "sympathy" originally meant "to resonate with," not "empathize with". The target's name and image also resonate with them. By naming the doll, you empower it to send energy to the focus of the spell. Although most movies depict voodoo dolls as instruments of evil, these dolls are often used as healing tools, the pins denoting where healing power goes into the body. The doll image is simply one of the most popular forms of sympathetic magick, but there are all kinds to explore.

Envelopes

Envelopes are a tool of binding. Write the harmful situation on a small slip of paper, fold it up, and drop it into an envelope with the intention to bind it. Lick this magical trap and seal it, completely trapping away any harmful energy directed toward you.

Colored Pens and Highlighters

As agents of color and light, highlighters, pens, markers, and crayons can be used much as food coloring is used. Use the magical properties of colors as a focus for your magick. If your intention is to bring happiness to someone in a depression, write his or her name out and then highlight it in pink. Take a copy of your bank statement and mark it with green arrows going up, to increase your prosperity. If someone needs protection, take a picture of the person and draw a bubble around it, to activate his or her own protection shield. Be creative when practicing your magical art.

Elastics

Elastic bands are tools of binding, used like thread. The only problem with them is that they tend to break over time. Only use them for temporary binding spells, as a stopgap measure.

Glue

Glue is an agent of binding, literally bringing forces together and keeping them together. Glue can bind you to what you desire. By using a symbol for yourself–say, your business card–and gluing to it a new title that reflects the promotion you want, you can bind that new title, that new identity, to you through a simple act of sympathetic ritual. By making it a magical reality, you manifest it in the physical world.

Paper Clips

The lovely thing about paper clips is that they are so pliable. The metal wire can easily be bent into a shape or symbol as the focus of a spell. Chapter 7 will go into detail about making magical symbols, but some symbols you may already know. The five-pointed star, the cross, the "X," and the circle are all potent symbols. Wrapping paper clips around pens can soften their straight lines into curves. If you have a problem making a sharp bend, fold the clip over the edge of your desk. Paper clip talismans are easily hidden in desk draws.

Scissors and Letter Openers

Both are extensions of the will, tools to focus intent. Each tool can break former bindings. Scissors cut threads and elastics. The dull blade of a letter opener can still easily open sealed envelopes. They both open up portals and clear obstacles from your path.

Pushpins

Tacks can temporarily bind something, getting it out of your way by symbolically sticking it to a board. The image is the office equivalent to the Hanged Man in the tarot, or the sacrificed God archetype. The pins can also be used as regular pins and needles, to stimulate points on a sympathetic poppet. I've used pushpins in rows to mark outlines of magical symbols on my bulletin board. They were far enough apart so no one could recognize the shape but myself. You have to be careful, however, that people don't randomly borrow pushpins from you. If they take the wrong one, they can break the symbol.

◎ OFFICE SPELLS ◎

Magick done to effect change within your working environment can be done with tools from that environment. You can simply use these spells with your office tools in the privacy of your own home, or, with a simple moment of intent, consecrate and charge these tools before using them in the office. Magick need not be elaborate, nor does it require a ritual circle. It helps, but these office spells remind me of the age-old kitchen spells, in which magick was disguised as cooking and busy-work. The kitchen was the home base of many witches. Now the office is home base for many practitioners. Magick is the little things you do in life to effect change. These acts can all be disguised as mundane work.

Binding Spell

Binding spells should not be entered into lightly. They should only be used when reasonable means of solving the problems are not effective. Use them when someone specifically means to do you harm on any level. If you beat someone out of a promotion fairly, and they now hold a grudge against you, you should not use a binding spell. If they actively undermine your authority, however, or denounce you to your boss and co-workers and generally try to discredit you, then a binding spell is appropriate. Talk to the person first. Talk to your supervisor, if possible. If all else fails, do a binding.

Take the person's name, or even better, a business card or something else he or she has handled, and put a big black "X" through it, with the intention of blocking and neutralizing any harm. Place it in an envelope. If doing this at home, get some salt and pepper. Charge it for protection. If at work, your office may have a kitchen or cafeteria. Sometimes, condiments are packaged in little paper envelopes, as at a fast-food restaurant. Charge the salt and pepper for protection and place them in the envelope along with the name. Seal it, with the intention of sealing away all harm, roll it up, and tie it with either string or an elastic. Put it in the back of your desk drawer where no one will touch it. As long as it stays sealed, the binding will be in effect and the person will not harm you in any way. As crazy as it sounds, I've done all sorts of binding spells and they really do work.

Removing Career Blocks

If you are in the business world or, better yet, in business for yourself, you probably have career goals. These may be based on title, company, pay scale, or job description, but, ultimately, you want to be moving toward the things that make you happy. There are many bumps along the road to career happiness. Many strong personalities and energies vie for their share of satisfaction in the business world. This can create a certain amount of office "static" in the magical worlds. Some feel their prosperity is blocked, often by circumstances of their own making. This spell helps you remove such blocks in general. It can also be individualized to remove specific abstracts. Be sure to do it in a spirit that is correct and for the good of all involved. You can do this inside a circle if you desire, but it's not necessary. Relax yourself and focus on your intent.

Take your own business card or a stiff piece of cardboard with your name on it and wrap some string around it. Each time you make a full wrap, think about what is blocking you. Once you cannot think of any more obstacles off the top of your head, tie the string in a knot around the card. Take a pair of scissors and cut each loop of the string, breaking that block. Cut every loop, until all blocks and bindings fall off the card. Then take a coin and charge it for prosperity. It can be any coin–a penny, quarter, nickel, or dime–and glue it to the back of the card to bring success and prosperity to you. Let the glue set and keep this charm somewhere safe to do your magick. This little act of folk magick can open a whole new world of possibilities to you.

Perfect-Job Spell

Everybody is searching for the ideal job. Everybody needs to make money and be self-sufficient–or even beyond sufficient to comfortable, getting the things they both want and need. At the same time, however, we want something that suits our personalities and is personally fulfilling and meaningful. It's hard to get all that in one package. Jobs seem to be round holes into which we, with our unique talents and ideals, try to fit as square pegs. To fit the job available, we often have to relinquish our comfortable "squareness," hiding some of our talents, personality traits, or needs.

Write up a little blurb about yourself, as if you were running a help-available add. List all your qualities and a general statement about what you want to do. Focus on things you want to be doing every day for a living. Be realistic. List qualities you have and your actual qualifications. If you didn't graduate from high school, don't try to sell yourself as a Harvard business school graduate. Include your expected pay range and benefits. Then write a statement from a potential employer. Don't make up or mention a company name. Just describe a position you would like to become available. Make the description match your own qualifications and desired position, including pay range, location, and any other details important to you. Get a newspaper classified section. Glue in both your ads, separately, adding them wherever they fit in this section. Type them out to make them look more "official" than handwriting.

Cast a magick circle, with the newspaper by your side. Invoke any of your patrons or totems who may help you in this endeavor. Then draw a circle in black pen or marker around each of your mock listings and draw a line connecting them. The line can cut across other ads, or gently follow the lines between them. Choose the path that feels right to you, literally. This is your new perfect-job symbol. Visualize it in your mind's eye, as you focus on connecting yourself and your talents to the job of your dreams, still staying in the realm of reality. At the end of the ceremony, burn the newspaper, releasing your intent. A few days later, look in the local listings and call your contacts to find the right job coming toward you.

◎ Techno-Shamanic Tools ◎

The tools of the trade are not restricted to the ritual tools of modern folk magick and arts and crafts. Reach out to the shamanic realms and all the devices that help lead you to the shamanic realms. Traditional practitioners use drums, rattles, blindfolds, chanting, and sacramental concoctions. You can use all of these techniques and tools, or any of them to which you are drawn. Experiment with modern rattles and sound machines, the new tools of the trade, as we have discussed in previous chapters. Here are some of the modern tools in a bit more detail.

Drum Machines, Sequencers, and Synthesizers
With the advent of electronic music, you can have a whole band within a box. A drum machine is a device that re-creates electronically

recorded drum and percussion sounds and preprogrammed rhythm patterns. You can choose different drum sounds, assign them to a pattern, or link several patterns together. You can even make entirely new beats. You control the tempo and balance. This mix can create shamanic trance music for the Industrial Age. Depending on how musically savvy you are, you can create a chain of complex primal rhythms, and you do not have to be a musician to do it. So much of it is preprogrammed, that a musical novice who just knows what he likes when he hears it can program the rhythms. A sequencer is a device similar to a drum machine. It can program beats and rhythms for drums, and for other instruments as well. Usually, sequencers contain a range of other instruments, from violins and cellos to electric guitar, piano, oboe, flute, and organ. The preprogrammed patterns contain chord changes for particular styles of music—funk, rock, country, and techno. You can also program your own original music or record your own melodies by playing an electronic instrument connected to the sequencers. The preprogrammed styles make sequencers easy to use, but this requires a little familiarity with music. Synthesizers are machines that let you electronically record a sound and manipulate it to make it sound different, often otherworldly. Many synthesizers have a keyboard interface and contain either a drum machine or sequencers that lets you compose your own recordings. They have the widest range of capabilities, but require the most knowledge.

With the desire to learn and some time to experiment, a good sequencer or drum machine can be an asset to the magical practitioner. You don't have to worry about finding someone to drum for you. You don't have to listen to the same CD or tape over and over. Each track can be created with a magical intent in mind, to fit the mood and goal of your journey. This is magical music, without the need to learn a new instrument. Don't get me wrong. As someone with a degree in music performance, I feel learning an instrument is wonderful and rewarding, but if you really want to journey and not play, then electronic music may be the road for you. This is an art form in itself. The electronic rhythms are conducive to city magick. I've used a Yamaha QY-10 sequencer that I bought in college. It is as big as a VCR tape and comes with headphones. It's fun and easy to use. Since then, I'm sure other models and brands have come out that incorporate advanced technology. Keep it simple, however, and get something you will understand and use.

If you are musically inclined and ambitious, good-quality 4-track home studios that allow you to record entire songs and mix live recordings with electronic instruments are relatively cheap. You can have your own power song recorded for any magical journey.

Stereo, Walkman, and Tape Recorder

These are the musical tools for the 21st-century shaman. Through them, you can play trance-inducing music that sounds like Tibetan monks chanting, tribal drumming, sounds of nature, white noise, taped meditations, personal affirmations, and rush-hour traffic recordings. All of these things may not be practical or even possible to have in your living space when needed. The CD and tape player bring them to you. A large supply of prerecorded material can be found, or, if you are so inclined, you can make your own.

Television and VCR

The television has already been discussed as a potential altar site. As a medium, it connects us to the world, albeit selectively. Not only can we watch images on it and feel a connection to them, but, through the VCR and video tape, or even a video camera, we can trap these images in an endless loop for our ritual purposes. The white noise of static can also be used to distract our conscious minds during trance work. Just be careful if you are a crystal collector. If you keep crystals on your television, as silly as it may sound, you run the risk of overloading the set. I've heard of it happening to the electrical devices of many careless crystal collectors.

◎ City Plants ◎

Plant magick is a time-honored tradition among sorcerers. We still take the puffy heads of dandelions and make wishes as we scatter the seeds. The witches of Shakespeare most likely were not killing off newts, toads, and bats, but taking herbs named after these animals and adding them to their potions. The folk names have changed and we don't know what they might have been using, but we have other plants, like deer's tongue, cat tail, bleeding heart, maidenhair, kangaroo paw, and, my all time favorite, dragon's blood. No dragons will be killed here. Dragon's blood is a red powdered resin, named after dragons because it is so powerful.

By knowing the power of each plant, you use the natural spirit helpers in the environment around you. The dried herbs and spices of the kitchen are powerful, but there are living plants all around you. If there aren't, there should be. Magick wielders are the secret guardians of the land, promoting the growth and health of all things.

The key to plant magick is to understand the nature of the plants. Each plant has a signature, through its color and shape, to indicate its medicinal and magical uses. Liver problems often give one a yellow complexion, indicating the dysfunction. Dandelion flowers are yellow, indicating a sympathy between them and liver disease. Dandelion root is used to aid liver cleansing and healing. This system of relationships is often called the Doctrine of Signatures.

Signatures also apply to the elements. Plants that are bushy, low to the ground, or have vast roots or large seeds are influenced by the element of earth. They are for healing and physical advancement. They can be used in money and home magick. Plants with sharp points or bright, warm colors are related to fire. They work with spirit, will, and passion. Tall plants, with starlike flowers or strong aromas, are related to air. They work on the mental process and bring clarity of thought and spirit. Plants filled with water, like many fruit and vegetable plants, or with leaves that hold water after the rain, are obviously water plants. They often have cooler colors. They work in the realms of emotion, healing, and love.

Plants can relate to any combination of elements, depending on the mixture of characteristics. Use your instinct to determine the powers of new plants, but also ask the plants themselves. Connect to and communicate with them. Attune yourself to them, much as you would to any other spirit helper. When you talk to a plant, listen and see if it answers in your mind. When you start talking to your house-plants, really talk to them, and listen for their answers.

Many traditional magick wielders lived in very rural places, ideal spots to collect a full apothecary of medical and magical herbs. City dwellers have a more difficult time. They are there, however, if you know where to look for them. Make the effort to include plants in your magick and in your life.

Start by noticing the plants already around you. Pay attention to them. Many office buildings, shopping malls, lobbies, restaurants, libraries, airports, and friends' apartments are decorated with house-plants. Some companies make a living by taking care of other people's houseplants in the city, particularly big displays in public areas. Notice the variety of life all around you. If you haven't taken the time before, it may surprise you. As with a lot of things, we tend to take plants for granted. Expand your awareness; go walking through the park. There is life hiding all around in the park. Notice the trees growing through the concrete sidewalks. They are alive, not just ornamental. Honor them and acknowledge them. They help clean the air in the city, providing oxygen for us. Very few people take the time to notice them. Let them know you appreciate them.

EXERCISE 15 – PLANT-SPEAK

❶ The first time you attempt this, start by doing Exercise 1 to bring yourself to a meditative state (see page 17).

❷ Sit in front of a plant. If you can touch it, do so. Feel your energy mingle.

❸ Look closely at the plant. Notice its signature and elements. Appreciate its simple beauty.

❹ Feel your energy reach out to the plant and communicate with it. Speak to it in words and pictures. Introduce yourself. Ask the plant about itself. Wait for and be open to the answer. You may receive a message in many ways. If mind-speak does not work for you, speak with your full voice. Plants like to hear us, too, but they are really reading our thoughts and feelings.

❺ When the experience is complete, bring your awareness back to ordinary consciousness.

You may want to bring more plants into your home. You can keep them by the windows, or in window boxes to let the more seasonal plants experience the outdoors. Develop a relationship with them. Commune with them before asking them to participate in your magick. Ask them what they need to grow well. In general, they need moderate amounts of water. Some thrive in direct sunlight, while others need less light. Soil types vary, too.

You can always buy cut, dried herbs and commune with the spirit and energy in them. Most cities have an herbalist shop or natural food store where you can procure all natural herbs for your magick and medicinal needs. Some occult shops carry a supply of the more unusual ones. And there is always the spice rack. I think, however, that working with living plants gives you a more complete appreciation for the plant kingdom. You will then be able to commune better with plant spirits from dried herbs and roots.

When actually using living plants in ritual, if you need to use a part of the plant, ask permission first. Then listen for the answer. If the answer is no, the plant may give you a reason or a better sugges-tion. You can dry out the part you take–perhaps a leaf, flower, or root–or you can use it fresh. Plant parts may be added to brews and potions. Check with a good herbalism and houseplant book for poi-sonous plants to make sure you don't use anything toxic. Never con-sume a plant or plant product without checking first. Many house-plants are toxic, so I suggest not consuming any. Here are some com-mon houseplants you can use in magick.

African Violet

The African violet can be a temperamental plant. People either have a knack for them, or they have a horrible time with them. I wonder if that's because of the magic involved. African violets raise the level of spirituality in the room, marked by its frequently blooming flowers of purple, violet, blue, and white. They take their light indirectly and tend to burn in bright sunlight. The soft fuzzy leaves hate getting wet. Perhaps this earth and air spirituality does not like to confront the water and fire aspects of its owners. Use African violets for working with the earth and sky energies in your body, like the axis of the Worldscraper.

Aloe

There are many varieties of aloe, but the one we are talking about is the houseplant with thick juicy leaves. You can break off the leaves and use the juice to heal burns, cuts, and other skin damage. The thick watery gel inside indicates an emotional component, but hidden, pro-tected by the tiny spikes. Aloe is a plant of protection for the self and home, used for healing and good luck. Some research indicates that its juice works, both internally and externally, to heal cancer. The spikes indicate it can be used both to cause cuts and holes, and to heal them. This includes external lacerations and energy holes in the aura.

Cactus

Cactus is a colorful desert plant, not in pigment, but in character. It is a stem succulent that holds its water in the center. The cactus is a survivor, storing water for a long time. It is the plant of the hearty traveler. The spines protect it from those seeking to take the water from it. Cacti in general are used for protection. The spines are used by witches to write out spells, carve candles, and as a substitute for iron nails in protection and binding spells. A variation of a binding spell is to fill a bottle with cactus spines, salt, and a paper with the name of the antagonist. This spell protects the caster. Cactus spines can also be used as voodoo-doll pins, both to hurt and to heal. Native shamans have used the cactus for healing. The sacred peyote sacrament, used to induce visions on shamanic quests, comes from the cactus family.

Fern

Lush, leafy fern plants are becoming more popular in home arrangements and office settings. In the wild swamps and woods, these are plants of protection. Legend says that their seeds can grant the power of invisibility. Those sitting near ferns in an office will often go unnoticed by their co-workers, as if camouflaged. They can be particularly useful if you don't have an office door and want to screen out unwanted visitors when working.

Hyacinth

Hyacinths are very magical flowers. The purple or pinkish flowers promote peace and love. Their scent helps alleviate grief over the loss of a loved one. They are named after Apollo's mortal lover, Hyacinth. Apollo created the flowers after her accidental death. The dried flowers or oil can be used in love potions and charms. Try adding it to a variation of the love oil recipe given previously.

Ivy

Ivy is a ground plant, reaching for the heavens. It seeks something higher, but doesn't always have the support to reach up. It needs structure to grow up toward the heavens, whether a building face or tree. Ivy is known as Gort by the Celts, and, although it is not a tree, it fits in the Ogham tree alphabet. You can train ivy to grow around a shape or form, mimicking our own ability to change, adapt, and learn new skills. Use ivy in magick when you need to adapt to new situations or seek and accept support from others. Traditionally, ivy is used for healing, protection, and good luck.

Jade Plant

Jade plants are my favorite plants. In the last office where I worked, I adopted an abandoned, mutated strain of the jade tree. Jade plants are bright green, like the mineral used for healing, improving eyesight, and love spells. I think the jade plant can do all those. The waxy leaf protects from dryness, while it holds in water. Emotions are present, but controlled. I feel the jade tree is a strong earth-and-water plant.

Mother-in-Law's Tongue

This long-leaved plant often has yellow stripes on the side of its leaves that look like giant tongues sticking up out of the ground. The obvious association is to the powers of speaking and communication. Mother-in-law's tongue can aid in all manner of family quarrels, easing tension, and promoting a peaceful resolution to the conflict.

Palm

Many types of palms live indoors, but they all have a lot in common. All are tall, topped with a fanlike leafy crown. They reach toward the heaven without need of support, unlike the ivy. They bring clarity, vision, and the ability to rise above petty concerns. They have been the source of fibers, waxes, oils, fruit, and sweets. They are fertile providers, used in magick for fertility, protection, and clear decisions.

Peace Lily

Peace lilies extend their white tropical flowers up through their green leaves like a point of white light. They promote peace and harmony, granting subtle illumination and insight into your environment. They work much like African violets, but are not as temperamental.

Philodendron

Philodendron has many species in its class. They are a low-light-level plant, preferring indirect light. Philodendron are ideal in an office with no windows. Magically, to me, they adapt to the darkness and carry their own light within. Use philodendrons in magick when you are in dark times and need to stay cheerful and happy despite difficulties. Many philodendron have heart-shaped leaves, indicating that they are used in love magick and healing the heart.

Spider Plant

Spider plants are another favorite of mine, just because they are so prolific. The long green leaves, often striped with white or yellow, reach out like a spider. When this plant runs out of room in the pot, it projects out and flowers with small white buds. The flowers eventually grow into baby plants, hanging down like spiders from a web. They reach down from the air to touch the ground. I find them good for grounding into the body and the material world from more lofty pursuits. They are very fertile and also help when you need to work on a problem from many angles. They just create more paths. They adapt to the situation. Use them for grounding or when you need to grow in a new direction because you feel trapped.

Peace Water

Offices are often places of high stress, tension, confusion, and sharp feelings. The mechanisms of office politics can play havoc with co-workers. It's hard to maintain an air of balance and tranquillity in the midst of all this, but some magick can help.

This potion is useful if you have office plants. Your magick can be disguised as a moment of watering the plants around you. Take the fresh flowers of either an African violet or a peace lily, or both if you have them, and let them soak in a bowl or bottle of water. Charge the flower to bring peace and tranquillity before setting it into the solution. You may visualize white, violet, purple, or blue light in the liquid. In this way, you are making something similar to a flower essence. You may even add a few pinches of some harmonious herbs from your spice rack, like allspice, marjoram, rosemary, or thyme. Let the mixture soak for at least 12 hours, if not longer. Then put it in a spray bottle and use it to mist your plants. You can add more clear water to the solution to fill up the bottle. Spray this mist on office plants when tension runs high, or water each office plant with a few drops. It will bring more calm to the office. Visualize colored lights spreading throughout the office. Even if you water only the plants directly around you, imagine the peaceful mist expanding to fill the entire building. The water itself doesn't need to be everywhere for the vibration to be carried.

Shake the bottle each time before using, to activate the energy within it. This solution will only remain potent for five to seven days, depending on how much intent you put into it. After that, you will have to repeat the process, or try to re-energize the existing solution with concentration and visualization.

◎ City Stones ◎

Gemstones have a long colorful history in magick. The most famous probably comes from the mythic high priest's breastplate containing the twelve birthstones, each one corresponding to a zodiac sign. All magical cultures have used stones in spells and healings. Quartz crystal points direct energy. Scryers use balls of crystal to gaze into the future. Turquoise and jade are used for healing. The magical value of metals and gems made them valuable, causing them to be used as the foundation of our monetary systems. Why was gold so valued in the ancient civilizations, and even in our modern world? It couldn't be used for weapons or tools. Even though it can be beautiful, society has placed an outrageous value to it. Gold is valuable because it is the metal of the Sun, full with life-giving powers. Even though we have forgotten that, unlike our Sun-honoring ancestors, modern society still places great value on it. We still use crystal magick disguised as traditions. Diamond rings as tokens of engagement carry their own spell for fidelity and a long-lasting relationship.

As cities are alive in their own way, so are all stones are alive. They are animated by spirit and energy. Each has its own personality. The chemical composition of the stone, along with its color, determines the uses of that mineral. Each stone has unique powers to heal and make magick. These systems of magical correspondences have generated many volumes on crystals and stones. They are all valuable and a great resource. Books like *Love Is in the Earth* by Melody (Earth-Love Publishing House), and *Cunningham's Encyclopedia of Crystal, Gem, and Metal Magic* (Llewellyn) are wonderful, but don't forget the resources on your own street.

If all stones are alive, they all have magick, regardless of whether they are found in a deep Brazilian mine or on your street corner. You can find magical stones on a walk through the park, at a construction site, on the sidewalk, or at the beach. You do not need to get expensive mined stones. If you are called to work with them, then do so. I have a rather large mineral collection that I use in crystal-healing sessions. Many of the stones come from places near my home.

When working in the magical vortex of the city, some of the most powerful stones you can obtain are those that have been dwelling in the city's energy. You need look no further. Go on a city walk, paying attention to the worlds between worlds. Go with an intention. If you need help with a material spell or meditation, think about that intention. Basic spells can be for healing, prosperity, protection, love, or happiness. Tailor the intention to your specific needs before you go out walking. Ask to find a mineral spirit to aid you in this intention. Be aware and allow things to happen.

On your journey, you may find a stone that catches your eye. These are your power stones. Don't pick up every pebble you see, but only the ones calling out to you, activating your psychic senses. Walk along your magical streets and park pathways. If you live near a river, lake, or ocean, search the banks or shores to find an amazing array of stones, usually smooth and polished. They are wonderful for magick.

Let the mineral spirit connect with you once you put your intention out into the universe. Some say you will only pick the stones who want to work with you. Practice hearing their voices. Some stones will not be able to help you, but may, rather, need your help. When stranded with a broken-down car on a New England highway, my friend and I waited for the tow truck on a hill by the side of the road. We both "heard" a stone. It was a small, rough fragment of quartz, probably from the granite abundant in the area. It was unhappy. It was not until we picked it up that we realized it wanted to be near its companion, a rock a few feet up the hill. It must have rolled down. We moved it and it seemed happy. At the same time, I found another piece of quartz that wanted to come home with me. I just knew it did. I asked it in my mind and got a yes to confirm it. Be open to the answers, in words, in pictures, or just by knowing. The stone is still on my altar and I meditate with it.

EXERCISE 16 – STONE QUEST

❶ Do Exercise 9, Sidewalking, but with the intention of finding a power stone (see page 79).

❷ As you walk, pick up the first stone that truly calls to you.

❸ Carry it with you and see if your sidewalking experiences and feelings give you an indication of the stone's use.

❹ Return home and quietly meditate with it.

Use your intuition for determining the use of the stone. Many city stones may not be easily identified mineralogically. There is no real place to look them up, because you don't know what they are. They are rocks, plain and simple. So keep it simple and use your senses, psychic and physical. The shape of the stone may suggest something to you. Some stones break in a heart shape, suggesting love magick. If the stone is more round or disc-shaped, like a circle, it may remind you of the protection of a magick circle.

Color is a great key for decoding the powers of stones. Even common street stones come in various shades. We each have our own color chart from personal experiences. Some colors mean love, while others mean peace. Use your own beliefs regarding the stones, as with all color magick. Look at any stone you find to discover color and shape combinations. Then use your nonverbal communication skills to connect with it and forge a bond. Here are some common minerals you may find and identify in the city, chipping off from building foundations and street corners.

Quartz

City quartz is usually found where granite has been used. After some weathering from the local elements, quartz will look like small white stones, sometimes semitransparent, but more often an opaque white color. Quartz pebbles are abundant in rivers and at beaches. Because of the color, quartz can be used for almost anything. It cures illness when used in crystal-healing layouts on the body. Others have used this mineral for shamanic journeys, meditation, increasing psychic powers, banishing nightmares, and general protection.

Granite

Granite is a mineral containing quartz, feldspar, and often mica, used in stonework for buildings and for curbs. Granite often chips from weather stress and imperfections in the rock, making a new home for the chips in the street. I happen to live in the Granite State, New Hampshire, where it's plentiful. Most of the major roads were cut out of granite hills, leaving shards of stone to be found and used in magick. Many ore deposits are found in granite beds, letting the stone pick up a wide variety of vibrations and powers. I see granite as a stone of balance and harmony, mixing different elements. With its quartz properties, it conducts magical energy and can be used for healing. Granite is a stone of foundation, grounding things in material, practical terms.

Marble

Marble is another valuable stone to architects, used in buildings and statues all over the world. As with granite, pieces often wear away naturally and can be put to good use. Limestone plays a major part in the formation of marble. Often, other minerals, including quartz and clay, mix with the limestone during the formation process, creating the different colors and patterns of marble. Because of this, marble is another stone of blending and balance, a stone of synthesis. Traditionally, marble is a stone of protection. Altars are often made of or covered with marble. In India, marble charms are used for protection. Success spells are more potent when combined with this stone.

Slate

Slate is a dark stone that splits naturally into thin plates. Because of this, it's often cut into rectangular plates and used as roofing material, tabletops, and other flat surfaces. Magically, we use slate in rituals to make a clean break from an old situation, job, or relationship. By using sympathetic magick, we empower the slate to represent the unhealthy connection. By breaking it and separating the pieces, perhaps by burying them, we break the connection. Slate can also be used for spells for organization, since it sections itself off into nice, neat pieces.

Tar, Pitch, and Asphalt

Tar, pitch, and asphalt are similar substances, each being a thick, black, viscous semisolid material. Tar is created from carbonization of coal or other substances like wood or peat. Pitch is made from tar or petroleum through a distillation process. Asphalt can occur naturally, or be created from petroleum. Today, in the cityscape, they are used mainly for roofing and road construction. Bits and pieces can be found broken off from newly hot-topped roads and driveways. They sound like horrible, nasty products, but each has its place. Their first property is that they are waterproof. Wooden ships were tarred to keep the water from seeping into the boat. Water is the element of emotions, and if you need to get some measure of control over your emotions, these substances in a spell can help you. This doesn't mean that I recommend blocking out or cuting off your emotional nature. On the other hand, it is not always fun to have a breakdown from your personal life seep into your job. If you feel the need to keep these things private, charge a piece of asphalt to help keep your emotions from overwhelming you. Carry it to work. Keep it in a plastic bag, since heat and pressure may cause it to soak through your pocket or purse. Plastic, vinyl, or some other nonporous container should help you transport it. Remove it when you get home and experience your emotional release. Don't carry the stone all the time or it will overload and cause an even greater emotional breakdown where you least expect it. Give yourself time to heal.

These substances often carry and absorb a dark vibration because of the way they are made. Some builders mix in all manner of construction rock and refuse. Neutralize any harmful substances in them.

Definitely do not work with them for long periods of time. Use new pieces, and neutralize and return the piece you are working with before getting another. As similar vibrations gather together, they can be used to draw and remove dark energy from a home, office, or other place. Charge the tar or asphalt to be a magnet, absorbing, holding, and neutralizing harmful energy. Let it work in your apartment for an hour, then remove it, putting the neutralized stone back where you found it. Complete the clearing using sage, copal, or frankincense incense. If you have any adverse reactions to using these dark substances, discontinue the practice.

Construction Rubble

Stones of any type gathered from a construction site have a very strong power stored in them, due to the world around them. They have been in an area where the old is being destroyed to make room for the new. They are strongly connected with the planet Pluto, a planet of elimination and transformation. Gather a small stone from a construction site when you need strong transformational action in your life. Make sure the small stone or pebble will not be missed. It's often best to wait until the construction is over. When you are ready to make these life changes, when you need to clear out the old to make way for the new, charge it in a ritual with your intentions. Obstacles will be removed, even obstacles to which you may be attached and that you may use as excuses in your life. Be specific in what you ask. Keep the stone on your altar as a reminder of its power working for you. Watch all that does not serve, and I mean all, fall away as new support systems come into your life.

Neighborhood-Clearing Spell

Magick can be used for personal gain, but it can also give back to the community around you. Giving back to others with your magick is a good habit to acquire. The more help you give, on any level, the more you will receive when you need it most.

Here is a spell to cleanse your living space, including your neighborhood. Eventually, it can be expanded beyond your neighborhood, to your district and the entire city. The cleansing occurs on all levels. First to be cleared is the physical, including the pollution we have created. Magick has a definite effect on reducing pollution levels, particularly if you work in a creative partnership with the devas of that area. This cleansing will help clear all pollution, not only the physical, but energy and astral pollution as well. You will cleanse the entire "vibe" of the place.

You will need a small quartz stone. A rounded river stone is best, but use any one you can find. Cast your magick circle. As you call upon your guides and guardians, call upon some additional beings. Call upon Mother Earth, the goddess Gaia. You should always be in contact with her when doing any form of Earth healing. Ask her permission to do the work before continuing. Wait to receive an affirmative answer. If you get a "no," there are other forces at work here, and it's best to leave things alone. If you get a "yes," ask to connect to the deva of the city and the devas of your neighborhood. Ask their permission to carry on. If you get an affirmative response, you will be in harmony with the city vortex. You may see it or the energy lines in a map in your head. You may not. You should only go forward if you feel you have Earth's and the devas permission to do so. Ask them to work in harmony with you and to help this ritual.

Charge the quartz stone at the center of your circle. Charge it for cleansing on all levels, in a manner correct and for the highest good, harming none. Put a lot of energy and intent into it. Feel the four elements enter and balance the quartz stone. Feel all the beings gathered in the circle there empower the stone.

The stone grows larger in your mind. Visualize the quartz moving out. It cleanses and neutralizes any harmful or unwanted energy it touches. Dark energy dissolves like fairy dust, like sugar in clear water. The stone expands farther out. It soon fills your circle with its cleansing energy. It moves past the circle into the entire apartment or

home. It grows to fill the entire building. At this point, it will probably start to contract. With some further practice and subsequent ritual, it may expand to cover the block. Eventually, it may be used to
clear the city. Be sure to ask permission each time you do this ritual.

Once it has contracted, thank all the powers gathered, one by one,
and release the circle.

Protection Charm

By wearing a good luck or protective charm, you let the magick
infused in the charm work with you, unconsciously, to fulfill your
objective. The fact that you have put on an amulet of protection,
however, doesn't mean that you won't get hurt if a truck runs over
you. The amulet works by subconsciously alerting you to danger, or
helping you to avoid the situation in the first place. This magick is
preventive.

Most spells casters use some form of protection magick. They may
say daily affirmations or activate their protective shields, as discussed
before. You can make a protection amulet for yourself or a loved one.
Gather up materials that have protective powers and seal them in a
charm bag.

Take a small, black, cloth bag, or make one by cutting a circle of
cloth, gathering the ends, and tying them once all the materials are
inside it. Charge each of these ingredients for protection before
adding them to the bag.

1 teaspoon salt
1 teaspoon black pepper
1 teaspoon chili pepper
1 teaspoon rosemary
1 teaspoon sage
Juice of 1 aloe vera leaf
1 power stone

The aloe juice acts to bind the herbal mixture. The power stone can be a piece of quartz or another stone found on your journeys. Charge the whole thing for protection and seal the bag. Carry this charm with you to increase your powers of protection, or give it to a loved one. Keep it in your car for protection when traveling.

Healing Spell

Healing is an important magical art. Each ritual and working is as individual as the "patient." The illness or injury often determines the course of action on physical, as well as magical, realities. Here is an overall healing spell, great for a cold, flu, or other temporary illness. You can adapt it to suit your needs. Place the following herbs in a large pouch. A small pillowcase will even do. The goal is to spread it out over an area of the body that is afflicted, usually the throat, chest, or abdomen.

1 part bay
4 parts coriander
3 parts dill seed
1 part orange peel
3 parts peppermint

Also put several power stones in the bag. They can be traditional quartz points, rounded stones found on your citywalk, or any other minerals you are drawn to use. Charge them all for healing and place them in the bag with the herbs. Imagine the sack filling with healing energy, bright, healthy-colored lights inside, glowing with health and vitality. Then place the bag or pillowcase on the person in need of healing, and visualize the body absorbing the energy, taking it in, and becoming more healthy. "Recharge" this pouch several times during the illness with your visualization. When done, throw out the herbs and cleanse the stones by dabbing them with your ritual oil, or smudging them with purification or temple incense. If they have absorbed any harmful energies, you do not want them to remain with you until they are cleansed.

◎ CREATING YOUR OWN SPELLS ◎

First decide what your intent is. What do you wish your magick to accomplish? Write it down. Language is a good key for materializing intent. Even if your ritual is not spoken, the very act of writing it down makes the exact intent clearer in your mind. Then decide what you need. If it is more of an inner transformation, perhaps a journey to the sky city or hidden city is appropriate. If you need a more phys-ical manifestation, a magical ritual may be right for you. You can design your own, or perhaps ask a god or guide to help you in mak-ing the spell that is correct for you at this time. Simply asking for guidance can bring your intuition to uncover the right techniques.

Choose the tools you want. Start by asking yourself some ques-tions. Will the ritual be all in your mind, working strictly with energy, visualization, and intent, or will you use physical tools? What tools will you use? Do any magick words, stones, or plants apply to your intent? Is this a long-term spell to be held in a charm, or a quick burst of magick for a specific, one-time intent? Will you cast a magick cir-cle, or perform a free-form ritual? Look at the examples above. Do they spark any ideas? Once you have these answers, you will have a clearer direction to follow. Just remember to get energy, either your own personal energy or from other helpers and tools, program at energy, and release it to do its work.

Chapter 7
The Language of the Streets

AS A WALK THROUGH THE WOODS brings out the voices of unseen energies–the voices of fairies, elves, and elementals found in the natural landscape–a voyage through city streets can bring out the city's own voices of power. Some, you may have noticed, appear on your sidewalking jaunts. Others need an intention and a different perspective to gain notice. These voices speak the language of the street, giving tools from the energy beings of the city, the consciousness of the city vortex, the buildings and streets, along with the nature spirits and elementals composing these forms. The language of the streets is another powerful tool, a resource for your magical bag of tricks. These words and symbols encompass a great deal of power in a single, seemingly small magical act, because they are in harmony with the city.

◎ MAGICK WORDS ◎

Abracadabra, presto change-o, and the rabbit is no longer in the hat. Everyone has heard something similar from a stage magician. Say the magick words and reality changes, although this happens through illusion and sleight of hand. But the tradition of magick words really originates with the more esoteric magicians.

Words, like pictures, are symbols of power. They stand for something else. They represent a force of the universe, a being, or a concept.

Many of the sacred languages, like Hebrew, Sanskrit, Greek, and Gaelic, have inherent power. Other sacred languages remain hidden, either by the contemporary practitioners, or in distant and tribal cultures, or they are obscured by time, like the ancient language of the Egyptians. The words and letters of these sacred languages, both spoken and written, carry great weight. Many cultures, including mainstream Christianity, believe the universe was created with a word. The word is God. Hindu traditions believe the word itself is AUM, more often seen as OM, the resonant sound of the universe. That single word, they believe, is the power of creation. Chanting it brings you in harmony with creation.

Even words we do not understand, or that do not fall into one of our known languages, have power. The tone and phonetic sound of the letters all have a resonance to them. The pitch and volume have an effect. Vibration is energy. Sound is power. Mystics have often spoken in tongues, using random sounds when in trance states. The words have meaning to our unconscious. This language, Glossalalia, is the primal language of creation. Since it speaks to the unconscious self directly, we all hear what we want and need to hear. When one hears a "prophecy" from a mystic speaking in tongues, they often hear their own personal message. The message can be a great thing, telling you what you need to know, but if you try to impose your own personal message on others, things become difficult. Everybody has his or her own message to discover.

Shamans, on their initiatory journey, often learn a new language from the spirit world. They either keep the words and pictures to themselves, making it a private, secret language, or share them with others, creating new magical traditions. I think magical alphabets, like the runes and Ogham, from the Norse and Celts respectively, were gifts from the Gods to the shamans of their people, much like the more modern Enochian language of the angels. By passing the magick on to the people, the Gods gave them a direct connection. Through the language, the powers of the Gods can be petitioned to help the people. The powers of the city work in the same way.

The power words revealed by the city do not often come in an obvious way. Many are voiced without speaking a word. No grand visions of extra-dimensional entities are needed. The physical city speaks to you in its own language. The written word is everywhere. Look for its messages. Look at the signs and graffiti in the city, on its streets and its shops and buildings. Everything is labeled. The magick is hidden between the lines. Look to see what letters pop out at you in the dazzling electric signs. Put those letters together and make something new. The word is already there, just waiting for you to see it. The city speaks with a secret power. What does it say to your inner voice?

For instance, in a sign saying

Annie's Books And Gifts

you may pick up on the letters A, B, A, and G, since they are capitalized. "ABAG" becomes your magick word. To me, this would signify receiving knowledge and wisdom, hence the book-shop association. But each of us interprets things differently. This interpretation is just the first thing I thought of when I saw the new word and where it appeared. You may put the letters backward–GABA–or rearrange them, coming up with a new word for you. Go with your first instincts and impressions, for they are the most important. Another sign saying

Grand Opening at McBurgers

reduces to "GOMB" in my mind. The round sound of the word brings a sense of satisfaction. You have what you need. I would use this type of word for prosperity magick. Again, the mood of satisfaction corresponds to our desire for fast-food satisfaction and eating on the run. Magick words do not always correspond in that way, however. Take the sign

> Restaurant
> Eat At Joe's.

I see "REAJ," but the image I evoke from that word is protection and strength, and that has nothing to do with restaurants. Go with your first impression. Some may be magick words signifying energy in the city, special code words to make things happen. Others may be names of entities in the city. They may be speaking through the signs to get your attention, spelling out an actual word. Or perhaps a few whole words will stick out as key to the message. You can do a spell and ask for a sign that it is working. On your sidewalking journey to gain a sign, the first place you stop at is "The First National Trust Bank," but "Trust" is the word that sticks out for you. There is your sign.

EXERCISE 17 – GAINING MAGICK WORDS

❶ Do Exercise 9, the sidewalking experience, but start with the intention of finding a magick word (see page 79).

❷ Once you think you have the magick word or words that are correct for you, write them down, along with any intuitive information you feel regarding their meaning and use. Some get a lot of information, others get only the word. Use whatever comes. Return home.

❸ Once home, get comfortable and prepare for meditation. Do Exercise 1 to enter a meditative state (see page 17) and Exercises 3 or 4, chakras and protection shield (see pages 25 and 27), if you desire.

❹ Chant the magick word or words in a slow meditative voice. Experiment with the pitch and tempo. Allow yourself to feel the effect of the words and tones on you. Be aware and observe.

❺ Chant only as long as you desire and feel comfortable. When done, write down your further impressions. They should give you personal clues as to how to use your magick words.

Once you find a word or phrase that resonates with you, if you do not have any intuitive information about it, do a journey or some more sidewalking to connect with this power and see what it wants and how you can work together. If you are uncertain about the nature of a word, invoke your protective shield and speak it before going to bed. Ask to receive and remember dreams and messages revealing its powers, or perhaps you will just awake knowing its true meaning.

By speaking or chanting such a word as "REAJ," with the association of protection, you are strengthening your protective shield. You can speak it quickly, like an affirmation of an energy or trait you need immediately. Chant it to raise energy for your spell in a ritual. Write it out and burn the paper during the ritual. There are a number of methods for working with magick words.

◎ SIGILS ◎

Sigils are written symbols used to evoke magick power. Magical symbols can be created all around us. Some have personal symbols that they wear as charms or tattoos to evoke their own personal power. The land abounds with them. Many relate to animals and trees, or to the cycles of Earth. They may relate to the Moon, the Sun, or the positions of the stars. Some come from ancient languages and magical systems. Ritual magicians have their magical squares, converting their intentions into numbers and then tracing the numbers across a grid to create a new esoteric symbol. New symbols can come from the city, traced from the lines of the city and paths where our personal power flows.

World Sigils

A modern, yet more traditional, method of sigil making is to take a statement of your intention and reduce it to key letters. These letters are then combined into one graphic symbol used for magick, either in ritual or to make a charm. The benefit of doing magick in this way is the ability to let your conscious mind forget the symbol's meaning, allowing you to detach from this goal. With detachment, you increase your chance of success, because your fears and worries about success will not detract from your spell. Once you use it, you can let the meaning go.

Here is a simple statement for protection:

PROTECT MY HOME

By crossing out the repeated letters, reduce the statement to its basic components.

P R O̶T̶E̶C̶T̶ M̶Y H O̶M̶E̶

This technique reduces the statement to these five letters:

P R C Y H

These letters can now be combined into a graphic symbol for home protection. They can be turned upside down, on their side, or arranged creatively. Use your imagination when making your own sigils. Once created, a sigil can be traced ritually or painted on your doors and windows, drawn in the air, visualized, carved on a charm,

Figure 8. Protection sigil.

or likewise empowered and placed in the home. Can you see the letters incorporated in the symbols shown in figure 8?

This is one simple and fun technique for making sigils. I enjoy it, and those who resonate with symbols in general seem to like it as well. A slight variation on this technique is to remove only the vowels and make your symbol out of the remaining letters. Other more obscure techniques use other systems of symbols, converting the intention into what amounts to be a foreign language before creating the symbol. They are fun, effective, and worth exploring as well, but a bit beyond the scope of this book. Here we will be focusing on city symbols.

Graffiti Sigils

City sigils are a bit different, although the basic concept is the same. Create a pictorial representation of your intent. Instead of reducing your intention and using the letters of an alphabet, use the language of the city. By using the energies in harmony with your environment, you create powerful magical designs.

The first technique is somewhat like the pictorial version of magical words. You search the city for symbols and designs that catch your eye. The most innovative place to look for such symbols is in our modern-day cave art, graffiti. A lot of the ancient symbols held so reverently in magick today come from primitive drawings and etchings on cave and temple walls, stones, and tools. Street artists hold the same function in our society, drawing primal symbols and scenes while marking their territory. Unfortunately, this doesn't fit into what the rest of society has deemed acceptable, so most graffiti is seen as a problem. When looking at it with a magical eye and as a potential tool for your own empowerment, the whole concept takes on new meaning. In some ways, these artists are like shamanic practitioners, flowing free-form with symbols that change the energy and effect of an area, even though most are unaware they are doing it. Are these symbols any more or less important to the universe than the ones kept in bound books for mystics? I do not think so. As you survey your local graffiti, you may be surprised to see how many themes there remind you of more traditional magical symbols. Some of the most primal symbols are artistic letter combinations that act as the "tag," or signature, of the piece.

Once you find a symbol that attracts you, you must decode it. At times, you may simply see its meaning, and all is clear. The words, symbols, and colors around it can give subtle clues. In other cases, you must meditate on the symbols to discover their meaning. Each meaning is personal to the user, as each symbol unlocks your own personal connection to the universe.

After a bit of research you may have a complete symbol system drawn right from the city in which you live, a system as powerful and important to you as any other symbol system.

Figure 9 shows some letterlike figures between what appear to be two bent spray cans (see page 178). Upon seeing this symbol, I associated it with forces that push or blow you in different directions. Notice that the straight-lined letters consist of two separate parts, roughly joined in a curve. To me, this symbol relates to dealing with forces beyond your control or liking, to bringing together different

Figure 9. Graffiti sigil to make peace. Photo credit: William Michie

parts of the self, or two different factions that have been fighting. Use this symbol to make peace, internally and externally.

Figure 10 contains a few interesting things (see page 179). At the bottom center is a heart with more stylized runes. This symbol can most certainly be used in a charm for love magick. To the right is the word "ki," a Japanese term for life force. Although probably not the intention of the artist, this marks a high-energy symbol site. To the left is a cross, a symbol of balance, riding a wave surrounded by three dots (two toward the bottom on either side of the cross, one at the bottom of the vertical stroke), perhaps marking the trinity of mind,

Figure 10. Graffiti sigils for love magick (bottom left) and health and balance (bottom right). Photo credit: William Michie

body, and spirit. This symbol can be used for health and balance on all levels of being.

The image calling to me in figure 11 is in the lower left corner (see page 180). At first glance, it looks like a person, like the symbol for woman or Venus, a circle atop a cross. Surrounding it is a chaotic swirl of lines. If the circle and cross were a person looking at you, the majority of the swirls would be on this being's left side. The left side denotes feminine attributes—receiving, opening, intuition, emotion, and going with the flow. The symbol resonates those traits to me, so

Figure 11. Graffiti sigil to bolster the divine feminine within.
Photo credit: Lena Garutti

I would use it in a magical ritual to bolster those traits and open to the divine feminine within.

Figure 12 is one of my favorite graffiti symbols (see page 181). The right-hand loop looks to me like a handle. The rest is a futuristic key. The symbol is almost astrological in shape and form. For my magical purposes, this symbol is used in information magick, to unlock the doors of knowledge, wisdom and mystery. When you need to remove obstacles from your path– whether mundane, as in a job, or magical, as in seeking out new information–use this symbol.

Figure 12. Graffiti sigil to remove obstacles. Photo credit: Lena Garutti

One of the more complicated symbols I found in my quest for graffiti magick jumped out at me as a symbol for higher guidance. In figure 13, buried between the lines, is a very modern symbol for an angelic figure (see page 182). I see a halo on top, swirls of wings, and several star shapes. Use this image when invoking higher guidance and seeking out a new guide in your meditations.

As you experiment with these techniques and symbols, you will discover your own magical insight to decode them. As with everything, practice and an open mind make all the difference. Once you have found a symbol, meditate on it, draw it in the air, write it down, or make a charm out of it. Charge it with your intentions.

EXERCISE 18 – GRAFFITI SIDEWALKING

❶ Do Exercise 9, the sidewalking experience, but start with the intention of finding a magical symbol (see page 79). Bring a notebook and pencil with you, or a Polaroid camera, so you will have a copy of the symbol immediately.

❷ Once you have found the symbol correct for you, write it down or take a picture of it, along with any intuitive information you feel regarding its meaning and use. Some get a lot of information. Others get only the word. Use whatever comes. Return home. Meditate, using the symbol as a focus. Write down all you can remember after your meditation.

Figure 13. Graffiti sigil to invoke higher guidance. Photo credit: William Michie

Map Sigils

The second technique for identifying sigils uses the very streets and pathways of the city itself. These pathways are a language of power, connecting people and places through lines of power. The lines you follow can be streets, subway tracks, waterways, or simply lines connecting important places. All pathways, whether natural paths or man-made are usually conductors of energy. Use the shapes of these paths to your advantage. This is geomancy, the study and manipulation of energy lines to create a harmonious environment in action. You are creatively using maps of these power lines to manifest your desires. What could be more in harmony with your environment than that?

Start by getting a map of the city where you live. You may have one already, used to trace magical power lines you have discovered on your sidewalking trips. This is your magical map, an invaluable city tool. Once you have the map, pick places and streets strongly associated with your goal. Decide your intention and, instead of reducing it to simple letters, reduce it to points on the map. Once you have decided what parts of the city can aid you, connect them. Use the city streets and subway lines as your guide, or simply cross conventional pathways and connect places separated by greater distances. Tracing paper is an important tool for initially creating the sigil, as it saves you from making a mess of your magical map. Here are some examples of my own city sigils.

For a time, I was in the music business, trying my hand at fame and fortune to become a rock star. My band came from New Hampshire and was desperately trying to break into the Boston club scene where no one knew us. Boston is a big club town, with many bars for the college kids to go out and hear music, but there are ten times as many bands floating around town as there are clubs. When you start out as unknowns, club owners expect you to get all your friends to fill the club. If you're from out of town with no real reputation, you may leave their club empty, no matter how good you are.

I made this sigil and used it in a ritual, asking for more shows in the Boston area. I wrote out my intention with the sigil and cast a magick circle. In the ritual, I visualized my desired outcome. I saw the club promoters getting our tape and calling me up to book the band. Then I burned the paper and raised the cone of power in a magick circle, releasing the energy to do its work.

The symbol in figure 14 is based on the locations of some of the clubs we were targeting (see page 185). I used Lansdowne St., Boston's infamous club row, Central Square in Cambridge where all the new bands play, The Paradise Rock Club back in the city, and Kendall Square, a more low-key artist area also in Cambridge. By connecting these points, I created my magical sigil in harmony with the intention.

Focusing solely on Cambridge, I based my next sigil on Harvard Square and used it as an amulet (see figure 15, page 186). I worked not too far from Harvard University, and found myself constantly doing errands there. There was a great occult bookstore in the Square at the time, along with a witch shop down the street. I found some other interesting shops and restaurants. Parking in Cambridge, and Harvard Square in particular, is horrible. Street parking is difficult and, frequently, the garages are full or very expensive. Even my usual visualization of parking spaces often failed me. Then I started doing city magick to get parking spaces.

The parking sigil in figure 15 is based on locations where I had had luck parking before: Church Street, Garden Street, and Mass. Ave. just before you enter the Square. I marked these locations as special sacred sites, because parking spaces are a special gift from the Gods. At least, that's how I felt. In this case, the locations were close enough to use the streets as the base of the sigil. I joined them, using the closest streets available. I liked the symbol, but found it lacking. So, in an artistic move, I doubled the sigil and mirror-imaged it, making it a bit more symmetrical (see figure 15 bottom). I painted the symbol on a flat disc of wood I bought in a craft store and consecrated it during a circle ritual to get me a parking space whenever I held it and said, "I have a parking space now." I say it silently to avoid freaking

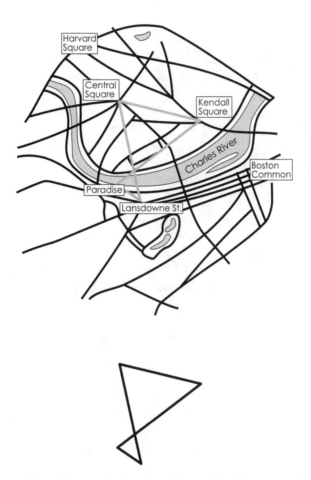

Figure 14. Map of Boston (top) with sigil for the band (bottom).

out my passengers. I have kept it in the car ever since and have found that it works not only for Harvard Square, but all over. I always thank it and the powers that be when I get the space.

Figure 16 (see page 187) shows a sigil I made for a friend moving to New York City. I have worked with Manhattan's energy a bit when I have visited there, but I have not really spent enough time

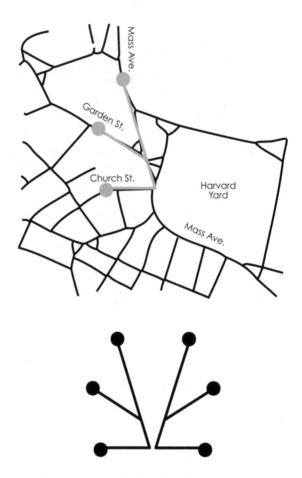

Figure 15. Map of Harvard Square (top) with elaborated parking sigil (bottom).

there to truly know the city intimately. You can, however, learn a lot about a city in a short time. Just be aware that a lot of it can still remain hidden. My friend needed an apartment because she was subletting and her lease was almost done. We marked on the map all the neighborhoods in which she was looking, and all the neighborhoods she had lived in where she wouldn't mind living again. By connecting

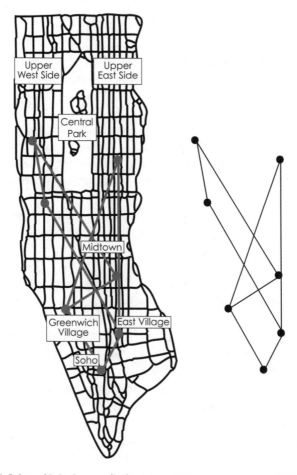

Figure 16. Map of Manhattan (left) with sigil for new apartment (right).

the spots, we created this sigil. She carried it around with her and visualized it before getting the newspaper real estate section. It gave her encouragement and a focus. She did finally settle in one of her chosen areas.

Exercise 19 – CREATING A PROTECTION CITY SIGIL

❶ Create your magical intention. That is the first step in the process. For this particular exercise, we are creating a symbol for your protection in the city.

❷ Get out your map and mark places important to you around your home. Include places you feel are safe and comfortable—your "turf," so to speak. Choose two to five spots. They can all be close together, surrounding your home, or spread across the city.

❸ Place tracing paper over the map and experiment with connections to these points. Create a symbol that resonates with you. Modify it artistically, as needed.

❹ Create a magical charm by drawing the symbol with intent on a piece of paper no larger than a dollar bill.

❺ Empower the symbol. You can simply stare at it and visualize your goal, or do a full ritual like the magick circle, inviting your spirit allies to join you. City sigils can also be empowered by walking the streets you've chosen, actually marking your symbol through your movements in the city. Your act of magical side-walking becomes the ritual of power. Carry the paper talisman with you in your wallet when you travel in the city. Know that its power and the power of the city are protecting you.

Now that you have a better idea how to find magick words and make your own sigils, you can use them anytime. Some practitioners have personal symbols or a group of symbols with which they work continuously, letting their power grow. Sigils can be carved on special tools and equipment. In the city, graffiti is another source of symbols and words. You can find them there or leave them. Marking your symbol on a place can infuse it with your own power, particularly for protection. If you use your personal symbol, however, it's as if you leave a magical and physical fingerprint that can lead right to your door. Be careful who you lead to your home base, both physically and spiritually. I am in no way condoning vandalism, but in places where graffiti is already prevalent, would you really be doing any damage? That's up to you to determine. I think the right symbol can add artistic and magical flair to an area. Graffiti magick to keep the peace and safety of the whole neighborhood can be a welcome act.

Chapter 8
20th-Century Runes

ANCIENT MAGICAL CULTURES each had their own systems of symbols and glyphs. They were carved and painted onto the rocks and trees, in temples and caves and on items of importance. These symbols embodied forms of communication, storytelling, record keeping, and magick making. Much of what we know from these cultures comes from such pictures. We all still recognize the stag dabbed in primitive paint on a stone wall. What we will never know for certain is the meaning the stag had to the people who painted it.

One of the most recognized systems of esoteric symbols, largely due to the influence of New Age mystics, are the Norse runes. The runes appear to be 24 symbols made up of straight lines. The word "rune" does not actually mean "symbol." Its meaning is more synonymous with secret, hidden knowledge, or mystery, much like the meaning of the word "arcana" from the system of wisdom known as the tarot. The mystery, the ever-evolving concept behind the symbol, is the true power of the rune. Each rune has an easily identified mundane meaning, like ox. The rune can simply mean ox, or the concept behind the ox. For the Norse people, the ox was a form of money, of wealth. Wealth leads to the concepts of desire, of those resources you have, and those you want. What you need, want, and have can be far removed from monetary measures.

Although the physical beginnings of the Norse runes are unknown, mythically, the system was discovered by the Norse God

Odin, who hung upside down from the World Tree for nine days and nights, until the branches revealed these symbols to him. The symbols were, perhaps, not the most important thing that Odin gained here, but rather, the mysteries he learned in this Hanged-Man position. The wisdom of the runes is making its way back to the world. Rune necklaces and bracelets are found in kiosks at most shopping malls. Hopefully, the fashion statement will later cause the wearers to seek out the lore and history of the symbols they wear.

As we pass the millennial milestone and look back on the culture of humanity as a whole, we see that we have created many new, almost universally accepted, symbols. Some are unique to a given society and point in time, but most people recognize that a green light on a street means go and a red one means stop. Another commonly accepted symbol is the skull and crossbones, marking poison or danger. This symbol is, hopefully, like a magical ward, barring all from danger. Other symbols come from our popular culture. A heart with an arrow through it is a familiar Valentine's Day love symbol. Golden arches indicate a particular dining experiences. If you look around your city streets and in your home and office, a whole pictorial language of labels, street signs, and everyday objects emerges. The range and scope of this language goes unnoticed by almost everyone.

Not only has modern society created these simple symbols to be easily recognized, they have created their own system of runic lore. These symbols all have their mundane meaning, the meanings most recognize, they also represent other evolving concepts. At least, for the city magician they do.

Modern magick has reclaimed old runic traditions. Primarily, they are used in two ways. The first is divination. Divination is the act of reading the past, present, or future. Scrying exercises, like looking into a crystal ball, are a form of divination. Divination with symbols occurs when we read tarot cards. Each symbol answers a question or series of questions, as interpreted by the diviner.

The second use of runes is to create magical items, charms created with specific intent. Through various methods of combining runes, much like creating city sigils, you create a power object that can be used for spells of protection, love, and success.

Now let's take these methods a step further, and create runic traditions from the modern symbols all around us.

◎ Modern Symbols ◎

Figure 17 shows a collection of symbols that can be used in modern rune rituals (see page 193). They are symbols with which I have experimented and had success. There are many more to be discovered. Ignore those that do not resonate with you and supply yourself with ones that do. The wonderful thing about creating your own tradition is that there are no rules. You can pay homage to the past, or simply create the symbols that feel correct for you. Most divination systems have a set number of pieces, a magical number resonating with the system. The traditional Norse runes, the Elder Futhark, has 24 symbols. The Younger Futhark has 16 runes. The I Ching has 64 hexagrams. The tarot has 78 cards. Use a number that is correct for you. You can add to it, as long as the symbol system does not become too complicated for you to use it easily.

Airplane

The invention of the modern airplane gave humanity a chance to master the dimension of flight. Metaphysically, the airplane obviously resonates with the element of air, both mastery, as signified by a "successful" flight, and a disaster. The airplane symbol on an outward and obvious level can mean travel by plane, or, more important, travel by mind. Place your thoughts, your worldview, into a new location. Sometimes, the journey is more important than the destination. Excitement and potential danger are signified by this marker, though the danger can seem exaggerated, since, statistically, travel by plane is much safer than travel by car.

Figure 17. Modern rune symbols.

Answering Machine

Of our many loved communication devices, the answering machine is a favorite of many. Acting as a personal secretary, it can simultaneously take messages and screen phone calls, allowing you to avoid those to whom you do not wish to speak. Only our modern world could simultaneously embrace the answering machine or voice mail to avoid people, and call-waiting to make sure we don't miss anyone important. For those who, when calling, get the answering machine continuously, it becomes a source of constant frustration. This symbol indicates miscommunication, avoidance, and the feeling that someone is too busy for you. It can also mean that the responsibilities you are avoiding are piling up.

Arrow

The arrow is a symbol of direction. It can point where you are going. At other times, as in a one-way street sign, it can indicate restriction. If you turn this way, you have no choice but to follow the arrow. There is no turning back. In a rune reading, the arrow symbol can point toward another symbol, indicating that those energies are unavoidable. It can also point to the pathway that will answer your question.

Atomic

The symbol of the atom shows great potential for creation and destruction. The atom itself is the basic building block of matter and, ultimately, of life. It symbolizes the knowledge humanity has gathered regarding the physical sciences in such a short time, and how much more knowledge it has to discover. The atom is a great symbol for the misuse of knowledge and power, whether in science or magick. The atomic bomb can be seen as one of the greatest misuses of power in the world. The potential problems deriving from atomic energy are also given this symbol. Remember, however, that the Sun's light also works on atomic principles, so all atomic energy is not clouded by the specter of the bomb. The atomic symbol truly denotes power, for good or evil. With that power comes the potential for misuse.

Balloon

Balloons go up and away, rising with gases lighter than air. The symbol is obviously connected to the sky realms and the idea of rising. For some, this may be a message of enlightenment, of continually expanding perspective, or gaining a greater vantage point. The balloon also signifies some potential problems. As you go higher, you gain a greater perspective of the whole, but may lose track of details and become detached from individual people and situations. Sometimes things rise without us. Think of a crying child accidentally letting a balloon go and watching it float away. Moreover, once something goes up, it usually comes back down, with no control over the location of descent. Balloons are battered by the winds of fate and have no control of the journey. Depending on your need for control and attachment, the lesson of the balloon symbol can be a blessing or a curse.

Boat

The boat is master voyager, a tried-and-true form of travel. Tales of magical boats and journeys by boat are plentiful in mythology. Water is not only the emotional or the astral, but also the gateway to the otherworld, the underworld in Celtic myths. A journey by boat is a journey of the soul as much as of the body. On a mundane level, the symbol can indicate an actual boat journey or time spent near the water. On a metaphysical level, it can indicate an emotional or magical journey, often for healing or transformative purposes. Like boat rides, emotional relationships can be smooth and steady, tranquil or turbulent, filled with sound and fury.

Brick Wall

Like many symbols, the brick wall has two interpretations. It can indicate a wall that is blocking you from going somewhere or doing something you desire. It can represent an obstacle with which you have difficulty. You could potentially climb over it, but you have no idea what is on the other side. The other possibility is that the brick wall is protecting you from something on the other side. It is a defensive measure you have put in place. Unlike a window, although it is strong, it does not allow you to see what is on the other side. You can climb to the top and peer over, but that action could reveal you to your enemies. Both these meanings share the common element of obscurity–the unknown on the other side of the wall. You may have created the wall, or it may have been created by someone else. In divination readings, look to see what is being blocked by the wall.

Car

The car is another symbol of elemental transportation. Driving over roads and highways, the car resonates with the element of earth. It stays close to the ground and relies on the land as its foundation. For many, car travel is a more practical method of travel, despite its obvious environmental drawbacks. The car symbol indicates a practical, usually short-term, journey, often in the mundane sense, by car. It also indicates the potential for people to humanize objects, giving their cars names or assuming they have a personality and disposition. Many spend a lot of time in their cars. Some live out of them, seeing them as a second home. Many keep little necessities in them, giving them a very lived-in feeling. In a reading, the car symbol can indicate travel, or a home away from home.

Clock

The clock, whether mechanical or digital, is the mechanism by which we measure out our days, hours, minutes, and seconds. Society works on an agreed objective division of time. Through this common language, appointments are made, schedules set, and things agreed upon. The clock symbol can indicate the necessity or importance of time and scheduling, or the lack of time. Many feel they are running out of time and this symbol usually indicates deadlines or missed opportunities, if you are not aware of time.

Computer

Computers are, to many, the modern miracle. Many jobs would be much more difficult without this invention. Computers indicate the ability to do many different tasks, and often to do them at one time. They indicate the potential for worldwide communication. Some see them as artistic tools for composition, music, and graphics. Others see computers in a darker light, as machines that take us away from nature and basic skills. Both are correct. As with the atomic symbol, there is a dark side and a light side to this technology. The ultimate extension of the computer symbol occurs in the world of AIs, or artificial intelligences–self-aware computers. Speculated about in many science fiction movies, this is the ultimate interface of humankind and a potential new life-form. Will these creatures be kind to their creators? Although they will probably be relegated to science fiction for quite a while, the potential for disasters still exists. The computer symbol will always carry your own personal interpretation. Do you see it as a helpful or harmful tool? What do you use it for, if at all?

Dollar Sign

The dollar sign obviously indicates money, but, on an esoteric level, it indicates the more subtle levels of prosperity, abundance, resources, and the talents and education needed to acquire wealth. Depending on what symbols are near it, the dollar sign can indicate where and how wealth will be made or lost.

Garbage Can

Garbage is the unwanted waste, refuse, and remains of our activities. The symbol itself indicates something thrown away, something discarded in life. For some, the symbol can aptly describe emotional garbage and unhealthy relationships, as well as physical refuse.

Sometimes, it marks things accidentally abandoned. Think of how many times you may have searched the trash bag for something you needed, like a receipt or a check stub. The search through the unwanted waste is never pleasant, indicating a need to deal with what you created, even if you thought you had thrown it away. In reality, there is no "away." There is only here and there.

Go

The green traffic light is a symbol giving permission to go forward. The road is safe and clear, proceed with your plans. When you are looking for permission to do something or go somewhere, the go symbol indicates you have the green light to proceed.

Gun

Guns and gun control are a hot topic in North America. Gun violence, particularly when children are involved, is a growing problem. Many, however, believe in the right to bear arms for protection. The lines are getting blurred in the types of weapons and responsibilities involved in gun ownership. For some, the gun symbol is an indication of protection, either present or needed. For others, the symbol means potential danger or attack. Many associate guns solely with the criminal element. For those living in the city, the chance of being robbed, or knowing someone who was robbed, is high. You can substitute the gun with another weapon that you feel is appropriate to your rune set.

Key

The key is the symbol of opening. The key unlocks barriers and obstacles. It can indicate a doorway through the brick walls around you. The key unlocks parts of your self that you hide or information you seek. A key without a lock marks a search for its match, or a quest, a desire to find your missing half, which can be interpreted romantically in a reading.

Lightbulb

In comic strips, a lightbulb above the head depicts an idea or inspiration. Similarly, in the runes, the lightbulb symbol shows a burst of insight or knowing. On a mundane level, it can indicate electricity. As an esoteric principle, it resonates with fire, spirit energy, and life force.

Man

This familiar symbol, found on many bathroom doors, means you are working with a masculine energy. Notice I did not say "man," necessarily. Though many men may be the living archetypes of masculine force, both good and bad, that energy is not restricted to people of that gender, or to people at all. Masculine energy indicates an active, electric, more aggressive energy. Many times, it is more mental in nature and more likely to project outward rather than look inward. Again, these qualities do not indicate men in general, just the energy described here.

Medical

The ancient symbol of the medical profession, the serpent and staff of the caduceus, is used here. If you prefer, a simple cross, like those found on ambulances, can be used as a modern rune. The caduceus is originally the symbol of the God Hermes, a founder of many of the arts and sciences of ancient Greece that became the building blocks of modern Western society, minus much of its esoteric content. On a mundane level, the symbol indicates medical aid or the need for it. Such a divination would indicate potential illness or injury. Sometimes, the medical aid is traditional, other times less so. Most important, the symbol marks the relationship between life force and the body, and the true roots of disease that lie in the spirit. If your spirit is relaxed and easy, it will experience no "dis-ease," unless you bring it out of balance through your actions, thoughts, and feelings.

Pedestrian

On the roads, a pedestrian-crossing sign indicates a potential danger in the area, danger that you, as a driver, can cause to someone not in a vehicle. The symbol indicates those who might be caught in the "crossfire" of your action, usually inadvertently. These people do not have the same situation or protection that you do. The crossing sign also points to a potential crossroad, where many paths lie before you. It may also indicate simply that you must cross one path before you can continue on your journey.

Poison

The familiar skull and crossbones tells us danger is near, and, more important, toxicity. Poison has the potential to make you sick or make you dead, and care must be taken around all toxic substances. The poison symbol in these runes is not restricted to physical substances and chemicals, but more often points to toxic or poisonous relationships. It tells us something or someone is poisoning us and often this slow poison is operating on an emotional level. When someone is angry or jealous of you, speaking badly, they are said to "spew venom," an animal's natural poison. Toxic relationships are the most difficult to break, for, at times, these harsh feelings become addictive patterns and we no longer realize they are harmful.

Prohibited

The circle with a slash, usually red, tells the viewer that the word or action depicted within the circle is prohibited, not allowed. The rune symbol means the same thing. An action you desire, or an action related to your question, is not allowed at this time, at this place. If you ask a question about starting a romantic relationship with someone specific, and you receive the prohibited symbol, the answer is not likely to be favorable.

Railroad

Railroad-crossing signs signify the opposite of the pedestrian symbol. Here, at the crossroad, you must be aware and cautious, because stronger, potentially destructive forces may be crossing your path. The magical image of the crossroad, the province of the Greek Goddess Hecate, is the image of a junction point between worlds and realms. The many paths between the worlds can lead you where you want to go. First, you must decide where that is.

Recycle

The recycling symbol is the rune of transformation. One substance, now useless and discarded, is transmuted into something more useful. As we learn to recycle our wastes to create our future, the concept behind the symbol becomes even more important to our survival. In magick, this rune indicates a transformation of old to new, whether physical, personal, or spiritual.

Rocket

The rocket is our last mode of elemental transportation. The fires of the rocket guide it out to the great beyond, beyond the realms of earth, air, and water. This method of transportation obviously res-onates with fire, but also with the undefinable life force that reaches beyond our earthly perception. Usually, the rocket rune does not mean travel by rocket, but a controlled spiritual journey upward. Danger is a potential, but growth and understanding are more likely.

Scissors

Scissors are a tool for cutting. This marker means that you are mak-ing a break or cutting things away, usually ties to people, places, and situations. The familiar image of cutting the apron strings is an exam-ple of this symbol at work. It can indicate cutting off unhealthy or healthy relationships. Sometimes, we push away those who could help us and maintain binding ties to unhelpful forces in our lives. The meaning of the scissors symbol in a divination depends on what is near it and on your own intuition.

Shoe

The shoe, or more important, the foot, is the sign of walking, travel under your own physical power, through no other vehicle than your own body. This symbol demonstrates the ability to be self-reliant. Walking journeys are introspective, a time to think things through and explore in a relaxed setting. All the aspects of the sidewalking exercise relate strongly to the shoe symbol. Drawing this rune in a magical work can indicate a need for some city sidewalking.

Skyscraper

The skyscraper is the image of the archetypal Worldscraper, the connective force between the worlds. It can be the mundane world of the street level, with its upper crust of business elite, or a symbol of the worlds within us, a connection of the middle self to the sky self (higher self) and the lower, hidden self, the unconscious or psychic self. The most important lesson of this rune is the connection between vastly different realms. Depending on what other symbols are used, the skyscraper symbol is the vast bridge between worlds, people, and self-images.

Stop

The octagonal red street sign means stop to drivers. The rune bearing the same image is a call to come to a complete stop. Then look around and proceed with caution. Such signs are there for your own safety, as well as the safety of others. When you receive this sign, take time to weigh your options and be cautious. Obstacles and injury can be avoided with some awareness.

Telephone

The telephone is a key to verbal communication, the medium of words. It carries the implicit drawback, however, that you cannot see the reaction of the person on the other end. The phone is a double-edged sword, giving the gift of easy communication over great distances, and the potential for miscommunication. Telephone wires are the metaphorical web that connects most households and businesses across the world. They are a symbol of unity, but, as with a web, make sure you do not get caught in the pitfalls. Most important, this rune indicates two-way communication, back and forth between people.

Television

The television is a one-way window on the world. The television symbol indicates information you are receiving and can react to, but does not indicate one-on-one communication. The information flows in one direction. You cannot send a message or an image back across the box to those you just saw. In a divination, drawing this rune can indicate absorbing information, or simply entertainment, but also the inability to communicate a response. It can mean a one-way relationship, one in which you feel more like an audience member than an actual participant.

Test Tube

The image of a laboratory fascinated me as I was growing up. The idea of discovery through actual experience, actual experimentation, was a magical concept. The test-tube laboratory is a place of wonder and science, of potential miracles, but also of potential dangers and poisons. Another symbol of the blessing and curse of science, the test tube rune stands for all these things and more. The symbol means medicine, elixirs of life and love, advances in science, and fertility for those seeking artificial means of conception. The test tube also stands for explosion, poison, and accident. The fragile glass can contain a miracle cure or the pox, and one wrong move can release it. You may see the vial as Pandora's Box, never knowing what is inside until you release it.

Woman

Another symbol found on bathroom doors everywhere, it indicates the female. For our purposes here, it indicates feminine energy, and not necessarily a person of the feminine gender. Qualities of feminine energy include intuition, emotion, grounding, nurturing, protection, and receptivity. Some say feminine energy is passive, but I see it as more receptive, going within for answers instead of seeking them outside the self.

Yield

The triangular traffic sign means you must let others go before you. They have the right of way; you do not. The rune also indicates that you are in a subservient position and must yield to another who has the right of way. The yield symbol does not mean that you will always be in this position, or that your efforts are completely blocked. It simply means you must let others pass until the right opportunity presents itself to you.

Here I have given you thirty-three modern symbols to get you started. You can use them as a complete system, or modify them as needed for you magick and divination. Add symbols specific to your own experiences, like symbols of totem animals you've encountered on your shamanic journeys. Use the names of beings you meet in these journeys. Your system of city runes does not have to be limited to modern symbols. One of the greatest modern traditions is borrowing from the past. If you have some favorite ancient symbols, use them. Add to the symbols or replace a few. The symbols for Venus and Mars can be used for woman and man, bringing the connotations of both gender and the planetary energies.

E_XER_CI_SE 20 – RUNIC SIDEWALKING

❶ Perform a sidewalking adventure, as explained in Exercise 9 (see page 79). This time, start with the intention to quest for magical symbols to add to your runic system. You can carry a pen and paper with you to write down these new symbols.

❷ Mark on your magical street map where you find these symbols, both new ones and the ones listed above. These can be additional places of power for you, particularly when making city sigils. You can combine the power of these modern runes with your streetwise magical symbols.

◎ CRAFTING RUNES ◎

To use your runes as a full system of divination and magick, you must actually create a rune set. Rune making is a fun form of magical craftsmanship. Traditionally, runes are made from wood and painted, most often in red ochre. Find a fairly uniform wooden branch and peel it, sand it, and cut it into even discs. Upon the surface of each disk, paint a rune, or carve one before outlining it in paint. Usually, a vertical line is placed on the other side of the disc, so the rune reader knows how the circular rune should be aligned when doing a divination. This vertical line allows the reader to flip over the disc, and reveal the rune upright or reversed, avoiding the difficult and vague interpretations of slightly sideways runes. To avoid this problem completely, some practitioners create runes from rectangular blocks of wood.

Modern rune makers can replace the branch with a wooden dowel, making more uniform runes. Craft stores sell wooden discs, squares, and rectangles that can be used for this purpose and for all manner of amulets and talismans. For more specific instruction in crafting traditional wooden runes, refer to *A Practical Guide to the Runes,* by Lisa Peschel (Llewellyn).

Although wood is traditional, I have made rune sets out of flat beach stones and acrylic paint. Although red is favored in the Norse runes, I used black outlined with silver for mine. Any color works. Some use purple for increasing psychic powers. Again, look back on your responses to Exercise 2 (see page 20) to see what colors work for you.

Flat glass beads are an excellent resource. They can be found in many import stores and in pet stores, as they are used to line the bottoms of aquariums. Clay is another medium you can use to customize your magical symbols. I have seen commercial rune sets in clay, plastic, glass, and semiprecious stones like amethyst and rose quartz. Small, inch-long bathroom tiles can be used as well. Whatever substance and style you choose, make sure it resonates with you. Many have strong rules against using plastic, glass, or clay, but if the medium speaks to you, use it. If it fails to produce results, try another medium.

When crafting your runes, make them as ritualistic as you can. Be mindful of your purpose, your intent. Reflect on each rune before making it. Meditate on each symbol before attempting to make the representation of this energy. You may want to reserve a special paintbrush as your magical paintbrush or marker, and use it only to make magical tools.

Once all the pieces are complete and dry, the final step is to obtain some container for them. Traditionalists use a pouch, usually leather or cloth. Urban mages can use a jar or box as a container. Now consecrate your rune set for use with ritual and intention.

EXERCISE 21 – RUNE CONSECRATION

❶ Start by casting a magick circle, as outlined in chapter 2. Make sure you have your rune set with you in the circle.

❷ Call upon the energy of your city itself, including any urban archetypes or totem animals.

❸ Take each rune, one by one, and hold it in your hand. Feel your energy mingle with it. Reflect not only on the meaning given in this chapter, but on its meaning to you. Let one idea forge a link to the next associated idea, until you fill the rune with your personal energy and interpretation. Each link helps create a magical chain of associations for the symbol.

❹ Complete the ritual by placing the runes in their container. Thank the powers who have joined you and release the circle.

◎ Divination ◎

Diving with symbols is much easier than you may think. The first step is to be familiar with all the symbols you are using. We are already familiar with the mundane meanings of all the city runes. Hopefully, through the construction of the rune set and its subsequent consecration, you will have some insight to other meanings for these symbols.

You will need an additional tool for divination–a rune cloth or other similar surface upon which to do your work. The cloth simply marks out different territories in which the runes can land. Each position will give the rune a different meaning when you interpret the rune cast for answers. Each division should be made from a different color material. Practitioners of Voodoo and Santeria sometimes use a tray for this purpose in their own divination systems. A tray with a raised lip is excellent, since it will catch the runes if they are thrown too forcefully. The tray can be painted with divisions or decorated with runic symbols or city sigils.

The division of this workspace can be with any symbolism you feel comfortable using. I suggest two different forms. The first is based on the symbolism of the Worldscraper, or the three shamanic realms. The cloth or tray is divided into three equal horizontal bands (see figure 18, page 208). The first section can be blue or white and

Figure 18. Worldscraper rune cloth, divided into three sections (sky city, visible city, hidden city).

represent the sky city. Runes falling in this section deal with the "higher" aspects of life, such as the mind, spirituality, guidance, and imagination. Direct aid is indicated here. The middle section is for the middle kingdom, the visible city. Marked by green or yellow, symbols in this section will relate to the world at large, money, career, home, physical needs, and other necessities. Your own resources and abilities take form in this space. The last section marks the territory of the underworld, the hidden city beneath the streets, set in black or red. Runes landing here yield information about the dark world, including power, trials, obstacles, initiations, family, and health. It indicates the unseen forces working with us, or against us. Read chapter 4 again to review the three worlds.

The second form is based on elemental symbolism. If you were familiar with other forms of divination and magick, before delving into these urban images, the elemental division may be more comfortable for you. In this form, the cloth or tray is divided into four equal sections (see figure 19, page 209). At the top is the section for earth, usually green or black. The earth section marks the physical, including home, health, and money. Earth is for your own resources, talents, and the things you can depend on. Moving clockwise, the section to the right is for air, for your mental aspect. Runes in the air quarter reveal your thoughts, what's on your mind, what you plan for the future, and what you reflect on in the past. At the bottom is a section reserved for fire. Fire reveals our spirit, our passions and ambitions. This is the quarter of action. Fiery romances, career ambitions, and potential conflicts all are revealed in fire. The left side of the rune cloth contains the water element. Runes in water point to your emotions, relationships, family, and loves. Water is all about how you feel, which may or may not coincide with what you think or what you are doing. Some reserve the middle space for spirit, marking the force

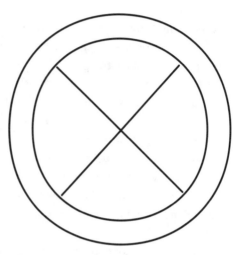

Figure 19. Elemental rune cloth based on the four elements.

unseen above the more human realms. It indicates fate, unforeseen changes, inspirations, karma, and divine aid.

Start any divination, whether for yourself or someone else, by getting in tune with yourself and relaxing. Do Exercise 1 before reading the runes (see page 17). As with many other ceremonies, Exercises 3 and 4 can be quite helpful as well (see pages 25 and 27). Hold your runic container and make an intention to read the symbols correctly and accurately for the highest good. Reach into the container without looking at which runes you are grabbing. Ask your question and then pick out a group and cast them on the cloth or tray. Let them land wherever they may.

Turn over runes whose symbols are not facing up. Leave upside down symbols that way. Then look at the symbols before you. Reflect on their meaning and position. Let one thought link to the next and then the next. Do not censor your thoughts, but do not let your ego or what you want to happen get in the way. Allow new thoughts to come suddenly, like a miniature epiphany. You may be surprised at the strange thoughts you have, only to find that they were completely accurate. The same principle applies to all divinations. In a tarot class I was teaching, everyone was paired off to read the cards. The first thing one student thought of when looking at a card was the *Wizard of Oz*. She mentioned it, but felt silly. Her partner, for whom she was reading for, had just rented the *Wizard of Oz* the night before. It no longer seemed so silly. Trust your gut instinct when doing divination work.

The process is quicker and easier than it may seem. Go with the flow. Once you have contemplated all the symbols and positions, you should have a potential answer to your questions. As with all skills and talents, practice improves your results. Since the process is difficult to comprehend until you have done it, I will lead you through a sample reading and its possible interpretation.

My question here is whether I should take a position that is being offered to me at work. The job description is not quite clear, but it could be a wonderful opportunity. I seek guidance from the city runes and meditate on the question, holding the container of symbols. I gather a few pieces and gently toss them onto the cloth, divided into the three worlds. I turn over all the runes to reveal the symbols, leaving those that fell upside down the way they are. The runes look something like figure 20 (see page 211).

In the middle world, or visible city, we have an arrow pointing up and a dollar sign. In the physical world, this shift "up," a promotion, looks likely and an increase in finances would be worth something.

In the underworld or hidden-city position, indicating my psychic messages or subconscious, there are scissors. Since they are alone, I interpret that to mean cutting away from subconscious fears lurking in the back of my mind.

In the sky-city position, we have the clock, television, airplane, and answering machine. The clock strikes me with two meanings. As a place of higher guidance, the message could be "the time is now." Conversely, it could be telling me to bide my time. Overall, however, I get a positive feeling from this rune. Television and answering

Figure 20. Sample reading on Worldscraper rune cloth.

machine concern me, since both indicate one-way communication. I fear my new supervisor would have that effect. The rumor is that he is difficult to reach for approval. My first thought, when looking at the airplane, is that the journey may not be as perilous as I may think. In fact, it is probably better than I would think, and I am spending too much time dwelling on the negative.

My overall impression of the signs is that I should take the job, since the good symbols, in my mind, outweigh the negative. Remember, the symbols are a personal interpretation, and it's difficult to separate your ego from your psychic mind without some meditation and a simple ceremony.

The next sample reading is for someone who would just like to see what messages these runes have for her. No specific question is asked. I ask her to focus on her life, if no specific questions are apparent, and to reach into the container, grab a handful of runes, and toss them onto the tray divided into four quarters, one for each element. Figure 21 shows the cast (see page 213).

On the earth quarter is medical and test tube. I immediately follow my intuition and feel she is ill and undergoing some medical treatment. She is possibly on a new medication and awaiting its results, or waiting for test results to start a new form of treatment.

In the air quarter are poison and man, indicating a less-than-supportive relationship with a masculine force in her life. I feel it is a husband and/or father figure. I also feel intuitively this has something to do with her medical condition.

In the fire quarter, the brick wall is on the line between fire and water. That indicates unknown obstacles in her life, her spirit and life force, and her emotions. The physical ailments probably have a deeper root, and fear of emotion is preventing her from connecting to the fire, or life force, she needs.

In the last quarter, for water and the emotional realm, I find the edge of brick wall and recycle, railroad, and lightbulb. Together, these indicate a change, or a need for change, in the emotional realm to deal with brick wall. Railroad indicates a crossroad–the time is now to choose where to go. Lightbulb guides the way and asks her to follow the guiding force in her life. Recycle means the old emotions and feelings must be transformed into empowerment.

Granted, these are both hypothetical readings and variations on experiences I've had. Their purpose is only to demonstrate how the runes work in different positions, in small groups, and how to let your intuition guide you through interpretations. Practice is the best teacher. While working with these runes, I suggest you do a divination at least once a week to keep the symbols fresh and growing new meanings in your mind.

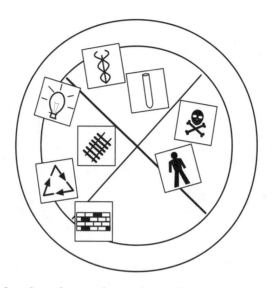

Figure 21. Sample reading on elemental rune cloth.

◎ TALISMANS ◎

Like the sigils created from city maps, the symbols of your new rune set can be used for magical intentions. The first step is to determine your intention. What is the desired goal or outcome of the spell? Once you determine that, you can choose your symbols appropriately. Talismans are then created by combining the symbols, either in a straight line, as if you were stringing letters together to form a magical word, or as a unified, new magical symbol.

To make a talisman to aid you in finding and purchasing a car, you can combine the car symbol with the dollar sign symbol and end with the arrow. The three together indicate the desire to have a car, purchase it, and then travel (see figure 22 top left, page 214). If you need more money, but feel your previous intentions for prosperity lacked power, combine the atomic symbol with the dollar sign. This will create a talisman of power (see figure 22 bottom left, page 214). For

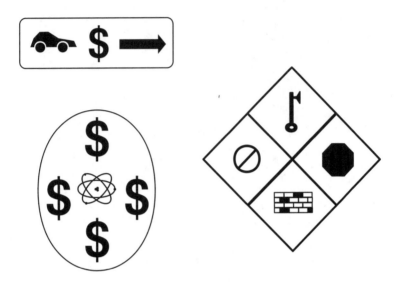

Figure 22. Modern runic talismans: new car talisman (top left); money/power talisman (bottom left); protection talisman (right).

another home protection charm, creatively combine the key, prohibited, stop, and brick wall runes for a defensive perimeter (see figure
22 right). Depending on what you use to protect your home, you may
also include the gun symbol, but I would not suggest it.

Once designed, the talisman can then be created, much as the
runes above were created. Choose a medium you favor and create the
individual charm, maintaining focus on your desired goal. Consecrate
the talisman in a magick circle, as if you were doing any other spell or
sigil. The talisman can be kept on the altar, buried, or carried with you.

Chapter 9
As the World Turns

ANOTHER PROBLEM CITY MAGICIANS, pagans, and witches face when feeling disconnected from the natural world is dealing with the seasonal holidays. The tried-and-true signs of the seasons shifting as the world turns and orbits the Sun are much sparser than for their fellow rural practitioners. Fewer trees mean fewer leaves to turn color in the fall. Less open land yields less grass and fewer flowers to rise up in the spring. The whole point of seasonal holidays is to celebrate the natural forces around you and attune yourself to the natural flow of life force as it changes. For a city practitioner, this is even more important.

Modern pagans, or neopagans, celebrate something called the Wheel of the Year (see figure 23, page 217). The Wheel is a cycle of celebrations based on the changing seasons and the myths–usually European–relating to each season. The image of the eight-spoked wagon wheel is used, ever turning as the seasons shift. Celebrants take an active part, working with the natural forces to turn the Wheel of the Year. The energy of the goddess is expressed through Earth itself, changing as the face of Earth changes with the seasons. The god-force changes form many times during the year, sometimes expressed as the Sun, sometimes as animals, vegetation, or the shadow.

Four of the holidays are solar in nature, based on the Summer and Winter Solstices and the Vernal (Spring) and Autumnal (Fall) Equinoxes, as celebrated in the Northern Hemisphere. Evidence seems to indicate that these holidays were most important to the Germanic, Norse, and Saxon traditions of Europe.

The other four holidays celebrate something called the fire festivals. The four fire festivals fall between the solar holidays, at the cross quarters. Their energy is less astrological and more seasonal. The Celtic tribes, who migrated west across Europe until they reached the British Isles, held the fire festivals sacred. Modern traditions have combined these customs and now celebrate eight major holidays.

Most pagan and witchcraft books contain information and material on these eight major holidays. Although drawn mostly from Celtic, Germanic, and Norse sources, these traditions are well represented in materials relating to other ancient cultures. If you are looking for traditional celebration material, it is best to look at more traditional resources. Here, we will be exploring celebrations for city dwellers, for those on the go, in apartments, and far from the fields and forests. The magick is all around you, as we've seen in previous chapters. You need only find creative ways to celebrate the energy and become attuned to the cycles of life.

Here are some modern, urban celebration ideas that are in harmony with the theme and energy of traditional holidays. They are simple to do in a small home or office, or during a lunch break. They require no groups or exotic tools, and they are not fully scripted rituals. Only you can decide which elements are correct for you to practice. Make your own rituals, using what you have and what you may already be practicing. Use your personal city totems and gods, and incorporate your personal mythology into the traditional framework. These archetypes celebrating the earth, sea, sky, and harvest are found in all cultures. In the city, the hard-to-find harvest may be the local supermarket for you. Without its bounty of fresh foods and all sorts of delicious (if not always healthy) foodstuffs, urban dwellers would not go to bed with full bellies. Now, that is something worth celebrating and a great way to remember that, even when not living off the land, you are still depending on it.

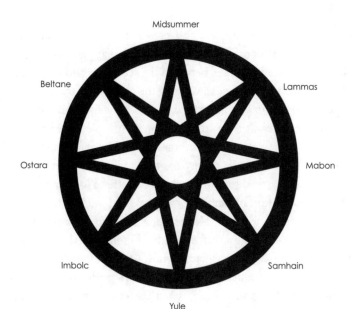

Figure 23. Wheel of the Year.

Find the heart of the celebration within you, and do what you can to work with any limitations you may have in location or tools. You will discover that celebrating the holidays in the city need not be limited, but can be filled with wonderful opportunities to be creative.

◎ SAMHAIN ◎

Samhain, usually pronounced "Sow-en," is my favorite of all the holidays. When I got involved in witchcraft, it was the first holiday I celebrated. This time of year, coinciding with the more modern celebration of Halloween, which is rooted in Samhain traditions, has always been very magical to me.

Samhain is the celebration of the Celtic New Year. On this day, October 31, the Sun is in the astrological sign of Scorpio, a sign of regeneration, power, and the occult. Here, the third and final harvest, the meat harvest, is traditionally celebrated. The first animals are slaughtered, salted or smoked, and preserved for the coming winter. Because of this slaughtering of livestock, Samhain is associated with the land of the dead. The veil between the worlds is said to be thinnest on this day. Stories of the dead walking the earth were the origin of our Halloween ghosts and goblins running wild. Originally, ancestors were revered on this day, as they still are by many people across the world. On Samhain, the god was in the underworld, regenerating from his summer death, and, in many myths, the goddess descends into the underworld, as marked by the slumber of Earth, to join him.

A city celebration of Samhain can best be done by combining the old traditions with the new. Now, young children walk the streets in costume, "trick-or-treating" for candy. Originally, these costumes were to scare away the misplaced ghosts for the evening. Now we celebrate cartoon characters and movie stars with our costumes. A Samhain sidewalking adventure, when the veils between worlds are thinnest, can be quite a celebration.

Materials Needed: Your altar, mementos from deceased relatives, your magical city map

❶ Start the celebration at your home altar, at twilight. Upon your altar, place anything you have as mementos from people in your past. Traditionally, these are from deceased relatives with whom you seek to reconnect, but they can be famous personalities you wish to contact, people whose lives resonate with you, like musicians or actors. Place items associated with them on the altar. Some leave out food for the deceased, on the altar or on a windowsill.

❷ Say a blessing for these people, asking them to be with you tonight. Now is a time to say things that were never said. If someone passed on with whom you were not on good terms, say what you need to say to make peace, for both of you. Forgive and let go.

❸ Do Exercise 3 and 4 to prepare yourself for your sidewalking jaunt (see pages 25 and 27).

❹ Do a sidewalking adventure through the city, as outlined in Exercise 9 (see page 79), before, during, or after the "trick-or-treaters." Be particularly open to information and psychic senses, but also be very careful. This night is wonderfully magical, but often brings imbalance to others.

❺ When you return home, take out your map and trace a sigil of your evening's walk. If you have any spell work to do that night, particularly for spells making peace with the past, releasing old wounds, or saying good-bye to the deceased, do it, and perhaps use the sigil as your vehicle. Or this sigil street tracing can simply be burned on your altar as part of your celebration.

❻ Thank all the powers who have joined you in this celebration.

◎ YULE ◎

Yule celebrates the rebirth of the god-force as the Sun. Honored on the Winter Solstice, usually falling around December 21, the Sun enters the sign of Capricorn. On this day, the light starts its ascension, growing stronger with each passing day. This signals the birth of the young Sun god, familiarly depicted on the Sun card from more traditional tarot decks. You will probably note that this day comes suspiciously close to the birth of another young god, one associated with light in the Christian faiths. Many feel the Christian holiday was moved to match the pagan one, in an effort to convert the pagans of Europe to Catholicism.

Many diehard pagans celebrate Yule outside, regardless of snow and temperature. Some friends of mine even do it barefoot. In the city, you probably won't have the luxury of privacy for an outdoor celebration, unless you have access to a rooftop. The holidays can be celebrated quite well indoors. Celebrate the birth of the new god with some simple tools and a ceremony.

Materials Needed: One fresh egg, ritual bowl or chalice

❶ Prepare your altar with anything you feel is appropriate and festive. Decorations of holly, mistletoe, and pine were originally from pagan celebrations, as was the use of the colors red and green. Modern altars can be decorated with tinsel, garland, candy canes, or Christmas lights if you desire. Have appropriate candles for a solar holiday—gold, yellow, and orange.

❷ Center yourself and get into a meditative state by doing Exercises 1, 3, and 4 (see pages 17, 25, and 27).

❸ Cast a magick circle, as outlined in chapter 2. Add any urban elements from chapter 6 that resonate with you.

❹ While in the circle, invoke the young god to be with you. Traditional images of the young god are Horus, the divine son from Egypt, Pryderi from Celtic traditions, Dionysus, the reborn son of the Greeks, or any other being who feels correct for you.

❺ Feel their life and energy enter the egg on your altar. Ask to help turn the Wheel of the Year and bring the light into the world once again.

❻ Crack the egg and drop the golden yoke into your ritual bowl or chalice. Bless this life force. Feel it illuminating you with life and light, filling your room. Give thanks to the new Sun god. Light any candles you have to bring light to the world.

❼ Remain in the circle as long as you like. Once the ritual is complete, thank all beings who have joined you and release the circle.

◎ IMBOLC ◎

Imbolc is the fire festival celebrated on February 2. Traditionally, it is held sacred to the Celtic goddess Brid, pronounced "Breed," a triple goddess of fire, light, healing, poetry, magick, and smithwork. Although she was later transformed into St. Bridget, and her holiday became Candlemass, her traditions are still kept alive.

This celebration is a feast of lights. Light is used to awaken the sleeping Mother Goddess, Earth. Light is also used to dispel the darkness remaining from winter and to purify your home. Brid is also the goddess of home blessing, infants, and the protection of both.

Materials Needed: Candles, incense, water, salt

❶ Imbolc is the true root of our spring cleaning—or more accurately, cleaning for spring, not cleaning in spring. To prepare for this ritual, clean out your home. Clean out the dust bunnies, and cobwebs. Take the winter staleness out of your house or apartment by cleansing everything, first physically, then spiritually.

❷ Prepare yourself by doing Exercises 1, 3, and 4 (see pages 17, 25, and 27).

❸ Since Imbolc is the festival of lights, start your ritual by lighting many candles in the goddess's name to purify, bless, and protect. Fill your home with as many candles as you safely can, making sure that they are all on nonflammable surfaces. Invoke the goddess of light to be with you in your home, among these lights.

❹ Feel the flame and light fill your home with magical, purifying fire.

❺ Take the salt, bless it, and call upon the beings and elements of Earth. Ask Earth for protection. Bless the water, calling upon beings of water for purity and cleansing, and mix the salt and water together. Using your fingertips, sprinkle some in each room. Outline all the doors and windowframes with this mixture.

❻ Bless the incense and call upon beings of air to purify your space, to raise your vibration. Use any incense comfortable for you. I suggest something like mixtures of sage/sweet grass/cedar, frankincense/myrrh, or lavender/cinnamon. Commercial sticks or cones are appropriate as well. Go from room to room, letting the incense burn. Bring it to each window and door.

❼ Repeat the steps above until you are confident that the space is cleansed and blessed. Thank all beings you have called upon and return to normal activity. Take notice of the differences within your home now.

◎ Ostara ◎

Ostara is the celebration of the Vernal Equinox, the resurrection of Earth through the spring vegetation and flowers. The equinox itself usually falls around March 21, when the Sun moves from Pisces to Aries. Aries is the sign of new births, new beginnings, being the first sign on the Zodiac wheel. As such, it is appropriate that it signals the rebirth of the land and the fiery awakening of the goddess.

Ostara is named after a Teutonic goddess of Earth, very similar to our images of Gaia, or Mother Earth. She is also a goddess of eggs. Eggs are a symbol of rebirth and resurrection, as noted in the Yule celebration above. Our modern customs of painting and hiding Easter Eggs comes from Ostara. Ostara is the time for spring planting as well. Seeds, like eggs, are another capsule of life. On this day, many ask that their seeds and gardens be blessed.

Materials Needed: Seeds, soil

❶ To prepare for Ostara, you need to acquire some seeds. Many markets and hardware stores carry seeds in the spring, even in the city. If you have difficulty finding them, organic grocery stores, often found only in the city, as they are a new trend, have raw, unprocessed seeds that will sprout.

2 You can do the celebration on the actual equinox, or the evening before. When you plant the seeds, however, you should do it during the daylight hours. It is so simple that you can even skip the full ritual and do it on your lunch break.

3 Do Exercises 1, 3, and 4 (see pages 17, 25, and 27). When doing the chakra exercise, focus strongly on your connection to Earth below you. Dig deep down below the city and touch the center of the world.

4 Put the seeds on your altar and, if you desire, cast a magick circle, as outlined in chapter 2. Add any urban elements from chapter 6 that resonate with you.

5 Call upon the goddess beneath your feet, the goddess bright and alive beneath all cities, beneath all stone. Call upon the heart of Earth herself.

6 Ask this goddess to bless your seeds. Ask them to bring new life. If you have an intention, some aspect in your life that you wish to grow, put one intention into each seed.

7 Thank all beings upon whom you have called and release the circle.

8 Plant the seeds with a little blessing. Thank this Earth goddess. You can use window boxes, indoor pots, or simply walk through the park and scatter the seeds. Many wildflowers bloom in the cracks of the streets, so you never know where your magical blessings will go.

◎ BELTANE ◎

Beltane celebrations are more commonly found in the guise of May Day celebrations, with people dancing around the May Pole, singing songs, and having a grand old time. What most miss is that the May Pole is actually a phallic symbol of the god, placed in the ground as part of his union with the Earth goddess. The god is seen here as young and joyous, celebrating the life of his mother and their union, before assuming more serious aspects of his appointed tasks. Beltane is a fire festival marked by good times, frivolity, and love on all levels.

The name Beltane comes from the Celtic god Bel. It means "Bel's fire." Not much survives of the myths of Bel. Some historians wonder if he was really a god at all, or if this story is simply a modern pagan convenience. Regardless, Bel is now portrayed as a fiery young man. The flames of sacred bonfires were lit from the remaining wood of the winter. Cattle, and often people, passed between two bale fires (fires made from sacred woods and bales of hay, used in traditional Beltane celebrations), letting the heat and the sacred wood purify them from the maladies of winter.

Beltane is flower time, when Earth abundantly blooms. Even in the city, her handywork is found—in the parks, flower boxes, and storefronts. Many of the seeds of Ostara bear their beautiful blossoms by Beltane. For this celebration, we reflect and meditate on Beltane.

Materials Needed: A flower

❶ To do this celebration, you need to find a blooming flower. Something still alive and in the ground is best, although you can use a potted flower or even cut flowers as a last resort. If you think it will be difficult to find a growing flower, think of this celebration as part quest. With a little ingenuity, I'm sure you'll find one somewhere.

② Do not cut the flower. Sit with it. Observe it. How many petals does it have? Does it make a shape? What color is it? How tall is it? How many leaves does it have? What shape are they? How does the plant make you feel? Does it evoke any sensations in your body?

③ Do Exercise 1 to enter a more receptive state (see page 17). Then ask to communicate with the flower. That's right, as crazy as it may sound to some, talk with the flower. If you attempted Exercise 15, Plant-Speak (see page 153), then you will already be familiar with the process. Talk to it as if it were a person. Let the answer come to you. Responses can come in feelings, intuitive flashes, pictures, music, or a little voice in your head. You may think you are talking to yourself. That's okay. You are doing fine.

④ Ask the flower the meaning of this time of year. What does Beltane, or May Day, mean to the flower world? Before your conversation is done, ask the flower if it has anything else to tell you.

⑤ Thank the flower for its time and depart. Beltane is a day of festivity and fun. Meet your friends and spend a day or evening with them, just to have fun. They do not need to know the occasion if they are not comfortable with your magical practices. If they are, or better yet, if they are practitioners, you can always invite them to join you with the flowers.

◎ MIDSUMMER ◎

Midsummer's Eve, or the eve of the Summer Solstice, marks the start of summer in our modern calendar. To the ancients, however, it was recognized as the day when the light started diminishing. The summer continued to be hot and humid, but the amount of daylight started to dwindle. The Summer Solstice is the longest day of the year.

Midsummer is much like Samhain, in the sense that the doors

between worlds seem to be open. Many celebrate this time with nature spirits and fairylike beings, or do magick to draw more solar light within themselves. On this day, some traditions claim that the light and shadow components of the gods do battle, and that the light loses, as seen in its waning strength. The light god must be sacrificed on Lammas and sent to the underworld on Mabon, to be there for Samhain. The dark god resumes his control of Earth and the kingdom finishes blooming and starts to wither.

As the god-force has a dual aspect, a polarity of light and darkness, so do we all. In this celebration, we observe our dual nature.

Materials Needed: Mirror

❶ This ritual is best done at twilight or at night, since it deals with shadows. Have your mirror on or near your altar and light your space only by candlelight. Keep things dim and evoke a feeling of the otherworld.

❷ Do Exercises 1, 3, and 4 to prepare for the ritual (see pages 17, 25, and 27). Pay extra attention to your protective shield. Although your shadow is a natural part of you, and not something evil, as many contend, it can be difficult or frightening to view. Being centered, grounded, and feeling well-protected makes the experience easier.

❸ Cast a magick circle, as outlined in chapter 2. Add any urban elements from chapter 6 that resonate with you.

❹ Ask to be aware of your shadow side on this day, when the shadow side is victorious. Ask it to come with "ease and grace," meaning it will not be traumatic for you. Remember, the shadow is not evil. It is simply the part of us we usually do not show to the world. Sometimes, we do not show it even to ourselves. When presented with it, the weight can be too much to bear. Gradual introductions like this are best.

5 Look into the mirror. Gaze deeply into the reflection of your eyes and your entire form. You may look or feel different. You may start thinking about all the things you push away, things about yourself that you try to ignore. While the shadow can bring emotions we want to avoid, it also brings strengths we may have forgotten.

6 When the process feels complete, stop looking in the mirror. Thank the shadow aspect of the god for showing you this about yourself. Thank all beings you have asked to be with you and release the circle.

7 Make sure to ground yourself fully and be centered and present. Write down anything you learned about yourself for future reflection. Pay attention to your dream on this night and keep a notebook by the bed for further insight.

◎ LAMMAS ◎

Lammas, called Lughnassadh in the Irish traditions, is the first harvest. It is usually celebrated on August 1, when the first grain is harvested from the fields and given as an offering to the gods. The rest of the grain will be stored for the winter months.

Since urban dwellers have difficulty relating to harvests and the fact that preparations for winter were once a matter of life and death, they should focus on the divine aspect of the harvest. Many traditions see the harvest as the sacrifice of the god in the guise of grain. The Sun's power is waning after Midsummer. Lugh, a Celtic god of light and grain, is often portrayed as the sacrificed god.

Daylight rituals are difficult for the modern person working nine to five. Lammas is not quite the same at night if you are trying to celebrate the light before the winter darkens your door. One year, I did this quick ritual to celebrate the harvest in my own way. During my lunch break, I sat barefoot under a tree on a pathway leading to the subway. No elaborate ritual tools were needed, and it was one of the best celebrations I've ever had.

Materials Needed: Fresh orange

❶ Sit somewhere quiet where you can see the Sun. Noontime is perfect, but, if it is too hot, sunset is another beautiful time. Do it whenever your schedule allows.

❷ Get comfortable and do Exercise 1 to enter a more receptive state (see page 18). Do Exercises 3 and 4 to connect to the earth and sky and to feel protected completely (see pages 25 and 27).

❸ If you want to cast a circle silently to yourself, visualizing yourself in the center of a ring of light and calling in the quarters, you may do so. I didn't, but it may help you. You don't have to speak it out loud. This celebration is quiet, internal, and personal.

❹ Hold the orange up, so that it covers the Sun. The light shines out behind it. In this ritual, you will be drawing down the Sun into the orange, much as witches draw down the Moon into a chalice. You are drawing down the power of the solar god. Feel the orange fill with light and energy.

❺ Invoke a solar god. It can be Lugh, or any solar/sacrificed deity with which you choose to work. If unsure, ask to invoke the energy of the solar god. Ask him to be a part of your ritual and inhabit the light of the orange. Thank the god for all the light of the past seasons. Thank the god for the light in your life and your own harvest, your own blessings in your life.

❻ While in the meditative state, eat the orange, consuming the life force and energy of the solar god. It becomes a part of you. You fill with energy as the god and your own energies mingle. Be very aware of the whole experience and any images or wisdom you receive.

❼ Feel the remaining solar energy within you drain out from the bottom chakra, the root, and into the earth for healing. Close the ritual or circle and thank all beings you have invoked.

◎ Mabon ◎

Mabon is the celebration of the Autumnal Equinox, usually falling around September 21, when the Sun moves from the astrological sign of Virgo into Libra. It is named for the young god, Mabon, who gets lost in the underworld until his mother, Modron, rescues him. The theme of Mabon is the descent into the underworld as the leaves turn and the scent of death and darkness fills the land. The sacrificed god from Lammas is descending. Here, the underworld is not a place of torment, but of regeneration, akin to the hidden city connected to the Worldscraper.

Mabon is also the second harvest, the harvest of fruits. The reward from such fruits is often wine, so Mabon has also become known as the winefeast, and is associated with gods of wine like Dionysus. Try this winefeast ritual to celebrate Mabon.

Materials Needed: Glass of wine, grape juice, or sparkling cider

❶ Do this ritual at home, privately, after you return from work. Prepare for the ritual by placing a glass of wine on your altar or another similarly fruity beverage, if you are averse to alcohol. Light any incense that will relax you and, in the background, play any suitable underworld music. I think almost anything by the musical group Dead Can Dance would be appropriate.

❷ Do Exercises 1, 3, and 4 to prepare for ritual (see pages 17, 25, and 27).

❸ Cast a magick circle, as outlined in chapter 2. Add any urban elements from chapter 6 that resonate with you.

❹ While in your ritual space, take the glass of wine and bless it. Ask for the sacrificed god, or god of wine, to be with you. Thank the earth for this gift of liquid, no matter what it is. All things come from the earth and, eventually, return to it. Feel the energy of the hidden city, the underworld, rise to meet you and fill your glass. The wine is simply a vessel for this energy.

❺ Drink half the glass, being mindful that it is your key to the power of the underworld. The remaining half can be used as a dark mirror in which to scry. Scrying is the simple act of looking into a reflective surface, like a crystal ball, and letting your mind wander until images form. You can ask questions of this under-world energy and receive images, symbols, and insights.

❻ If you choose not to scry, this time and space is excellent for a shamanic journey, as outlined in Exercise 11 (see page 91). You descend into the otherworld to receive your information, or to be initiated, or simply to celebrate this energy with no specific goal in mind. Let the journey lead you where it will.

❼ Once the journey or divination is complete, thank all beings invoked in the ritual and release the circle. Write down any infor-mation you received.

Chapter 10
The New Urban Temples

MANY ANCIENT CULTURES, from the Mediterranean to Central America, revolved around religion. Magick was part and parcel of these ancient religious ways. Cities were dedicated to gods and goddesses. Temples lay in the heart of cities. The priests and priestesses had power in the community. Citywide celebrations lasting days or even weeks were held in honor of these deities. Such national holidays were celebrated with a passion that our modern "Monday-off" holidays lack. I wonder if these ancient people would have been as religiously zealous if they had grown up with television, radio, and video games?

In modern Western cultures, religion has been downplayed. Changes in worldview, embracing scientific paradigms, and the invention of new forms of recreation have taken the fervor out of a once strongly religious culture. The rise of Christianity was meant to be an embracing, unifying force, but it seems to have done anything but unify. Different factions have split off from its central doctrine in response to attempts at control by individual groups. Now there are so many brands of Christianity that it is hard to keep track of them. I think that this lack of unity and organization is leading to something far better—the resurgence of individual spirituality instead of dogmatic religion. We, as a society, both magical and mainstream, will continue to splinter, until everybody has his or her own practice. Each of us is finding ways to connect to the source on our own terms.

Modern society has not given up many of its religious and social customs. We, as a whole, have merely transformed many of the pagan practices and adopted them as part of our social customs, without even knowing their psychological roots. Many have destroyed the old icons, or kept relics around as works of art without understanding the ceremonial meaning of these tools of worship. For the modern gods of this urban magick, we have created new temples where we worship, petition, and work our craft.

◎ Homes and Offices ◎

The first of the new temples is the home. Home altars have become important components of urban magick. In essence, these altars are not new, merely reclaimed from the traditions of the past. In many ancient cultures, the home shrine was not only accepted, but commonplace. Home altars are a place to do magick, and a place to be reverent to the deities of your life and fallen ancestors. You don't have to go to a church building for spiritual rejuvenation. Spirit is all around you. By creating sacred space in your home, you make your home into your primary magical temple.

The office is the next magical urban temple. In the cultures of the past, most worked in or near the home. The concept of "going to work" had no meaning for them. The home held much of the work, in the form of farming, raising livestock, preparing food, or making clothing. The primary temple, the home shrine, was therefore never far. Later, as civilization developed, "work" moved farther away, to the meeting places of merchants and the state houses of ancient cities. Even then, however, the people were usually united through common beliefs, and the temples of the city were not far from either the home or the workplace.

We now spend much of our lives at our jobs. Now, however, there is no common bond of belief to unite us at the workplace. People would find it strange if you took a meditation break or ran off to a local sacred spot, whether it was a conventional church or your own outdoor space. Modern industries only observe spirituality by sometimes begrudgingly giving employees time off for religious holidays. Our daily observances must, therefore, be done in private. Our places of renewal can be hidden among the items in our offices as nondescript office altars and shrines.

◎ Nightclubs ◎

If business places are where we spend much of our time working with the gods of prosperity, then nightclubs, bars, and taverns are where we go to worship the gods of ecstasy, music, wine, dance, love, and sex. Here, we spend our special recreation time–when we are not in front of the TV, that is. Friday and Saturday nights are spent searching for some nebulous enjoyment we seek to make tangible. They are part of the magical power of the city, coming alive when the conventional world slows down. As we come to see the city itself as a partner and patron, a living pool of energy, the life it breeds at night becomes a potent setting for magick and exploration. In many ways, the hidden city, our urban shamanic underworld, literally consumes the visible, waking city of the daylight hours. By exploring these habitats, you can walk the underworld paths, eyes wide open, here in the physical realm.

Venues for our nightlife come in all forms. Following the "birds-of-a-feather" principle, similar people tend to gather at each place. There are local bars with friendly faces and pool tables, and more traditional lounges, often with singers and piano players for live entertainment. Some are jazzy, while others have a more "Las Vegas" flavor. All are magical in their own right. Las Vegas is a magical city of light, wonder, and illusions. Anyone gambling there will agree. Live entertainment also comes in the form of rock clubs, with guitar-heavy bands trailing the circuit searching for fame and fortune. Other musicians and wanna-be rock stars frequent this club scene. Some come

City Magick

in support of their brothers, while others salve their egos, ripping apart their peers' creative endeavors. The revival of coffee houses can be included here. They may not be clubs, but they can foster a similar environment. Live music, poetry readings, and the ever-present social exchange over a caffeine-rich liquid constitute a sacrament peculiar to these venues. Perhaps most important to the shamanic world are the various dance clubs, offering everything from top-forty hits to underground and illegal raves, where primal beats are pounded out, often shamanically taking others to a place within, even if they know nothing of magick or shamanism. These clubs serve that higher purpose in a very unconscious way, unknowingly letting patrons explore the frontiers of consciousness. By going to them with a purpose, knowing full-well their magical qualities, you can reap even greater benefits of self-knowledge. Ultimately, self-knowledge is the goal of the modern magician.

Like an ancient initiation, we pretend to descend into the underworld, a dark regenerative place where we meet all manner of strange beings. These rituals mimic some of the most sacred myths. Many gods and goddesses descended into the underworld, the hidden city, to return transformed. In Celtic myths, we see the recurring theme of a child abducted and taken to the underworld. Most familiar are the tales of Mabon and Pryderi. The child usually returns steeped in underworld magick, while the mother undergoes some tragedy. In Greek myth, Persephone, as the maiden Kore, is abducted by the lord of the underworld, Hades. There she sheds her maiden persona and assumes the role of Queen of the Underworld. She returns to the surface for part of the year, and, with her mother, the grain goddess Demeter, signals the growing season. When Persephone retires to the depths, the land again goes fallow. An earlier version of Persephone's myth tells us that she was not violently abducted, but willingly seduced. A goddess who, no doubt, descended of her own free will is the Sumerian goddess Inanna. Deciding to claim the power of her sister, Ereshkigal's, underworld throne, she traveled to each level of the underworld. At each level, Inanna was forced to shed one of her belongings, her clothes and jewelry, until she reached the lowest part of the underworld completely naked. Though her bid for power ultimately failed, her story teaches a more important lesson. To descend to the darkest places of these hidden cities, you must shed your old identity, the very traits, characteristics, and objects on which you base your self-perception. Only then can you arrive at your true, essential self, even if only for a short time. Then you can claim the underworld magick.

Descent into the nightlife is not always as dramatic as this, but it does have similar connotations. In this place, we wear unusual costumes of power to attract the right attention. We undo our usual, nine-to-five identities to become something new. By shedding the old and trying on new roles, we hope to discover the core, essential being within that is beneath all outer identities. This transformation is part of the descent. This dark world operates under a whole new set of rules. The norms of behavior may not apply, depending on what section of the underworld we visit. Strange customs are invoked. By unhinging our own identities, it is easier to move and operate in this realm to complete the tasks at hand.

Some of our experiences lead us to a being who has just the right words, attitude, or insight that we need, both on a mundane and an esoteric level. I've had many wonderful conversations in such places, with people whom I barely know, who happened to tell me exactly what I needed to hear when I needed to hear it—as if my guides were speaking through them, and perhaps they were. These recreation centers have become new holy ground, where elaborate rituals occur and words of power are exchanged. There we may renew passion or vitality from these encounters, or we may fail the initiation and leave more broken than when we started. If this all sounds silly to you, on your next sidewalking trip, with your magical senses open, step into a club and see what happens. You may be surprised.

◎ Invocation ◎

Invocation, the process of identifying with a pattern and personality of a spirit, is the most direct way to transform your personal identity into something new for such adventures. Invocations can be specific, drawing the force of a particular god or goddess into your body, or they can be more nondescript, drawing on certain qualities and general archetypes you wish to embody. Magical traditions are rich with invocations. When a priestess invokes the goddess during a ritual, she is the embodiment of the goddess for that ceremony.

Our modern city invocations have the same effect, yet are outside the bounds of normal ritual. Therefore, we must make them into our own rituals. You may be doing this already without even knowing it. When you go to a party or a club where no one knows you, you have the opportunity to say whatever you want, do whatever you want, and be whomever you want, with no expectations. In a manner of speaking, you are invoking and creating a new identity, to learn and explore. In traditional ceremony, there is a point of invocation and a point of release or banishment from the essential self, followed by a return to "normal" consciousness and "normal" identity. At your party or club, there are no such formal points of consciousness shifting. The process is gradual, and, for some, it is easier to lose themselves to the new identity. I suggest working on creating such points through your own rituals, using tools such as visualization, glamours, makeup magick, ritual sacraments, and invocative dance.

◎ Face Painting, Glamours, and Riding ◎

Tribal people all over the world recognized the shift that occurs in consciousness when donning a new identity through mask and paint. Not only does the pigment paint your body, it alters your spirit, allowing you to take on new characteristics. Different symbols, colors, and materials can be used, depending on the occasion. The face-markings for a harvest celebration will be different from those used when going to war. Celtic warriors charged naked into battle, painted only in blue woad pigment, believing the symbols and plant dye would protect them from injury. Makeup and face painting in general have lost their magical charm. Movie magick uses makeup to effect transformations of actors for the silver screen. Women, in particular, use makeup as a part of their own daily transformation, creating a simple mask for the world. There is magick in face painting and it is time to reclaim it.

Ritualize the process of face painting when preparing for your sidewalking journey to the underworld. Getting ready through clothes and makeup is the start of your invocation. Taking the makeup off is the banishment. Depending on what kind of establishment you plan to seek out with magical eyes, makeup may not be restricted only to women, though in America at this time, it is more socially acceptable for women to wear it than men. Alternative establishments are perfect places to experiment with face painting, including symbols and designs drawn on the body with makeup, regardless of your gender.

When you are getting ready, either by dressing in special, unusual clothes, washing up, face painting, shaving, or any simple act of transformation, the mirror is one of your most magical tools. Prior do doing these exercises, you should consecrate your mirror, charging it to be a magical tool, as described in chapter 5. The mirror, like any scrying device, allows you to see beyond the physical. In this case, you are looking with your magical eyes at your aura, the persona you project. Like Inanna, you are stripping away your outer accoutrements and then slipping into your new identity.

Glamours take makeup magick one step further. They are like illusions, but nothing quite so holographically real. They are ideas, attributes, and images subtly projected for others to pick up. They are like magical masks, but not in a physical sense. By altering your aura, your energy field, you can project the qualities you want other people to recognize. Your illusions won't necessarily turn a five-foot brunette into a six-foot blonde, but they can help a rather demure five-foot brunette project the image of a dressed-up demi-goddess or demi-god for the evening. They work in the realm of presence. When actors project a certain character, not only acting like the character, but thinking like it, they unknowingly provide a glamour of sorts. Here we do it with a magical purpose in mind.

Think about the kind of identity, the qualities, you wish to invoke for the next exercise. Meditate on how these qualities are different from your normal persona. Would you like to learn more about them, and perhaps, at some point, incorporate them into your everyday life? Or do you simply want to experience how the "other half" lives? Whatever your personal motivations, seriously reflect on what you wish to become before attempting the next exercise. Have a side-walking destination in mind that is appropriate for the new qualities you have invoked.

EXERCISE 22 – GLAMOUR

❶ Charge the mirror you will be using to be a magical tool, to aid you in this ritual. It can be your bedroom mirror, bathroom mirror, or a full-length mirror. Charge all the mirrors you will be using.

❷ Start with Exercise 1 to get into a more meditative state (see page 17). Then affirm your protective shield as in Exercise 4 (see page 27). This is particularly important when doing any invocation, even when you are not working with a specific spirit or deity. You do not want to invite the unwanted into your being. Spend a simple moment visualizing your shield of protection.

❸ Go through your normal routine for "going out", but be quiet, meditative. Put on some appropriate music in the background to set the tone, but nothing that will take you out of the light meditative state you are in. Take a shower or bath, wash up, and stand before the mirror.

❹ Visualize the persona you want to assume. Look at yourself in the mirror with your magical sight, adding the qualities, quirks, and appearance you want to project to the world tonight. As you gaze into the magick mirror, imagine and allow yourself to change. At first, it's a lot like playing dress-up and pretending. If you feel slightly foolish to start, you are on the right road. Keep it up until you feel you have adopted this glamour as your own for the evening. You are still you physically, but, magically, you are adopting a new face for the world. We all wear many masks, often subconsciously created. This time you have a conscious choice in the construction of your mask. Understanding who you want to be, even in fantasy, gives you great insight into your own personality, your soul's own ego mask.

❺ As you imagine and allow these things to come into being within you, dress the part. Put on makeup, cologne, perfume, clothes, and jewelry that are appropriate for this new guise. Mark yourself, even if the symbol is only worn under your clothes. You will know it is there. Put all the finishing touches to the ensemble to make it as real as it can be. Believe it. Know it. Live it. Be it.

❻ Do your sidewalking journey, as described in Exercise 9 (see page 79), with a nightlife destination in mind, a goal for your journey. As you enter the establishment, shed any final vestige of your former personality, at least for this evening, and adopt your new guise completely. This is an adventure, but remember the role of safety and common sense in every magical exercise. Do not let this new guise lead you into foolishness. No matter the guise or persona, you are always solely responsible for your actions and their repercussions.

❼ Experience the place in this new role. On the journey home, start to reflect on what you learned this evening, about yourself, about the city, and about the world.

❽ When you come home, go through a similar dismantling process, reversing the glamour and resuming your normal mind-set. Shed the clothes and jewelry. Take off the makeup. Complete the ritual by looking back into the mirror, letting go of the new attributes, and invoking your normal self-image. Wash up and get some rest.

Another method for shifting your persona is reminiscent of the voodoo practices. Invoke a god-form and allow it to "ride" you. You are not being possessed, but rather are asking a specific god or goddess to merge part of their essence and consciousness with yours. This is very similar to more traditional invocation processes, in which you invoke a specific deity. Here, you are simply invoking the god's or goddess's qualities into your body. Sometimes, if you have the gift of clairaudience, or psychic hearing, you will hear the voice of the persona as part of your own inner dialogue. For these new temples, you will probably stick to inviting the more rousing or powerful deities, tricksters, or those who simply like a good party. Dionysus, Pan, Kali, Loki, and Erzulie come to mind. Dionysus is the god of wine and ecstasy. Pan is a Greek satyr-god, full of lust and sexuality. Kali is the devouring mother, the dark goddess whose dance destroys all obstacles. Loki is the Norse god of mischief. Erzulie is the voodoo loa whose eyes are red from weeping that no man can love her enough. She is a particularly fun goddess to be with when an ex-partner is in the club. By looking through the eyes of these beings, and, more important, letting them look through your eyes, you view yourself and your world in a different way. This different perspective can give you insight into your thoughts, feelings, and beliefs.

The spirit experiences movement in the physical world, and the person experiences the essence of a deity within. This can range from union, which I advocate, to total control. Control is a difficult issue and, personally, I choose to co-create with my gods and spirit allies, instead of giving up control and responsibility. You will be the one held responsible for the actions of your body, regardless of who or what is in control.

Before attempting the next exercise, research a deity or spirit with whom you wish to work. If you have met one that resonates with you in previous practices and exercises, then choose that one. You may choose a unique city being or a more traditional mythological figure with whom you are intimately familiar. When starting this exercise, invoke those who feel most comfortable to you. Later, you can turn to beings with whom you do not resonate, as they can be valuable teachers. Until you are thoroughly familiar with the process, however, stick to those who resonate with you.

EXERCISE 23 – RIDING

❶ Start with Exercise 1, to center and balance yourself, and Exercise 4 for spiritual protection and activating the auric shield (see pages 17 and 27). As in the previous exercise, activating the shield is a very important step. You may even want to perform this exercise in the center of a magick circle.

❷ Ask to connect to the being with whom you desire to work. State the name three times. Then, invite the deity into you, asking to invoke it in a manner correct and causing no harm. Ask only for energies that come in perfect love and trust, causing no harm.

❸ Be with the spirit. At first, you may feel silly, as if you were playing pretend, but, as the process continues, you will identify more with the spirit. As with the glamour, you can feel your aura, your magical presence change. As you blend with the being, you can feel its qualities become a part of you. Some feel the presence

241

as a simple blending of two wholes. Others identify solely and completely with this new being, until the invocation is completed.

❹ Continue to work and be with this entity for as long as you are comfortable. Perform a sidewalking jaunt, a descent into the nightlife world, or simply stay where you are and experience life from this new point of view.

❺ At the end of the session, you should thank the spirit and bid it farewell. Ask to release it completely and safely, harming none in the process. Feel the presence leave you. Perhaps leave an offering to it on your altar the next day, or light a candle in its honor.

◎ Magical Sacrament ◎

Temples and initiation mysteries often use a sacrament, something to consume or a ritual to conduct, to change you through the worship process. We have carried this tradition over from pagan sacraments to the Holy Communion of the Catholic Church. We have even created new sacraments in our new temples, imbibing substances from the psychotropic to the mundane to embue us with ritualistic power when descending to the underworld. Sacraments mark a start to a special time, a special place for ritual.

In the new temples of nightclubs, bars, and dancehalls, the ancient barley water of the Elusynian mysteries in Greece—sacred, secret rites of life and death—is replaced with other sacraments, like beer and other alcoholic beverages. Even though alcohol is technically a depressant, since it depresses your body's systems, it often makes us feel better. Sometimes, suppressing other systems can open the doors to new worlds and new systems. Abuses of this sacrament, however, like any other, can bring problems. Alcohol alters your body chemistry and changes your mood. Some people become more psychic after having a drink, then continue drinking, thinking it will increase these new senses. They miss the window of opportunity and lose coherence. Tobacco is another widely abused sacrament. Native people used it sparingly because of its power. It was a sacred rite for them. Taking a pack of cigarettes a day, on the other hand, including all the chemicals and tar, can do horrible things to your body. Even so, cigarette smoke has become the high-powered, noxious incense of the new temples. It alters your mood as soon as you enter a bar. Coffee is another, often abused, sacrament. Coffee beans, soaked, were eaten as a ritual sacrament by Central and South American cultures. What modern westerners drink as a beverage was the refuse of this ritual preparation, but it has its own power. The custom has grown and now many cannot continue without their daily ritual of morning coffee.

Other sacraments in the new temples become more exotic and illegal. In some club scenes, recreational drugs are used as a trial by fire, a rite of passage into a new group. Sharing an experience of that level with a new member forges bonds. Unfortunately, many of the bonds are unhealthy and moderation is not practiced. Use of such substances for recreation, rather than as a sacrament, often leads to abuses and dysfunction in daily living. This is by no means an encouragement to abuse alcohol and tobacco or to participate in any illegal activities. I am a firm believer that the magical practitioners should be able to do all these things without chemical stimulation, but, realistically, you cannot talk about these modern rituals without at least mentioning these tools and trends. Be careful in choosing what sacraments you wish to take. You can choose a specific drink, alcoholic or not, that you reserve for shamanic ritual when entering a nightclub. If you are only relaxing, and do not seek to open up these senses, then do not order that drink. The sacrament becomes a physical symbol to your body and spirit that there is magick to be done.

◎ Dance ◎

Many magical ceremonies use the more exhibitory method of dance
to get into a trance. These techniques are more physical and include
all types of dance and movement. Dance clubs have replaced these
ceremonies in our culture, providing the beat background for these
magical mindscapes. If you really get into dancing, have you ever
noticed how it seems to take you someplace else? Your entire worldview changes, as when someone unexpectedly throws a ball at you.
In that moment, the world stands still. You have time to react and
grab the ball. Your interaction with the universe changes for that
time. A new point of view opens. You enter a gnosis, or meditative
state, in a completely different way. Through dance, you can enter a
similar, but extended, trance state in which the world changes.

Modern dance music, like techno-music, has a beat roughly double
the human heart rate. Many think that to enter a trance state, the
music has to be slow, lowering your brain waves, but modern research
into sound, however, has shown something shamans have known for
a while. The beat needs to be fast—usually around 120 to 160 beats
per minute. When shamans do their travels, their spouses or protégés
beat the drum. The shaman rides the sound of the drum into the other
worlds. It leads them to a World Tree or mountain, helping them on
their journey. DJs and musicians have that role for us now, keeping the
steady beat of the universe while we travel. Let the new music lead
you to the rapture of these temples. Find your own journey.

At first, the experience can start by simply opening your perceptions, much like your sidewalking adventures. Energy becomes more
apparent, either through second sight, or through sensing the shift in
vibrations. Auras and spirits can become visible. Sometimes, you are
vaguely aware of being somewhere else. You are working on a higher
level, and the music facilitates this shift. If you are not consciously
aware of the shamanic journey, it usually shows up in dreams, or the
memories can be triggered by a word, picture, or name.

Some of the journeys feel like bi-location–being in two places at once. You know you are still in the club, but you are aware of some-place else. You feel as if there are two of you, and you are more con-scious of the total experience. You will probably remember this open-eyed trance and all the experiences associated with it. At first, it can be quite disconcerting to feel as if you exist in two places at once. In truth, we are all multidimensional. We all exist in many different places and on many different levels of existence. You are opening to the endless possibilities.

During a dancing trance state, you open up the lines of communi-cation to the spirit worlds. I have had some of my best conversations with spirits while dancing. They entailed no journey or invocation, just a simple message in my head. There's no telling where ecstatic dance magick can lead you, if you let it. Though it can be done in the privacy of your own home to start, there is something magical about being in a crowd of people, each on their own journey, whether they realize it or not. The sound, lights, smoke, and crowd all play an important factor in such magick.

Whenever you start any kind of journey, it's good to have an intention in mind. Is there a goal to your journey? Make one. It can be knowledge or insight about a particular situation in your life. It can be for the simple purpose of seeing what happens. Just make an inten-tion. You only get what you put out to the universe. If you ask for nothing, quite often you get nothing. Once you have an intention, continue on to the next exercise.

EXERCISE 24 – DANCE MAGICK

❶ Start by firmly repeating your intention for this magical, eyes-wide-open journey. Reaffirm your protective shield, as in Exercise 4 (see page 27). After experimenting with it once, you can com-bine this dance magick with the previous glamour or riding exer-cises, enhancing the overall experience. Before dancing, you may want to take a ritual sacrament to set the tone for your work.

❷ When you decide you are ready to dance, go out onto the floor and basically follow the simple guidelines found in Exercise 6 (see page 34). Let the music carry you away, until you are no longer thinking, no longer acting from the ego, but acting only from instinct.

❸ Allow your perceptions to open up at first, and take notice. You may see aura or patches of energy with your magical sight. You may see spirits and other people's invisible guardians. Enjoy this voyeurism for a time. People are there to be noticed. You are simply noticing them with a different pair of eyes.

❹ Accept whatever thoughts, sensations, feelings, and images come to you. The journey will not be as all-encompassing as a shamanic journey you take with your eyes closed and focused completely on the second reality. Here, you will be playing with both realities. The journey, or information, can be more disjointed and jumbled. You may travel to the sky cities and hidden worlds, or go to unfamiliar terrain. Do not try to intellectualize it. Simply experience. You can figure it out later.

❺ When the experience comes to an end, slowly bring yourself out. Come off the dance floor and relax for a bit. Look around. Think about what you have experienced. Ground yourself and feel back in the here-and-now. Thank the powers that worked with you for the journey and leave when you are ready, or continue on with the night.

One final thought for rituals in these club temples. You can work with all manner of spirits, those in a body, those without flesh, and those inside yours. You can journey to them and they can come to you. Know the banishing techniques from chapter 3 and feel confident working with them. Use care, common sense, and intuition when dealing with any unfamiliar spirits. Stick with those you know until you are comfortable in your own power and the process itself.

◉ Museums and Historic Sites ◉

Museums are like cemeteries. They are temples of the dead. While graveyards honor the individual, museums honor whole cultures. We go there occasionally to honor the dead, those cultural ancestors who have passed before us, and to mourn the lost secrets they have taken to their graves. Museums honor dead technology, dead customs, and dead art. We invest a lot of time and money in preserving what we have, and in learning from those unknown secrets, so we do not make the same mistakes.

Historic sites are preservations of legend. What is history now may someday be legend. Tales of battles between continents and countries, weapons, and bombs will one day undoubtedly become as mythic as the wars of gods and ancient men. We still have time to help determine if Uncle Sam and Mother England will be the heroes or villains of the tale. The parks, museums, and sites are rich with this mythic energy. Churches, archaeological sites, old buildings, and memorials all have it. You may feel a shiver where a world-changing event occurred, etched permanently into the etheric records of the area. You may feel spirits of the deceased or unavenged. Time plays tricks at these important places, and we place more power in them as each traveler passes by. Make sure you not only honor, but also understand, the past.

Add a museum or historic site to your next sidewalking jaunt. Most cities have them. The talent of psychometry comes in handy here. It is fairly easy to learn, but difficult to master. Psychometry means to psychically read an object's past or future by interpreting its energy. Most people use touch to facilitate this process, but you don't have to touch an object. In most museums, you can't. You need only connect with the energy. From it, you can glean information, images, and words from the past, present, and future.

EXERCISE 25 – PSYCHOMETRY

❶ Start your sidewalking adventure and go to your intended historic site or museum.

❷ Initiate pranic breathing, as described in Exercise 12 (see page 104). If you have been practicing it, the process is very easy to start and get flowing.

❸ As you exhale the energy through your heart chakra and into your body and aura, visualize the field expanding out further from your body. When you exhale, exhale the prana a bit more frequently than usual to expand this energy field. Make the energy fields reach out and envelop the object of your psychometric exercise. If it is a place, simply expand outward. If it is an object, go far enough for the pranic field to touch the object. If you can physically touch the object, that is even better.

❹ As you breathe in energy from the crown and root chakras, imagine a strawlike tube sucking in energy from the object or place. Imagine it coming into your energy field and passing through your chakras. As it passes through your head, you can see and hear images associated with it. Intend to read the object and let the first thing that wanders into your mind take root. You may get a word or phrase. You may see an image or a series of images. Many see the object through the eyes of those who have held it in the past. Some have a strong sense of intuitive knowing, without any other information. You can have a date, time, name of an owner, or complete history of the object, from how it was made, to its uses, and how it ended up in the museum, or anywhere else. You may even get a glimpse of its future fate. Some talk to the item or the spirit in the object, as if they were talking to any other spirit or being. Sometimes asking for information is the easiest way to get it.

❺ When the process feels complete, retract the energy field around you. As you inhale, feel it get smaller, returning to the normal size of your aura. Disengage from the object or environment. Continue to do the pranic breathing, flushing your entire system of any energy remaining from the psychometric experience.

❻ Ground and balance yourself. Feel your perceptions return to the normal, physical world.

Chapter 11
Techno-Temples

THE LAST OF THE NEW TEMPLES do not even occupy a physical space. This sacred site exists in what is now known as cyberspace, a nonphysical "place" created through the vast networking of computers called the Internet. Through the Internet, we have access to a wide array of information and services. People can communicate through electronic mail, whose letters are sent over the computer with no physical paper. Material can be published on Web pages, creating electronic manuscripts through which anything can be shared. Once posted, anyone with Internet access and a Web browser can view them. You can "talk" with other people in real time through the use of chat rooms. Here, in these virtual, electronic spaces, words are exchanged. Some claim that this lacks the personal, face-to-face contact, or the tone of voice of a phone conversation, but there's no doubt that, with the Internet, you can reach people you would not otherwise see or call. Discussion can also take place through mailing lists, mass e-mails to large groups of people who join the list, and through bulletin boards, places where lists of messages on various topics can be posted for all to see. It is in these virtual meeting places—truly "a space that is not a space and a time that is not a time"—that many of similar interests meet, discuss, share, argue, and, now, even do magick.

The computer itself has grown with modern culture. Starting as a simple tool, it has become to many an indispensable part of daily living,

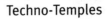
like running water, electricity, and heat. It is not a necessity of life, but try telling that to people who do their communing over the computer and telephone wires. The phenomenon once attracted only computer-philes, but now entices average students, businessmen, housewives, accountants, and artists, right down to nature-loving pagans, witches, shamans, and other spell casters. The Internet is a simple way to network and Web-weave with your peers across the globe.

Many draw their sense of community and well-being, not from those physically around them, but from the computer. Mailing lists, groups of people who share one large discussion on a mutual interest, can create a great sense of community, support, and even love. Particularly for those interested in magick, witchcraft, and off-beat spirituality, the on-line community can be a safe outlet through which to explore new experiences they feel can't be shared with those physically around them. Kundalini experiences, alien abductions, and witch coming-out stories bond people of similar backgrounds because they feel no one else can understand. If you want to be a witch, but have no one around to teach you, much of your learning can take place through the Internet. You can get more feedback from real people than from books. You can ask questions. The Internet is really a temple of information. I've learned a lot about magick and even many life lessons from my Internet communities. Some of us have met in the flesh and had wonderful experiences. Some will always remain electronic friends, so to speak, but their advice and opinion is valued more than that of many other people in my life.

Modern spell casters often use computer terms to describe psychic powers and magical phenomenon, showing how pervasive the seeds of these symbols have grown in the fertile mindscape of our collective consciousness. When learning about auras, I was taught to act as if your psychic abilities were computer programs. Bring up the aura program and there it is. When consecrating and charging magical tools, bring up the charging program. Keep it simple in your mind and the reality will be simple. Spells are often seen as analogous to a computer virus, a self-replicating program that goes out and grows, until it completes its function. Although most modern computer viruses are programmed with harmful intentions, they don't have to be. The creation of thoughtform entities and constructs, often known as servitor spirits, through such things as protection spells, are akin to the creation of computer programs or even artificial computer intelligences. A construct is a spell lasting indefinitely, one that will perform a set of instructions when given the proper stimulus. The spells can be simply to shield the home when someone threatens it, much like a program written, "If $x = y$, GO TO . . . ," completing the next set of instructions. The group consciousness of a coven or other ritual group can be seen as a collective program that each member taps into during ceremony.

The age of the magical computer is upon us, whether we like it or not. This section is not meant to be "Computer and Internet 101" for those unfamiliar with the World Wide Web and the possibilities of the Internet. That would require a whole book in itself, with little room for magick. Nor is it an argument to do all magick on-line and break away from normal human contact and traditional ceremonies. Like many traditionalist who might be reading this, horrified at the prospect of computers and magick mingling, I, too, prefer face-to-face contact in a physical space. I prefer to hear someone's voice next to me, not to read typed words. But I cannot deny the impact that discovering the on-line magical community has had on my life. For many, this is not only their sole outlet for magical interaction, but, arguably, a preferred way. Everyone has his or her own personal preferences. This is only a resource for those looking to explore the possibilities of techno-magick in its early stages. If you are unfamiliar with computers in general, perhaps this will persuade you to look at them a little differently. Look at them for a moment with your magical eyes.

The strongest archetypal trait of the Internet is its vast potential for storing and sharing information, cutting across geographic lines.

Perhaps only in the fabled library of Alexandria did we ever have such information. The sheer volume of information on so many top-ics in the modern world has doubled and doubled again, many times over. The most wonderful aspect of the Internet those involved with magick is the accessibility of this information. No longer is magical wisdom and specific information obscured from our sight. No longer do we have to study in far-off places and join unusual groups. Much of their information is now shared freely, available to those who know where to look. We live in a vast sea of information. The Internet is just one way to navigate this sea. It is a way to both give and receive treasured secrets.

The beautiful chaos of this cyber world, where anyone can share anything, leaves us with another, perhaps less fortunate, archetypal aspect of the Internet, that of the trickster. Quite literally, anyone can tell you anything, truth or fiction. People can lay claim to any title, any experience, and there is no way to verify it. On the Internet, a ten-year-old can pretend to be a nuclear physicist, and, if that ten-year-old knows more about nuclear physics than you do, perhaps you'll believe him. In magical communities, many claim to be the mas-ters of centuries-old magical traditions and secret societies. Some may very well be. But if they are so secret, and you have never heard of them before, then why are they revealing themselves to you now, over the Internet? In the best of circumstances, many share informa-tion they believe to be correct with novices in magick, witchcraft, and ceremony. The problem is that they either do not have correct information themselves, or they lack the skills to explain it correctly to others over such a medium. There are no "truth police" in the techno-world, and I, along with most others, prefer it that way. To whom would we give the right to determine what can and can't be shared and said? To no one, is my answer. To do so would only start a computerized inquisition, and I think our civilization can do with-out another inquisition, computerized or not.

The trickster aspect of the Internet teaches us one of the most important lessons we can learn in life, both on and off the computer–discernment. As magical people, we have to cultivate our powers of intuition and discernment to be able to distinguish falsehood from truth. We need to learn how to differentiate between a potential fool and a potential adept, and be able to learn our lessons from each. In some ways, the fool has more useful life lessons for us all. In general, you must critique all experiences and people in this cyberworld, just as you do when joining any new group or community. You may lack the advantages of eye contact and hearing the voice, which for most of us are the tell-tale signs, but you can learn other techniques as you delve into this realm. If you are there now, you have probably already learned some of your own methods for to discerning fact from fantasy on-line.

◎ WALKING THE WEB ◎

The first tool of navigation in this sea of magical information is the World Wide Web–a series of electronic documents, called Web pages, that can be viewed from something called a Web browser. When you type in a location, called a URL–usually one of those names starting with a "www" and ending in ".com"–of the Web page you want to visit, your browser brings you to it. The Web browser usually comes as part of your Internet Service Provider (ISP). Each Web page contains "links" or connections to other pages. Some pages are by the same author, others connect you to different locations, by different authors, that may be of interest to you. Moving from page to page is called "Web surfing." I love the image of an actual electronic web, since I resonate with the spider totem so strongly. It generates images of creativity and magick within me.

All kinds of Web pages exist out there in the magical world. Some are personal pages, people sharing their lives and traditions with the world. Others are teaching pages, giving out general information on magical traditions or specific lessons and techniques. You can find pages on covens and lodges, stores, and community networking.

These pages are found through the use of a search engine, typing in key words to get pages containing those words in their descriptions. There are many search engines, and new ones are being created all the time. Your Internet Service Provider (ISP) often has a default search engine. Some are even strictly related to pagan or magical groups.

Usually, the information exchange is one-way on Web pages. You can read the pages published. Often, authors will provide an e-mail address so you can communicate personally with them. If you want to have your voice heard, you can publish your own Web pages. You simply have to get a space on which to post them. Many groups give access to such space free or at a nominal cost. Then you either learn a Web publishing language, like HTML, or use a program that will convert your graphically created pages into a publishing language. You, too, can publish anything you would like on the World Wide Web.

Search Engines

A search engine is a page that links you to a database of Web-page listings. When you type in some key words for a search criteria, the engine brings you all the listed pages that match your criteria. Most people on the Internet have a favorite Web engine for general surfing. Some engines are topic-specific and have more on a given topic than the mainstream engines. Some engines are strictly pagan, spiritual, or occult.

Web Rings

Web rings are groups of Web sites, some commercial, some private, that are linked together by a particular topic. This allows more traffic between sites, exposing them to more viewers who are interested. It's a great way for many personal sites to be seen that might otherwise end up lost on the larger search engines. Once you find yourself on one page, there will be a link to the Web ring where you can move to another site, or two sites, or sometimes five sites along this chain of Web pages. All you know about them is they will all be on a general topic. There are many active Web rings in the pagan and New Age communities.

Messages in Electronic Bottles

The information exchange on Web pages is usually one-way. You read a page, you receive the information. For those looking for something more interactive, you have many choices. Two of the most popular are newsgroups and message boards. Newsgroups are simply electronic "places" dedicated to a particular subject. Those interested in the subject can post messages about various topics within the larger category. Others visiting the newsgroups can read these messages and post their responses or start their own topic. The collected responses to one topic are often called a "thread," creating a string of related messages you can follow like a discussion. Some are moderated, meaning the moderator or owner of the group removes messages that do not pertain to it, while others are a free-for-all, where the topics serve as a guideline, but anyone can post anything. Message boards are very similar to newsgroups except in location. Some are located on a specific Web site, making that site more interactive. Others are located within a particular service provider's area, such as America Online (also known as AOL), and are for members of that service only.

The advantage of such groups and boards is their interactive aspect, which allows questions to be asked and answered. The disadvantage is that the process is much like sending a message in a bottle, casting it out to the seas and not knowing who will receive it. It goes to no one specific and you are never sure who is responding. Such posts and responses can truly provoke your powers of discernment and your own thought processes on the topics at hand, forcing you to think about what you truly believe and why, because you may have to explain it. Here are some newsgroups for the magically orientated practitioner:

alt.magick
alt.magick.chaos
alt.magick.marketplace
alt.magick.order
alt.magick.sex
alt.magick.tantra
alt.mythology
alt.pagan
alt.pagan.contacts
alt.pagan.magick
alt.religion.asatru
alt.religion.druid

alt.religion.goddess
alt.religion.shamanism
alt.religion.wicca
alt.tarot
alt.tarot.friendly
alt.traditional.witchcraft
alt.witchcraft
soc.religion.paganism
soc.religion.shamanism
talk.religion.newage
tx.religion.pagan

Magical Mail

Taking interaction a step further than newsgroups is e-mail. E-mail simply means electronic mail. It is a new way for people to converse, much like writing a letter, but the delivery is instantaneous. The only delay is in waiting for the person to go to their computer, sign on, and retrieve their e-mail. Most do it fairly regularly, from once a week to once an hour, and everywhere in between. No longer do you have to wait for the world's postal services. With the click of a button, your note can be halfway around the world.

To be able to send e-mail to someone, you must first have their e-mail address. People now trade e-mail addresses at parties as they do phone numbers. Some people, myself included, are far easier to reach via e-mail than by phone. If you know the person, they can simply give you their address. When surfing the Web, many page creators create a link at which you can mail them. Some have guest books where you "sign in" with your name and comments and can leave your address for others to contact and network with you. When posting to newsgroups, usually your e-mail address is printed. When responding, you have the option of responding to the group, or to the individual that posted the message. You can thereby make new contacts for individual discussion. Many service providers give you the opportunity to fill out a member profile and others can search this directory of profiles for people with similar interests, locations, or needs. Some of these directories are for members only, while others are open to the public.

Personally, I've found that the best way to "meet" people on-line is to join a mailing list. A mailing list is a group you voluntarily join by subscribing to the service through a list server, a computer server dedicated to maintaining the functions of one or more lists. Through this list, a large group of people can discuss and share information on a given topic. All new "posts" and responses are sent to the list server, which automatically duplicates the e-mail and sends it to all subscribers. As with newsgroups, groups of messages pertaining to one topic are collected into threads. Most lists are organized around a specific topic, enticing those interested in that topic to join. Some lists are closed, however. New members must be recommended by current members and go through an approval process. Like newsgroups, some lists are moderated and some are not. I've found moderators, also called list managers, to be extremely beneficial on such mailing groups.

Internet mailing lists are as varied in topic as everything else, ranging from comic books to precious gems. Many spirituality, pagan, and magical lists exist. My own particular attraction to mailing lists came from a spirituality-based mailing list. While all mailing lists can foster a sense of community, I feel that spirituality-based lists foster that feeling even more. Through these groups, people share very intense personal experiences and look for validation, to know they are not alone, that someone is listening, that someone understands. If you are studying anything even remotely considered "New Age" or "alternative," and know absolutely no one in your area, you can feel isolated. For those having shamanic or psychic experiences, questions of sanity can start to arise. To find others with similar feelings and experiences is a true blessing. Those further down the path can help those just awakening, and many find peers on the same level of experience.

New tricks, techniques, spells, and meditations are shared. Through this intensely personal work, bonds of friendship, and even love, form. This is not typical, since all lists, spiritual or otherwise, are not always like this. When it happens, however, it is truly magical. As silly as it sounds, I've felt as close to some of my on-line friends as to my "in-person" friends. Some I have later met in person, some I will probably never meet in the flesh, but that doesn't change our relationship.

Lists have grown, flourished, and withered away. Some I've been on for years. Others have moved out of my life as my own path has changed. Some have been a support, while a few have been a source of aggravation and learning. The gifts I have received from the process, however, have made the journey worthwhile. I recommend it to anyone, at least for a time.

Although some Web sites sponsor their own mailing lists, the best place to look for new mailing lists fitting your interest are certain sites that manage a variety of mailing lists on various topics. You can search each site to find a list that is good for you, or you can start your own. With the growing popularity of paganism, witchcraft, magick, and shamanism, the number of such lists is sure to grow.

Space Beyond Space

One of the most interactive forms of electronic communication must be the chat room. The chat room is, quite literally, a space beyond space, a nonexistent, nonphysical room residing somewhere in cyber space where individuals can log on to "see" and "be seen" by others currently in the room. Here messages scroll across the screen in real time to be read by everyone in the room. Discussions take place with no delay. The trick, of course, is to get everyone involved to log into the room at the same time. Some rooms are open, allowing anyone access. Others are private, by invitation only. Like mailing lists, chat rooms are often organized by topic, so that only those interested in such topics enter. Some rooms are sponsored by the Internet Service Provider, for members only, while others are, in general, free to the public. Some of the very private rooms are hosted by the moderator of a mailing list, and information on how and when to enter the room is sent only to those on the list. This synchronous chat gives a real-world feel to those who have been corresponding solely through e-mail. It provides a great way to share even more.

Magical Netiquette

"Netiquette" is a new word, meaning etiquette for those on the Internet. As mentioned before, there is no Internet police force, or any agency for controlling the Web, for that matter. Users are bound only by the rules to which they agree, and by stipulations put in place by service providers any any on-line groups you may join. For this reason, lists of proper etiquette, codes of conduct, and behavior can be found on the Internet. In this way, the on-line community polices itself. If someone breaches this netiquette, or just ignores it, others in the community simply send a polite reminder. After repeated breaches, the notes may not be so polite, depending on the individuals involved. Although some of these courtesies may seem obvious, some address perils and pitfalls particular to magical communities. As with everything else, these are simply suggestions, like the magical redes of many pagan traditions. They are ways to conduct yourself–guide-lines. Ultimately, it is up to the individual.

FAQs

A FAQ is a collection of Frequently Asked Questions that contains information basic to a group. Most newsgroups, message boards, and mailing lists have some sort of FAQ file. Read it before participating in a group. It will answer your easy questions and let you know what is acceptable. It should give you a basic goal or mission statement for the group. Once you join a group, it is always polite to "lurk," or lis-ten without participating, for a bit, until you get a feel for how it works. Then introduce yourself in your first message so people know that you are a new participant, who you are, and a little of your background. FAQs read now can save a lot of future trouble.

Flaming

When someone is "flaming," they are posting information intended to upset others, to antagonize, and, often, to ridicule. Baseless arguments between two or more individuals, leading nowhere, are often called "flame wars." Most moderated groups do not allow flaming. Be respectful of the communities you join. In many ways, spiritual groups should be shining examples of tolerance, respect, and love. Too often, however, they quickly devolve into arguments containing the sentiment, "my God is better than your God" or "my tradition is older/better/more authentic than yours." Such words are reminiscent of the childhood taunt, "my dad can beat up your dad." Remember, there are many paths up the mountain, many roads to enlightenment and power. What is correct for you is not correct for all. There is no need to disparage someone else's beliefs. If someone is a phony, they will reveal themselves in time, usually by the things they say. They don't need you to unmask them, since such attacks simply make you look foolish. For those on the receiving end of such messages, don't take it personally. Many say on-line what they would never say to someone's face, since no one can see them, touch them, or hold them ultimately accountable for their words. It is easy to get involved in such dramas, easy to succomb to the need to prove yourself and your line of thinking. If you start getting wrapped up in the experience, remember, it's only a game. You wouldn't get angry at a book if it expressed an opinion you didn't like. You would simply stop reading that specific book, or that author, and move on to another. Do the same thing here. Let it go and move on.

Sources

When discussing anything with a measure of authority, cite the sources of your information. This is not to turn all magical discussions into high-brow intellectual banter, but rather to lend credibility to what you say. If your source is a book or article, name it, so others may confirm your point. If your source is your own experience, that is just as valid–if not more so, in my mind–so tell people that. No one can call your own personal experiences invalid. On-line discussions should be an opportunity for education. When you document your sources, you give people the chance to educate themselves and avoid the guru-seeking mentality. You also give credit where credit is due, and what goes around, comes around!

Ask Questions

By the very nature of magical work, much information is kept hidden, kept secret. Occult means "hidden," information not for the general public. People can come from many different magical backgrounds. If someone is talking about something of which you have not heard, but acts as if it is elementary, ask about it. What is the source, where did this person learn it, and how is it used? A basic foundation stone in one magical tradition may be completely alien to another. There is no shame in asking questions. Sometimes, you may even get a good answer. Often you won't, so be prepared. If someone is asking you a question, remember what it was like to be a novice and have no experience or knowledge on which you can draw. Remember, as well, that there are differences in traditions and that not everyone uses the same words for the same concepts. Be open to other people's experiences.

Age

When discussing topics like spirituality, paganism, witchcraft, shamanism, and magick on-line, try to be aware of the age of your conversational partners. Although there is no way to verify your impressions, most people are intuitive about age in general. Be sensitive to the fact that discussion of such topics can cause sparks among parents. Intelligent teens everywhere are getting involved in witchcraft and paganism, but there are also those interested because they saw it in the movies or on TV and want to be hip and cool. When young people seek you out and start asking questions, it's hard not to want to give them the truth about what you know and practice. Most reputable teachers and coven leaders will not teach minors. Minors are only allowed to participate in ceremonies and rituals if their legal parent or guardian is with them. I've been lucky enough to teach quite a few Introduction to Witchcraft classes to which mothers brought their teenagers to learn more about it. If a parent is unaware of such education, however, problems can arise. I think such matters should be dealt with in the home, in a family setting. I'm always happy to answer questions, but only when asked.

◎ CREATING THE CYBER TEMPLE ◎

Until now, we've talked about the Internet as a place to learn, exchange information, explore, and even build a community. One of the keys to building a community is to do things together. On-line chats and discussions suit most people of most interests, but those involved in magical communities know that celebration and ceremony play an important part in community. If you have no physical community around you, then the on-line community is the only place you have to do group ritual.

How can this be done? If people are not in the same room, the same physical space, can they really hold a ceremony? My experience tells me they can. I am fortunate to have a community on both sides of the computer. I've participated in wonderful loving group rituals with friends and family in the woods, on the beach, and in my parents' backyard. I've also had the pleasure of being part of worldwide meditations and on-line rituals with people who understand and share aspects of me that those physically around me might not understand. They are very different and I don't think I can equate them in any way, but both kinds of experiences have had meaning for me. The entire medium is ripe with magical possibilities. Since on-line rituals are a fairly new format, there is no real protocol for them. The sky is the limit, but the technology has some practical considerations for simplicity.

The first thing to decide is whether the ritual will be truly on-line or simply synchronized through on-line communication. If it is not on-line, usually an announcement is made—including the date, time (in several time zones, so those across the world know when they will be participating), and a basic format, including a group invocation to the powers and the intent of the ritual. Many worldwide "meditations" calling for peace during war times and to send spiritual support to those in disaster zones are popular. The information can be printed out and the ritual done quietly in a very introspective manner. Groups can gather at the appointed hour, or individuals can perform the ritual separately. Even when you work physically alone, you realize that others all over the world are echoing your sentiments, hopefully in synchronization. While this is going on, some groups can gather on-line.

Rituals on-line are usually done in chat rooms. There, everyone knows what is happening and when, unlike when they follow solitarily and blindly in a worldwide meditation. While in the room, you see the words cross your screen, invoking powers and energies. You know what each participant is saying and doing. You can choose your level of active participation, whether via the computer or through mental, emotional, and magical energy.

The steps in organizing any ceremony are similar, no matter the venue. Certain details should be decided prior to starting the ritual. The first problem to surmount in any ceremony, physical or virtual, is who will organize it. One of the reasons magical groups fall apart is lack of direction and organization. This is a fundamental need in virtual magick as well. Otherwise, people will be logged on with nothing to do. Is an individual or organization hosting this ceremony? If so, they are responsible for making those involved know the date, time, and all necessarily information to get into the chat room.

The next question is how to get this information out. Whom do you "invite" to this ritual? Is this "members only" for a mailing list or other group of acquaintances? Is it open to all who want to join in? If so, you can post the information on a mailing list, or to newsgroups and message boards, asking people to send the message out to their personal mailing lists of others who might be interested. Completely open circles can be difficult if someone who wants to make mischief and disrupt ceremonies comes into the room. Someone who disagrees with these beliefs and feels that all participating are damned souls could, potentially, be a very big problem. You may want to consider some sort of e-mail screening process by which those interested mail the organizers for the necessary information.

The next issue is to determine the purpose of the ceremony. Is it simply a celebration of community, or a specific act of magick? Is there a common goal, a chance to manifest things in your personal life, or a more altruistic goal for the world? None of these options is better than the other. They are just different. If there is a goal, it should be known to all who participate. Preparation work, such as preparing spells or intention, should be done prior to the ritual.

Is the ritual to be lead by one person or a small group, while the other participants simply observe actions on-line and lend spiritual support? Will everyone have a part in the ritual, even a simple response to invocations? Dividing the work makes everyone feel they are participating, instead of simply watching it on a screen. This builds a feeling of community. Will the ritual be written out word for word so that everyone knows what will be happening, or will the participants only have a general outline of the ritual and no specifics? Some prefer the mystery of not knowing what happens next, but I like to be completely prepared. If you are going to participate in rituals on-line, please learn to type quickly and accurately. Nothing is more frustrating than waiting for someone to type out the next invocation of the ritual. Delays like that can slow the momentum of the ritual and diffuse the group consciousness. In many ways, learning to type is the first requirement of on-line ritual netiquette. If the ritual is completely written, you can simply cut and paste the text before sending it to the room. In this way typing is no longer a problem. Some rituals are completely free-form, letting all participants add whatever words and intents they desire. Such free-form rituals are wonderful in small intimate groups, but in larger groups they can become a bit messy.

The first time you become involved in an on-line group, particularly if the group has been running before you joined, it's probably best to take a more passive role in the ceremony to learn how things work.

Once you have the technical information—how, where, when, the ritual format, and who is responsible for what—the more magical aspects of the ceremony can be contemplated. For many, the on-line ritual experience consists of simply sitting in front of a screen and watching messages appear. If your own experience starts out that way, do not be discouraged. In some ways, to have a very magical experience on-line, you must be even more skilled at visualization and energy work than for physical rituals. The true heart of the experience is multitasking, being able to do more than one thing at a time.

Most of us visualize and "see" with our eyes closed, usually in a dark room. Sometimes, a candle is lit and incense burning. These are great tools to set the mood for off-line and on-line magick. Continue to use them if you already do. The idea of typing during a ritual, and looking at a screen during a ritual, seems distracting to most. How can I close my eyes and "be there"? If you can multitask, the answer is simple. While you have your eyes open, you are still aware, in your mind's eye, of being someplace else. You are aware of part of your energy being projected across the cosmos, or, even better, across the Internet, to join with your fellows in the ceremony. The visual experience may not be as strong as a deep trance with closed eyes, but the feeling of being with these people in a sacred space is more important than anything else.

If someone is doing the majority of the ritual duties, the actual words of the ceremony can include guided imagery, much like a guided meditation, so that all participants can focus on a particular image to connect them, to add to a collective thought across this virtual circle. Having members visualize a network, a web of light connecting them, is helpful. If you are doing a variation of the magick circle ritual, members can visualize the circle going from member to member. A list can be created determining who is "standing" next to whom in this virtual circle. The order can be based alphabetically, on the order of entering the chat room, or even on geographic location, if people desire to share such information.

Guided imagery can also include creating a virtual temple. Much as guided meditation can create an astral temple, a home base so to speak, in which a coven can meditate, do dream work, and connect during ritual. Techno-mancers can create virtual-space temples, through collective imagery. Each member of the group adds thought and power to the collective image. It can be dismissed and dismantled after the ceremony, to be built anew, or kept together for future works. In many ways, it is just as with more traditional shared spaces that exist on the astral plane, but growing from seeds planted on the Internet. Once created, these spaces are accessible by all members, both when on-line and doing ritual, and in more meditative and dream states.

The last hurdle to surmount is the mechanics of spell work. If your intent is not a simple community celebration, but magical work with a goal in mind, you need a vehicle to focus the group, raise energy, and send out the intent. This is not an easy task for an on-line community. First, as a group or as the leader of the group, determine the goal of the spell. Is there one individual spell, or does everyone get to do their own? If it is individual, everyone could write out his or her intent (prior to the ritual) in a similar format. When it comes time to do the spell work, each person can send the intent to the chat room for all to see. Everyone can then focus on it and visualize the goal. The order can be determined before the spell. If you are using the circle imagery, simply go around the circle. Some practitioners accustomed to releasing an intent in traditional rituals through burying the intention slip or burning it may need an action to release the spell. One innovative way around this virtual problem is to send an e-mail to a "dummy address," one set specifically to receive such spells at the end of the ritual, thereby launching them out into the cosmos, literally launching them into the Internet. Many Internet Service Providers let one account owner set up several mail boxes. Others, search engines like Yahoo.com, for instance, let you have free e-mail addresses. You could devote one specifically to this use.

For group spells, having a common symbol on which to focus is very effective. Use the techniques in chapter 7 to find or create an appropriate symbol. You can use graphics programs that draw and paint to create the symbol as a computer file. In this way, you can work on your magical skills as well as your computer and design skills. The symbol can easily be shared by posting it to a Web page and having all members go to the page prior to the ritual and save or print the graphic. The symbol can also be shared by e-mailing it to every individual in the group in a common file format, usually as a JPEG or GIF file. Most browsers can read these types of files with no problem. Graphics programs usually give you a SAVE AS option, under which you can choose an appropriate format. Most applications can open JPEG and GIF files.

Instead of typing your intention during the ritual, you can simply send the sigil out to the group prior to the ritual and tell them to focus on the symbol at the appropriate point in the ceremony. Some feel strongly that everyone should know the intent behind the symbol, making the magick more powerful, while others truly feel that detachment from the outcome is more effective. Although, truthfully, I've found detachment a very effective tool, I have a hard time participating in a magical goal of which I am not completely aware, unless I trust the creator implicitly. Follow your own preferences and intuition in such matters.

EXERCISE 26 – ON-LINE RITUAL

This is a sample of an on-line ritual. Use it as a guide, outline, or inspiration when doing your own. Even for the most experienced traditional magick practitioner, the idea of on-line rituals can seem overwhelming. What is second nature in the physical world becomes awkward in the cyber world. This exercise is written more like a script, with words that can be typed and shared in a chat room. The ritual can go exactly as written, or it can be shared to allow for personal touches, creativity, and spontaneity. The visual cues can be a specific part of the ritual, or shared only in the preview sent to all members, assuming that all will visualize these things without re-typing them in the chat room.

For simplicity's sake, I've divided the roles into leader and participants. The role of the leader can be further subdivided between a small group, at the discretion of the group. This ritual is based on the magick circle.

LEADER: Everyone take a few moments to calm and center themselves. Light any candles or incense you like. Take out any ritual tools or crystals that you would like to have near you. Take a few deep breaths and focus your attention on the task at hand.

LEADER: We create this circle across the Web to protect us from all forces coming to do harm. We ask that only those energies coming in perfect love and perfect trust, in complete harmony with our magical intentions, enter this circle. We create a sacred temple beyond time and space, between the worlds, where our magical intentions will manifest. So mote it be.

PARTICIPANTS: So mote it be.

LEADER: Visualize the circle of light moving across the Web that connects us all. Feel yourself connected by the ring of light, stretching across the world to envelop all members, stretching across the world.

LEADER: To the north, I ask the element of earth and watchtowers of the north to be with us, to guard, guide, and witness this magick. Hail and welcome.

PARTICIPANTS: Hail and welcome.

LEADER: To the east, I ask the element of air and watchtowers of the east to be with us, to guard, guide, and witness this magick. Hail and welcome.

PARTICIPANTS: Hail and welcome.

LEADER: To the south, I ask the element of fire and watchtowers of the south to be with us, to guard, guide, and witness this magick. Hail and welcome.

PARTICIPANTS: Hail and welcome.

LEADER: To the west, I ask the element of water and watchtowers of the west to be with us, to guard, guide, and witness this magick. Hail and welcome.

PARTICIPANTS: Hail and welcome.

LEADER: We invite all spirits who come in a manner correct for our intentions. We invite our personal Gods, guides, and guardians.

PARTICIPANTS: (All can individually welcome their personal patrons by typing their deity or spirit's name.)

LEADER: In this space, we create a temple. Our work today is prosperity magick and the temple is filled with the colors green, blue, and purple, to bring abundance in all our lives. The temple is filled with the finest of luxuries, gold and silver fixtures, fine silks, and all the modern conveniences you could desire. Everything you desire is in this temple.

LEADER: As we do our spell work, each member, in order, will send the group his or her intention for prosperity and manifestation. As a group, we will all add our energy for a few moments, visualizing the outcome while we work in this temple together.

PARTICIPANTS: (Each person, in order, sends his or her intention to the chat room.)

LEADER: We release all these intentions to manifest for our highest good, harming none in the process. So mote it be.

PARTICIPANTS: So mote it be.

LEADER: Everyone take a few moments to ground themselves and bring themselves back to center.

LEADER: We thank and release all beings who have been with us, to aid us in our work.

LEADER: To the north, I thank and release the element of earth and watchtowers of the north. Hail and farewell.

PARTICIPANTS: Hail and farewell.

LEADER: To the west, I thank and release the element of water and watchtowers of the west. Hail and farewell.

PARTICIPANTS: Hail and farewell.

LEADER: To the south, I thank and release the element of fire and watchtowers of the south. Hail and farewell.

PARTICIPANTS: Hail and farewell.

LEADER: To the east, I thank and release the element of air and watchtowers of the east. Hail and farewell.

PARTICIPANTS: Hail and farewell.

LEADER: We release this circle across the web of life to manifest our spells. So mote it be.

PARTICIPANTS: So mote it be.

◎ THE FUTURE OF CYBER MAGICK ◎

No one can really know where such techniques are leading in the magical world. They may be simple experiments that are later abandoned in favor of traditional techniques as part of a world backlash against technological advances. On the other hand, cyber magick may be the start of a whole new magical revolution, turning many ideas and techniques on their collective ear. It is simply too early to tell.

With the advancement of virtual-reality technology, in which the human mind interfaces with the computer world through visual and sensory cues, the idea of group rituals may become something much closer to traditional circle-standing and hand-holding. In virtual space, you will be able to "see" computer-generated representations of your peers standing by your side. When you draw a banishing pentagram in the air of cyber space, everyone will see it, shining in computer-generated flame. For those with difficulties visualizing, this seems like an amazing feat. Detractors may feel that this is the very reason why such technology should not be used. It lets our "magical muscles," our inner vision, atrophy and lets the computer do the work for us. Where is the strength in that? Only time will tell. Personally, I'm torn between seeing the best both worlds have to offer, and the worst. Obviously, I don't feel that technology is inherently evil or I wouldn't use it. All machines, including computers, are tools to be used with wisdom. Our modern 21st-century tools are so different from those of centuries past, however, that it's hard to keep track of their potential abuses.

Another interesting point to ponder is the very medium we are using. Does the Internet go beyond the traditional definition of a rit-ual tool and grow into something more? As magick workers, witches, and pagans, we personify everything in life. Everything is living, from the obvious animal spirits and trees, to rocks, the clouds, and water. Many of these natural forces are tended by deities, cultural God-forms responsible for humanity's interaction with the elements. Some mages see the Gods and spirits as tools, a means to communicate with the vast unknowable universe. In the exploration of city magick, the city itself is personified as a living vortex of energy, of life force. The beings and structures occupying this space also exhibit the traits of personality, of individuality, and of uniqueness. Could the Internet not exhibit those same traits? This new entity is simply the embodi-ment of information, of knowledge, of raw data from everywhere and everything. Imagine invoking such a being. The possibilities are stagger-ing. As research into computer intelligences proceeds, the potential goes beyond the simple archetype and into the realm of literal possibility.

Our science fiction points to possible magical and technological medleys, where both arts are honored and combined. If science fic-tion is simply a map to our possible futures, then such a reality may exist. Remember, however, that the science fiction foretold a country controlled by "Big Brother" by 1984, a Moon-base hurtling through space filled with fantastic aliens in 1999. Far better to pay attention to the reality here and now, and consciously choose what our future will be. Is that not the heart of magick—the creation of your own destiny?

Chapter 12
Our Town

CITIES ARE NOT ONLY VAST SOURCES of power and spirit energy. They are, first and foremost, homes. People do make their livings there, but what they really create is life. Lovers and spouses are found, and families, in all shapes and sizes, are created. Some of the best families have no blood relationships. As the home of our daily and our magical lives—which aren't as different as some might think—we should strive to know our cities well. Cities are like big houses. You have to explore every nook and cranny of your home before you really know its potential. If you stay in one room all the time, you may know it very well, but you are forgetting the rest of the house. Better yet, cities are like friends. Each friend has many facets. Some are familiar and comfortable. Others are farther away, deeper and darker. We do not see these hidden parts unless we explore.

Each city has its own personality. Each has a distinct energy, as unique as its people. Every one is built over a unique vortex, an individual power spot. No two are alike. They change over time, with changes in population and social trends, but some core traits remain the same. Each city has its different facets, as we do. People act differently at work than when relaxing at home. The "face" we present to family can be different from the one we present to friends. Cities have similar facets, expressed as similar districts, but each one is a little different, just as each person in astrology has all the signs and planets in his or her chart, yet the expression of these similar energies is different. Cities are a lot like people. They even have astrological birth charts. Their birthdays are the day they were founded. States and countries can have astrological charts too. You can learn a lot about a city and the people who settle there by studying the city's birth chart.

Here are some common expressions of these traits, found in many cities, particularly in America, as it is more ethnically diverse. They are expressed as different districts, both official and unofficial. Each district may have a different character and history in a particular city, but they share many common traits. There are many more than the ones I've listed. Many are based on the various nationalities settling in the area. Others are based on the industries and activities of the city. Some are more magical than others. Explore on your own and discover the magick in your own city.

Downtown

Downtown is the center of town, where people come to meet, greet, and shop. Downtown storefronts were the scene of commerce before the invention of the mall, and many fine stores, shops, and restaurants have remained in the downtown areas with no intention of moving. Often, these more unique stores help give the city its own personality. Energetically, downtown has a lot of strong, direct energy. The feel is very electric and masculine in many ways. People are always running around. Although it may not be a pure, natural prana site, often people frequenting the heart of the city leave with a strong "buzz" of energy. You may physically or psychically feel a subtle shift in your vibrational level. Your energy rises. At other times, the energy may be very muddy and stuck, particularly around holiday shopping time. The high energy, the frenzy of the day, has no outlet. At these times, such areas can alter your mood for the worse, and often cause tension-related illnesses like headaches and stomach pains. The next time you are running around the city, if you are prone to headaches, notice where they start.

Financial District

Most major metropolitan areas have a financial district. This is an even more concentrated form of electric, masculine energy. The very nature of finance is electric, direct, up and down. One day the market is up, the next it is down, like a lightning bolt, it jumps to all points in between. There are no soft curves to it and the people working with it. Things are very black and white, profit or loss.

Thoughtforms and energy constructs are unconsciously made from the hopes, dreams, fears, frustrations, and failures projected by the movers and shakers of the business world. Spell casters consciously create their own thoughtforms in magick, with the intention that they dissipate once the spell is fulfilled. Many financial wizards have as much personal power as sorcerers, but lack an awareness of it. Because they don't understand true personal power, they don't realize what they are creating. Many thoughtforms exist in the financial district. Some have taken on a life their own, like little spirits. Often, the ones created from darker thoughts seek out and join others, and there are a lot of dark thoughts in the financial district. Much of the business is run on greed and control. Physical sickness often comes from thoughtforms, both of our making and from others, intruding upon our energy body. They can cause an imbalance in our energy bodies that manifests as disease.

On a brighter note, many of these financial superstars create beneficial thoughtforms for prosperity, luck, and success. Since they don't realize they are creating something either, these forms often stick around and can be used. By charging a charm for prosperity in the financial district, and by being on guard against unhelpful thoughtforms, you can attract a spirit of good fortune. You will give it a home and function, as it may be seeking one, and it will give you greater powers of prosperity, since it was created by someone with a stronger power in the financial world. Some spirits that exist on other planes, spirits that were never created by humans, may also be attracted to these places. Strong emotions and thoughts attract them.

What is stronger than the potential of making and then losing a fortune, with the possibility of making it again tomorrow? For some, that is the ultimate emotional roller coaster, an addiction as potent as any other. Like thoughtforms, some spirits are helpful, and others less so.

Uptown

Uptown is the land of high society, where the elite meet, so to speak. Homes here are posh penthouses or venerable estates where those considered "upper class" dwell. The vibes of uptown areas tend to fit the culture residing there. Tradition plays a strong role. There is an air of sophistication, of worldliness. If there are any retail businesses, they are high-priced and sell only top-quality merchandise.

Most would consider such a place to be devoid of magick and magical people. Not so. A close look at our modern magical history reveals that many of the old lodges, guilds, temples, and secret societies are maintained by those in the upper echelons of society. The upper crust work in this world because they have the resources, the time, and the inclination to do so. Working-class people are traditionally known for doing "low magick," or common folk magick, to fulfill their needs. They have more immediate concerns. The urban magical orders have the desire to organize, network, spread out, and maintain an intricate level of high magick. Their lifestyle permits it. You may be surprised by what is going on behind closed doors in uptown areas in a city near you.

Low Town

Low town areas are the dark shadow of the city—the "not so nice" neighborhoods where poverty and potential crime are more prevalent. The magical vibrations of such a place are difficult to assimilate from the "outside." The feeling that greets you can range from unwelcoming to menacing, particularly if the residents live in fear of gangs, theft, and assault. The important thing to remember is that many people make their home here out of necessity. Yet many wonderful things go on in these places, things not reported by the media because they are the simple kindnesses of life. In any case, be careful on your sidewalking trips through these areas. Always be conscious of your environment and the danger level inherent there. But do not write off a place simply because it does not conform to your ideals. Such low-town haunts are the best places for seeking magical images embedded in graffiti.

Chinatown

Not all cities have a large Chinese-American population, but some of the major centers do. They are worth investigating. The various Chinatowns hearken back to an Old World charm, juxtaposed with modern trappings. Many residents are immigrants from Asia, or first-generation Americans. Foreign customs, traditions, religious ceremonies, holidays, foods, and medicines are common. In some ways, life in a place like this reminds me of being a witch, being different from most of the people around you, hearkening back to the old ways of the world. In Chinatown, however, you have an inner community. The energy in many Chinatowns is more magnetic, creative, feminine, and secret. Old secrets, particularly of medicine, herbs, balance, and the mind/body/spirit connection, are honored. Great healing can be done with these energies, whether in your own rituals by drawing on the energy, or by truly honoring these customs by seeking a knowledgeable practitioner of Chinese medicine.

Little Italy

Little Italy is a region where Italian immigrants and their families have settled. Half of my heritage is Italian, so these areas hold a special place in my heart. The energy is strongly electromagnetic, balancing male and female energies. Even though the culture is stereotypically male-dominated, in truth, I find it more balanced than some groups. Men seem to be in control of the family, but many of the women are really in charge. They have just come to an arrangement. Most Italians are devout Catholics, but they belong to a branch of Christianity that strongly honors the goddess through the Virgin Mother Mary. Yet even some outwardly mainstream residents hear the call to the old ways, honoring both god and goddess through the Strega witchcraft traditions. What others call superstition is part and parcel of their culture. Some have forgotten the roots and reasons, but I've had relatives called upon for blessings, removing curses, giving the evil eye, and divining the future with tea leaves or oil. The magick of this culture has been woven into the religion, superstitions, customs, and cooking. The energy of these neighborhoods tends to reflect their nature, pushing and pulling between the two extremes.

Hispanic Community

Regardless of their divergent points of origin, Hispanic communities are quite possibly the most magical of all. Along with African communities, they retain an almost unbroken link to their magical traditions. Santeria and Voodoo are commonly accepted beliefs, shadowing more traditional forms of Christianity. They contain a sense of magical mystery to them, since, until recently, almost none of this material was committed to print. The charms and magick are passed through families and community lines. Go into many shops in the neighborhood and you will find thinly disguised magical tools. Everyone who lives there knows what they are. Even the grocery stores have seven-day candles marked with the images of patron saints and gods. Home altars are more common here than anywhere else.

Irish Neighborhood

Community settlements of those from an Irish ethnic background are quite prevalent in major cities. The energy here tends to be more male-dominated, with a strong sense of community and unity, often with a strong work ethic. In some ways, such neighborhoods are a bit like closed communities. Everyone knows everyone else. Everyone has a similar background, magnifying this unified tightly knit feeling. I have a special affinity for Irish culture, not through genetics, but more from their ancient history and magical traditions. My original training in magick and witchcraft was very strongly Celtic-influenced, and drew a lot from Irish and Welsh myth, magick, and poetry. Some modern descendents are reclaiming these traditions in their own practice of magick.

Gay Town

Many cities seem to have a district where the queer folk live, love, and party. Some dominate the entire town, while others tend to be more restricted to a single section. They go by different names—Greenwich Village in New York City, Back Bay in Boston, or Boystown in Los Angeles—but they have some traits in common. Obviously, they tend to be more open and accepting of those in nontraditional relationships. They tend to be the center of new art and theater. Shops there often have the newest trends and styles. The vibes in these places are high-energy and exciting, but in a more relaxed way. They rhythmically range from the electric and direct, to the magnetic and feminine. This is probably an effect of the greater concentration of androgynous people in the area. Even though these areas are high-energy, they are centers of fun and recreation, not power and control, although some people in unhealthy relationships would argue that fact. Magick for creativity and balance tends to be fruitful when drawing on energy from these places.

Theater District

Many cities have a concentrated area of theaters for dramatic and musical plays. The energy in such spots is empathetically wonderful, being very up and exciting. Think of all the adrenaline flowing in the actors, musicians, and directors, the renewed excitement with each performance, and the audience anticipation. For many visiting the city, such performances are once-in-a-lifetime treats. The local neighborhood usually supports the theater environment, with restaurants and shops staying open until the shows get out. There is a feeling of electricity all around. Those who pick up on emotional environments may get a contact "high" from such places, or even be emotionally overwhelmed by such strong feelings surrounding them on all sides. The protection meditation in Exercises 4 (see page 27) can definitely help build your inner defenses against such unintentional assaults. Magical jump-start spells, to increase excitement and activity, or spells for practitioners who are also performers of some kind, are potent in such areas, because there is so much natural ambient energy present there.

Club Row

If there is any type of nightlife occurring in the city–clubs, music, dance, or comedy–it will tend to be concentrated in focused little areas. As in the theater districts, there is an electric feeling of energy here, but the flavor of it will depend on the local "scene" and the types of performances occurring. These areas also tend to exude a predatory feeling. Many singles clubs are known for their "meat-market" mentality. Others are only hang-outs, places to gather and have a good time. Club Row is always an excellent choice for magical sidewalking adventures.

Red-Light District

Here you find adult bookstores, sex shops, and strip clubs. Such areas have a reputation for prostitution and drugs, so the predatory atmosphere found in the club area can be amplified here. Ultimately, this is a place for fulfilling your desires, no matter what they are. Strong thoughtforms run rampant through this section, giving many people creepy, eerie feelings. The true lessons of the area lie in the desires uncovered here and our shame connected to such desires. As long as everything is between consenting adults, there should be no problem. Indeed, the attraction of such places often lies in their forbidden and secret nature.

The red-light districts in the United States are slowly dying out due to zoning laws. People living in the neighborhood simply do not want such sleazy activites in their area. Crime often seems to flourish in such places. If handled well, there can be a happy medium. My first visit to Time Square in New York City scared me to death. Each subsequent visit, however, showed me a more "cleaned-up" environment. You can still get whatever you wanted there, but you feel a bit safer walking down the street.

◎ SURVEYING THE CITIES ◎

As each district has an energetic personality, so each has an overall personality coloring it. If you are drawn to a particular city, you resonate with its energy. On a higher level, you know you have a lot to learn from it. People either head toward the familiar, or they head toward what they desire to become. This can be an act of transformation. You hope to change by embracing the very thing you are not. Change by association. Many timid people head for the big city to gain more confidence, control, and power for themselves, and to increase their sense of self, their identity, and independence. If you can make it there, you can make it anywhere.

I have only listed a few modern cities, because these are the ones I feel I can write about with authority. I have opened my senses and explored these areas. Some information has been gathered by friends and fellow practitioners across the country whose opinions I trust and value. As with everything else, you need to explore you own environment and find the energies and spirits who will work with you.

Boston, MA

Boston is a very historic city, the first hub of the New World. Though not ancient by any stretch, for America, its history runs deep, from the landing at Plymouth Rock and the initiation of Thanksgiving traditions, to the witch trials, the Boston Tea Party, and the cradling of the heart of the American Revolution. Many sites, museums, and monuments in the area commemorate these events and record their energies on the etheric level. Many different cultures have come here. Each has staked out its own community, bringing different energies to this setting. Boston still has a young energy to it, as a premier college town. Many modern initiations go on there, with students going away from home for the first time, coming to Boston, and drinking and bar-hopping for the first time. The music and art scene is alive and well in Boston and its outskirts.

Boston is right on the Atlantic Ocean, with a harbor opening to it. The Charles River divides Boston from its sister city, Cambridge. The element of water is the undercurrent for what has traditionally been a stoic community. Emotions run deep, but are often hidden under a veneer. Much of the Back Bay area was built on swamp and someday waters will reclaim it, thus the whole city is very magnetic. The streets are curved and jumbled. There are few direct, straight paths along which energy lines can flow. The vast majority of the city was organized around walking paths for animals, leaving modern urban planners little room for street parking. Through these winding streets the energy flows. The paths are more natural, following the contours of the land and vortex, even though it can be hell to drive there. For those resonating strongly with magnetic energy, Boston can be even more magical.

Burlington, VT

When you first arrive in Burlington, you see a quaint New England city. The drive there is beautiful, and the scenery inspires a strong wonderment of the natural power surrounding the place. The natural power is not disrupted or spoiled in any way. Because of this harmony, I've often thought of living closer to Burlington. The city itself blends the new with the old, with a cobblestoned marketplace filled with the latest shops. As cities go, it's clean and neat, and the people are friendly. Its most striking feature is the lake. Lake Champlain has a lot of natural magnetic power just sweeping off it into the town. In fact, I would guess that the lake, not the town, is the center of the vortex. The city just grew next to the vortex. I'm sure the altitude has something to do with it as well, as the city is quite close to the mountains. I found it very easy to make magick by tapping into the natural ambient energy all around. Waves of energy come across the lake and bathe the city.

Cancun, Mexico

If you ever visit exotic locales, take the time to introduce yourself to the goddesses and gods of these lands. If you are doing magick, it's only polite to make yourself known to the ruling lords and ladies of the land, even those who rule in shadow, in the secret layers or forgotten times of the culture. You can find yourself with allies in cultures you were never drawn to before. Even if you intellectually see all deities as extensions of universal archetypes, you are really opening yourself up to a new experience. While visiting Cancun, I did a meditation asking to speak with the Mayan and Aztec gods who were appropriate for me at this time. Later, I traveled the peninsula that comprises the tourist area of Cancun. On the inside of this projection is a large lagoon, on the outside, the crashing ocean. The dynamic flow of the energy from the still water to the waves required a short period of adjustment. Ultimately, I found it empowering–this mixture of water power and the hot Sun beating down. The energy of this place, and I think perhaps of Mexico in general, is a dynamic polarity between water and fire, goddess and god. Next, I visited the Mayan ruins of Talum, experiencing the energy of these ancient people and their beliefs. The city, perched over the ocean on cliffs had a distinct, timeless feel to it. Once I had acclimated to the energy of the land and the culture, my partner and I called upon the Aztec rain god, Tlaloc. The news reports predicted rain for the rest of our vacation. We asked Tlaloc to hold the rain back, respecting him and his authority over this province and power. I think he accepted our offering, because it was sunny until the day we left. At home, I lit a candle in his honor on my altar. It is great to cultivate divine friends and allies across the globe.

Chicago, IL

Chicago is the classic windy city, and can be thought of as ruled by the element of air. Air denotes intellect and the power of the mind. Ideas are moved forward, and Chicago has brought to fruition a lot of ideas, being a major manufacturing center. The ideas of the mind are given physical shape. This city is also a major architectural center, home to the Sears Tower, and a pioneer in the upward growth of cities. In some ways, Chicago is the first archetype of the urban Mecca. After the Chicago fire, the city, when rebuilt, was one of the first to have a fire department and to replace wooden buildings with stone. Most cities have followed suit.

Even though Chicago is noted for wind, the element of water plays a strong role in its development. The wind comes off Lake Michigan. Even though the port is used mainly for shipping, the element of water, as represented by the lake, aids in making a connection to the realm of emotion and the heart chakra.

Hong Kong, China

Hong Kong started as a British colony and, while under British rule, developed into a world capital of industry and finance. The magical correlation I discovered here was the aspect of high town and low town, paralleling the mythical images of the upper world and underworld. The main city of Hong Kong, the upper-world model, is the Mecca. The streets are clean and everything is very modern. In many aspects, it rivals New York City, which I didn't expect. The area, for all its urbanization, has an almost pristine quality to it. Even the poorest and oldest sections have a feel to them quite different from American slums. The peninsula of Kowloon was the low town, the underworld. I know that my tourist's view of the open markets and shops just skimmed the surface of the social world there. I think if you looked hard enough, you could possibly get anything, legal or not, there. The upper world, Hong Kong proper, was very Westernized. English was a main language. In Kowloon, Cantonese was the main language.

Although many people spoke English, there was more symbolic communication transpiring. I don't judge one as better than the other on
the basis of language and culture. I enjoyed Kowloon immensely and,
in my mystical travels, I enjoyed the underworld. My point here is to
remark on the widely different worlds separated by a short ferry
ride—a modern incarnation of Charon, the ferryman of Greek myth,
taking the dead and brave heroes into the underworld of Hades.

Honolulu, HI

To me, Hawaii has always been one of the most magical places in the
world, even when I didn't really know what magick was. There is an
energy there that is apparent to all who visit. Some debate on the
purity of each island and, although I've never had the pleasure of visiting the big island of Hawaii, which I'm told has the most mana, the
Hawaiian equivalent of prana or life energy, the islands I've visited
seem very vibrant with life force to me. The energy comes from the
fiery volcanoes mixing with the ocean water to create new earth, as
the gentle trade winds flow over the islands. Perhaps it's the balance
of the four elements that makes it so magical for me. Some feel the
islands are the remnants of the enlightened continent of fabled
Lemuria. Everything seems so alive, but at the same time like a story-
book fantasy, from the looming volcanic mountains to the crystal-
blue waters of the coast. The vegetation, even in the more urban
areas like Honolulu on the island of Oahu, is breathtaking. Also on
Oahu is Pearl City, and, more important, Pearl Harbor. Travels to the
memorial of the sunken *U.S.S. Arizona* truly give you a connection to
the spirit world. The feeling is very palpable, mystic or not. You can
feel or sense things trapped in the ethers in this place. My father, who
is not what one would call psychic, could feel the presence. Modern
pagan interest has brought Hawaiian magick and myth to greater
notoriety. Some of my students have taken a liking to the volcano
goddess Pele and work with her, even though they have not physically traveled to the islands.

London, England

London, the capital of the United Kingdom, resides it a very magical land. Not far from this metropolis are some of the most ancient mystery sites. Many consider this place a hub in the energy grid of Earth. The countryside is marked by standing stones and such powerful structures as Stonehenge, Glastonbury Tor, Avebury Circle, and the carved chalk hills. The power lines cross the hills and valleys and seem to converge in these places. The city itself was founded by the Romans as Londinium, on the banks of the River Thames. The modern city houses everything under the Sun, from manufacturers to museums, and royal palaces, financial districts, monuments, and institutions of higher learning. London is another quintessential archetype of the urban Mecca, containing each facet of city life and built on ancient power. I have found that most magical practitioners who visit there either enjoy London immensely or have tremendously odd experiences. They report feeling "dizzy" or not quite grounded in the body while on the trip. All experiences, even the most mundane, become adventures in sidewalking, in which visions, ghosts, and strange sensations occur.

New York City, NY

To me New York is one of the most magical cities. When I think of the word "city," I think of New York. This land needs to be seen to be believed. When I first took a bus there, at age 17, I couldn't believe the skyline. The place did not look real to me. The magick comes in the form of hopes and dreams manifesting, music, art, and modern thought. I know that view tends to downplay crime, pollution, muggings, and murders, but so be it. Within the city are many modern miracles and achievements of man. From the Empire State Building and the Statue of Liberty, to Cleopatra's Needle in Central Park, they evoke the wonderment humanity is capable of creating. Each of the neighborhoods and boroughs has its own cultural and energetic flavor. The magick there is patchwork, like a quilt. In the city's center,

Central Park, you have what some would argue is a small forest–a place of enchantment and danger, the mythic forest of fairyland where you can be blessed and cursed. If you need to reconnect with the land while living in the city, go there.

The island of Manhattan is a strong phallic symbol, the heart of a fertile masculine Earth vortex, celebrated by the native people long before the arrival of the Europeans. For the most part, its strong, straight lines run up and down, directing the energy and current. It is surrounded by two rivers, symbols of the life of the goddess, the lifeblood of Mother Earth. The whole area is reminiscent of ancient mysteries like Isis and Osiris by the Nile.

The very act of moving to the Big Apple has been like an initiatory journey for many of my friends. Some find what they are looking for. Others discover what they seek to be elsewhere.

Los Angeles, CA

I have a bit of a negative bias toward Los Angeles. I was there as a child, when my sensory perception and psychic skills were pretty much dormant. It didn't bother me. I wasn't crazy about it, but it was okay. When I returned as an adult on a business trip, however, I experienced a very strong reaction. I felt that many of Earth's grid lines collapsed and grew weak around Los Angeles. I'm not sure why. If it related strictly to pollution, I'm sure many other cities would have the same effect on me. Los Angeles is on the Pacific Ocean, and, although oceans tend to be more magnetic and healing, the Pacific Ring of Fire tends to be more electric and masculine. Those qualities may have something to do with my response, along with the shifting fault lines. On the positive side, I found Los Angeles to be a strong spot in which to work with spirits. Perhaps the weakening of the grid opens up communication with other dimensions. Mediums and psychics may gather there for that reason. I found more spirits and allies popping up out of the woodwork, often at inopportune times. Here, more than ever before, I found the need to be discerning about the spirits with whom I worked. Use your judgment when working with unknown beings. Ask if they come in unconditional love and for the highest good. Use love and laughter with them. Dark spirits will think you are mocking them and will soon tire of you. Affirm your protective shield daily, if not hourly, in LA, for both spirits and other dangers.

Montreal, Canada

Montreal, built on the island of the same name in the St. Lawrence River, has some unique properties as an energy center. The city sits, for the most part, on this island, but spills out to some of the adjacent islands and partially onto the mainland as well. It is a city almost surrounded by flowing water, making it a very magnetic site and a good place to work with the element of water and the principle of flow. It is Canada's leading port, but the harsh winter can bring problems with ice. At times, the energy does seem a bit stuck or frozen in the area. The area is also dominated by the volcanic Mount Royal, extending some fiery and electrical aspect to the city. As a foreigner, what seemed so remarkable to me on my visit was the cleanliness of the city and how, unconsciously or intuitively, the people respected each other and the power of the city, honoring it quite a bit more than was characteristic in American cities.

New Orleans, LA

Though I must admit that I have never visited New Orleans myself, I'm a great fan of the contemporary gothic authors who base many of their stories in this wonderful city. A discussion of magical cities would be remiss not to mention New Orleans and I have loved the opportunity to talk to those who have practiced there. New Orleans is the place of gentleman death, a little underworld within the world. Since the city is prone to taking on water, being built in swamp lands, the graveyards are often built above ground, with stone crypts, a constant reminder of mortality. The dead hold a particular charm here. The entire city is permeated with the dark world energy–very watery, magnetic, and working well with the images of the dark devouring Mother Earth, instead of the more benign Mother Nature image. And this is a land of magick. Voodoo traditions are common here, both out in the open and keeping to the shadows, and have been for a very long time.

Salem, NH

Although my hometown would hardly qualify as an urban Mecca, I felt the need to include it for myself. In the northeastern area of Salem is America's Stonehenge, a mysterious megalithic site on a scale much smaller than England's Stongehenge. Its construction is tentatively credited to a Native American culture or migrant European tradition. No one knows for sure, but many artifacts have been found there. Like its British counterpart, it has many energy lines that intersect at its center, and these lines cross throughout the town. I've had the pleasure of attending workshops and conducting rituals there. With your psychic senses or divining rods, you can find the lines running throughout the complex. They flow throughout the town and sur-rounding areas. There are energy lines everywhere. Some areas are more concentrated than others. You can probably find them in your own town as well, if you are determined enough to look. Place the intent to find Earth energy lines into your diving rods and walk around your block. See if they cross anywhere. Those places may indicate high concentrations of energy and a potential line or crossing of lines.

San Francisco, CA

San Francisco is another magical city, nestled by one of the most beautiful natural bays in the world, but teetering, as well, on the edge of a powerful fault line. Here, a polarity of energies is at work, the giving mother ocean and the unforgiving San Andreas Fault. This sometimes-volatile mix has made this land to be a center of creativity, arts, and tolerance, a pioneering city in the dawn of the Age of Aquarius. San Francisco was the home of such unusual groups as the

Bohemians in the 1890s, the beat poets of the 1950s, and the hippies and flower children of the 1960s. The city was the womb of these brief, but revolutionary, social scenes. Even now, it is regarded as one of the most tolerant and accepting places in the world, hosting movements in civil rights, particularly gay, lesbian, and transgender rights, woman's rights, and public acceptance of pagans. I think the dominance of the watery bay marks a loving and accepting nature of feminine, motherly energies.

The city itself is marked by its diverse cultures and districts. Its maze of streets is lined with unusual architecture and office buildings. The city definitely has its own character, matching its unique population. The skyline is distinguished by the Transamerica Pyramid building, America's own pyramid right on the West Coast. Pyramids, by their very shape, are a place of power, magick, and initiation. Razor blades placed in pyramids do not get dull. Fruits stay fresher, more energized, in a pyramid. Many healing tools are charged in pyramid structures. You can buy or make miniature pyramids from copper tubing, wire, or glass. All the ancient cultures built pyramids and mounds, from Egypt to Central America. Although not in the perfect traditional shape, perhaps this pyramid can be used in such a way. By visiting it, you can tap into your own pyramid-power experience, and judge its benefits for yourself.

Seattle, WA

Seattle is the largest city in the American Northwest. Named after Chief Seattle, a peaceful Native American chief, this city lies on the hills between two bodies of water, Puget Sound and Lake Washington. Not far from the city there are mountains all around. The Northwest is on the edge of the Pacific Ring of Fire, a ring of volcanic and seismic activity that surrounds the Pacific. Mount Saint Helens, a once-dormant volcano that erupted as recently as 1980, is located there. Seattle is known for its rain, but according to a friend living in the area, that reputation has not been as well deserved in recent years.

Perhaps this unusual balance of energies, of elements, makes the Northwest so attractive and magical. Seattle has a bustling pagan community, of organized groups and many solitaries, probably inspired and drawn to the beautiful landscape all around them. A key signature of the city is the Space Needle, reaching up to the heavens like a modern-day futuristic Tower of Babel.

Sedona, AZ

Some argue that Sedona is the New Age capital of the world, with all the good and bad connotations that title carries with it. The town is booming with tourism, growing by leaps and bounds. People seem as attracted to the Native American cultures and ruins and the breathtaking red-rock cliffs as they are to the New Age classes and vortex tours. Like all cities built on energy sites, Sedona is no exception, but individual vortices have been located and isolated, each with different properties. There is one near the airport and another by Bell Rock, along with many others. Some residents feel these are some of the most powerful vortices in the world. People travel there to do ceremonies, meditate, and chant, and hoping to learn about Earth's energy field. Many tour guides genuinely know what they are doing and go to these sacred sites with reverence. For others, it's just another job. A friend has actually speculated that all these visitors have energetically polluted and clogged the vortices. New Age centers and shops have sprung up to cater to the spiritual seekers who come to the vortexes. Again, some are genuine, others less so. Friends have complained that those who come to Sedona are so involved in the New Age that they tend to shun pagans, witches, Druids, and ceremonial magicians. I didn't experience that myself, but I could see it happening. Sedona is a special place, and Native American prophecies have centered around the world's different people coming together in this land of red rocks. You can't drive through the rocks without truly feeling the touch of the divine running through you in their beauty.

E_XERCI_SE 27 – MEETING THE CITY

If you have been following these exercises, you probably have a fair idea of the urban energies around you. Start this exercise by making a list of all the qualities around you, where you live. You can restrict these qualities to your particular neighborhood and district, or use the entire city. Write out the qualities of the area, personalizing them, personifying them. Do they feel feminine, masculine, or androgynous? Do they evoke an archetype, a parental or godlike figure? Does one of the classic four elements dominate the environment? Take all these things into consideration. You should then have a fair idea as to the personality of the city, or at least of the face it chooses to show you.

Now create your own meditation, similar to those in Exercises 10 and 11 (see pages 86 and 91), but instead of choosing a particular location, let the location choose you once you enter the image of the Worldscraper. You may end up in the hidden world, the sky city, or the more visible middle kingdoms. Use the tools and talents you have gathered through this work and start with the intention to meet the spirit of the city, a personification of the energies you are using. During the shamanic journey, you may actually meet a being or find yourself in the presence of its energy. Many will know this being or energy already, since it pervades the entire environment. Communication can be verbal, visual, or intuitive. Make friends with this energy as you would with any other spiritual ally. Cultivate this relationship while working with city magick.

End the meeting and complete the conversation, as in any other journey. Bring yourself back through the use of the Worldscraper image, exiting in the middle world and returning your awareness back to the physical.

◎ SACRED PILGRIMAGES ◎

There are times when you need a change of scene. You need to make
a journey, physically and spiritually, to effect the proper change in
you. You may need to go deeper than you normally do in your magical journeys. Traditionally, many mystics go to spiritual sites, traveling far and wide in search of this new awakening. Shamans go off
into the wilderness for training they can get from no physical, human
teacher. They go questing for their power. The European wild-
man/magician goes off to the woods for a bout of madness leading to
sacred enlightenment. Some say Merlin went off on such an adventure before returning as a mage. Priests and priestesses, sacred orders
throughout time, have cloistered themselves from the world to seek
spiritual expansion. The idea of removing oneself from the normal,
waking environment for a magical quest, a sacred pilgrimage to commune with the forces of nature, is common in both myth and reality.
Such an adventure greatly benefits the city magician.

Think about taking your own journey. What is the goal of the
retreat? Does a particular land call to you? Meditate on where you
need to go. You can travel to the more famous sacred sites–Stonehenge, the pyramids in Egypt, the ruins in Mexico, Jerusalem, the temple of Delphi in Greece, Sedona, Arizona, or Mount Shasta in Cali-
fornia. Many spiritually orientated tours are available for those seeking to visit the sacred sites with like-minded people and possibly be
involved in ceremony or meditation at the sites. Many spiritual-retreat
weekends and festivals are available, offering classes, workshops, rituals, and drumming circles, along with and a variety of recreational
activities. They offer a great chance to recharge your psychic batteries
and commune with a new environment and a new community.

For those with a specific spiritual goal in mind, travel alone is best.
You may simply leave the city you live in for its outskirts, the surrounding wilderness, driving only a few hours. Change your environment. Most major cities are not far from a beautiful area near a

lake or mountain to which the urbanites retreat for much-needed vacations. Go camping or rent an isolated cabin. Live off the land, if you have the skills needed. Devote the day to your magical pursuits, making it a learning retreat. The level of intensity and commitment is up to you. Hardcore vision-questers will spend the majority of their days trancing, speaking to spirits, and working magick. Speak to your guides and totems. In the woods, you may find a different totem from the one who guides you in the city. Go with it. Seek out new things and new experiences. Create and, most important, have fun. Seeking spirituality may bring enlightenment eventually, but it brings joy first.

◎ SUBURBS, TOWNS, AND THE BOONIES ◎

If you've been drawn to this book, you probably resonate with a lot of the information and want to try it out. If you live in Smalltown, USA, however, what can you do? The whole point of this material is to modify traditional magical works for the urban setting. Experiment. Living in a suburb, small town, or way out in the boonies is not a bad thing, if that's where you are happy. In many ways, it's preferable. Go where you need to be–city, country, or anywhere between. You can modify these practices to fit any setting. I worked with a lot of these techniques while working in Cambridge, Massachusetts, and living in the suburbs. I went home to a relatively quiet neighborhood, with trees in my backyard and a small altar outside. I found myself taking lunchtime walks, or hanging out in Boston after hours, waiting to meet with friends or business associates. I felt a lack of spiritual connection, particularly in times of unhappiness, so I set out to discover the magick all around me, inside the office and out. That is your one goal–to discover the magick all around you. Try some of these techniques and exercises right in your hometown, or save them for a meditative jaunt into the city. Take the essence of this book to heart, and find your own practices.

Chapter 13
Futurama

WHAT DOES THE FUTURE HOLD? That's what all psychics are asked. Most people can't trust in the universe or create their own future, so they need to know what is next. Where do we go from here? An assurance of happiness and health is needed, or a warning to avoid disaster. As a community, family, tribe, city, country, or even planet, we are all co-creating our collective fate. What I do affects you, and vice versa. What we do as a group affects all other groups around us and all these groups affect life on every different level. Not many of us consult with the animal, vegetable, and mineral kingdoms before taking action. Not many ring up Mother Earth to ask what's best for the planet. Perhaps we should. We all have a responsibility to each other. What kind of future do you want?

Before we reach up to the stars, or even out to a new level of existence, a new dimension, we need to remember all the important things right here. Before we engineer new environments in sealed bubbles on the Moon or Mars, if we haven't secretly done so already, we need to learn balance in this vast living biosphere called Earth. Here, we have a closed system that used to enjoy a natural, balanced state. Its resources were renewed, all things depended on one another, and life continued in a manner almost assuring that life would go on indefinitely. At some point, we took steps to change that slate. We marched out of a homeostatic balance and into something else. Now we have reached a point at which we are literally punching holes in our little biosphere, through pollution, ozone damage, and nuclear testing. No one knows how this shift toward imbalance started, but it did. Some may rightfully say that cities led the way.

Perhaps cities are like a virus, demanding the sacrifice of all resources to replicate itself, like a viral attacker in the body. Viruses use up everything, regardless of the cost to their "host," and then move on to the next victim. We have already discovered that cities are like living beings, communicating with those who would listen and understand their power. I don't think, however, that our potentially fatal misstep occurred with the building of the first city. It came a bit later.

When the ancient cities were created, they were temples of learning, art, magick, and commerce. When we look at our records of Egypt and Summeria, arguably some of the oldest civilizations, we notice that marvelous cities seem to have sprung up from nowhere, very advanced and evolved by our standards, even today. The logical progression leading toward these civilizations is nowhere to be found. Boom! Suddenly we had marvelous pyramids and temples. These cities are far older than many in traditional archaeology wish to admit. The archaeological records mark, not the rise, but the steady decline of civilization. Somewhere, we had a really advanced society, embodied in a city, but observing and honoring the life force in Earth, and even the cosmos. It was led by philosopher kings who honored magick, astrology, and the gods who created it all. Fervent religious devotion was the manifestation of this honoring. As the society declined, however, people grew accustomed to the comfort, and forgot to honor these powers, or, worse yet, were forced by the ruling parties to observe ceremonies that had lost meaning for the people. Different cults and factions grew up, instigating the "us-versus-them" mentality, the "my-god-is-bigger-than-your-god" idea. Conflicting mythologies reflect that difficulty. Through these squabbles, which devolved into to holy wars, many forgot the one central spirit running through everything. I think most of the world has forgotten it since. We continue to make war, war on religion, on territory, on ethnicity, and a war against the planet that we think we need to subjugate. Even as we lost the true majesty of these special learning and spiritual centers, we continued to build more, trying instinctively to recapture the lost spirituality of first civilizations. We didn't know what was lost, only that cities were good at one point, so we continued to build them, searching for what was good in them. As each declined, we, as a people, spread out and made more. Some wise ones returned to the land, to the jungle and forest, to find what was lost. There, they could reconnect with the spirit. Perhaps that's what happened to the native people in the Western Hemisphere, the Anasazi of North America and the great Mayan city builders. They disappeared when the city model no longer worked for them. Most people living in a city, ancient or modern, do not want to give up the lifestyle they have grown to know, even though it might be missing something. Many proclaim the higher realms and dimensions to be cities made from gold, silver, crystal, amber, and white light, glistening in perfection. Our modern fascination with Atlantis, a real or imagined place, stems from our desire to reclaim the perfect city, the golden land of Utopia where we lived in harmony with all. Everyone had what they wanted. The myths tell us, however, that Atlantis eventually degenerated into a feuding war-torn country, plagued with internal and external struggles. Atlantis was first noted by Plato for its attacks on Greece. The Atlanteans' abuse of power led Earth herself to rise up and use the seas to swallow them.

The repeated attempts and failures of all these cities may prove that the model is flawed. No one in recorded history has gotten it right and kept it right, so why do we think we will? They may be correct. I think the answer goes back to a fundamental flaw in our collective civilizations. They forgot the spirit running through all. Everything is connected. Everything is alive. Everything affects everything else. Everything must be honored. If we remember and teach that to every generation, I think we have a chance, even if we live in cities.

City Magick

Our cities have been built over our Earth's energy vortices. They are intertwined now. We can change our cities from the model of a virus, sucking the energy up. We can transform the parasitic image to one of symbiosis. Everything evolves. We gain from a co-creative relationship with life on all levels. If we honor our creations, they will change with us. We can adapt our cities from the overpopulated pollution- and crime-filled zones many of them have become and head them in the direction of light and love. We have the technology, the will, and, now, the magick. We can do anything we choose. What do you choose?

The practice of city magick is a step in the right direction for many. Awareness is the first key to understanding our situation. By becoming aware of the living forces around you in all forms and understanding that they must be honored and respected, you can move toward the future. This book is only the start of a new magical journey. It gives the modern mystic new ideas for practice and raises more questions than it answers. How those questions are answered depends on your individual tastes, desires and personal tradition. Hopefully, your eyes will see things in a different light, one in which magick is a growing, evolving system, not a static relic. Older traditions and translations of the oldest magical works are great resources, inspirations, and wells of knowledge, but they were written for another time, for another people. Modern magick is for modern people, taking the tools from the past and carving out a new future— exploring, discovering, sometimes making mistakes, but ultimately learning from all. Urban magick will shift and change as society changes. Technology, music, and cultural symbols will be dramatically different, even in the next ten to twenty years. Whenever a culture changes, the magick and mysticism associated with it change. When the climate for magick was difficult, the country witches used their brooms and kitchen knives as tools. When mysticism became more accepted, seekers used separate ritual tools from their household items. The direction our world is taking is still to be decided. By exploring the life force all around you, by discovering that magick is not restricted to certain locations or certain types of people, but the birthright of everyone everywhere, you help determine the course of our collective future. Magick is a part of everything.

Some simply wish to sweep all this under the rug–modern magical traditions and our modern society–and return to the Stone Age to recapture what we once had. Barring the invention of a physical time machine, we can never go back, truly, only forward. So we must deal with what we have created, here and now. Many magical traditions hold the idea that you reap what you sow, what you do comes back to you in countless variations. Part of your spiritual growth is learn-ing to deal with what you've sown. Those who don't learn, or at least remember, these somewhat karmic lessons are destined to repeat them. This is where evolution and responsibility cross paths. As a world, we must deal with our own creations in concrete, steel, glass, and circuitry if we are to ever learn. As you can see from this book, they have much to offer. Go out and create, explore. Find the voices of the spirit connecting us all in everything. Learn all you can from the world around you, city and country, street and forest, fountain and lake. They all have words to share with you. Only then can you take these lessons and create a new world.

As we approach the dawn of the New Age, what many prophesy to be a new Golden Age, we must go forward and create a new world, not try to recapture the past. We can incorporate the best of ancient and modern wisdom to create something new. Will we move into partnership with our environment, transforming the model of the city from virus to symbiote, a healthy relationship for all? Will we move forward and create a lasting Utopia, a true shining bright city? Like the psychic reader being asked questions, the future holds infinite possibilities. The future holds what we want to create. We are all our own psychics, holding the answers to the future. What do you choose to create?

Bibliography

Andrews, Ted. *Animal-Speak: The Spiritual and Magical Powers of Creatures Great and Small.* St. Paul, MN: Llewellyn, 1993.

Belle, Maureen L. *Gaiamancy: Creating Harmonious Environments.* Greenbank, WA: White Doe Productions, 1999.

Beyerl, Paul. *The Master Book of Herbalism.* Custer, WA: Phoenix, 1984.

Black, Jason S., and Christopher S. Hyatt. *Urban Voodoo: A Beginner's Guide to Afro-Caribbean Magic.* Tempe, AZ: New Falcon, 1995.

Cabot, Laurie with Tom Cowan. *Power of the Witch: The Earth, the Moon and the Magical Path to Enlightenment.* New York: Dell, 1989.

Conway, D. J. *The Ancient and Shining Ones.* St. Paul, MN: Llewellyn, 1993.

Cooper, Phillip. *Basic Magic: A Practical Guide.* York Beach, ME: Samuel Weiser, 1996.

Cowan, Tom. *Fire in the Head.* San Francisco: HarperSanFrancisco, 1993.

Clow, Barbara Hand. *The Pleiadian Agenda: A New Cosmology for the Age of Light.* Santa Fe: Bear & Company, 1995.

Cunningham, Scott. *Cunningham's Encyclopedia of Crystal, Gem and Metal Magic.* St. Paul, MN: Llewellyn, 1992.

——. *Cunningham's Encyclopedia of Magical Herbs.* St. Paul, MN: Llewellyn, 1985.

——. *Incense, Oils and Brews.* St. Paul, MN: Llewellyn, 1989.

Farrar, Janet, and Stewart Farrar. *Spells and How They Work.* Custer, WA: Phoenix, 1990.

Flashmaps Boston. London, England: Fodor's Travel Publications Inc., 1998.

Fodor's '96 New York City. London, England: Fodor's Travel Publications Inc., 1995.

Gabriel, Peter. *Passion: Music for the Last Temptation of Christ.* David Geffin Company, 1989.

Grolier Mutltimedia Encyclopedia. Grolier Interactive Inc., 1997.

Harner, Michael. *Shamanic Journey Multiple Drumming,* vol. 7. Norwalk, CT: Foundation of Shamanic Studies, 1993.

——. *Shamanic Journeying Solo and Double Drumming,* vol. 1. Norwalk, CT: Foundation of Shamanic Studies, 1993.

——. *The Way of the Shaman.* New York: HarperCollins, 1980.

Hart, Mickey. *Planet Drum.* Salem, MA: Rykodisc, 1991.

Hine, Phil. *Condensed Chaos.* Tempe, AZ: New Falcon, 1995.

Judith, Anodea. *Wheels of Light: A User's Guide to the Chakra System.* St. Paul, MN: Llewellyn, 1987.

Kenyon, Tom, and Virginia Essene. *The Hathor Material.* Santa Clara, CA: Spiritual Education Endeavors, 1996.

King, Serge Kahili, Ph.D. *Urban Shaman: A Handbook for Personal and Planetary Transformation Based on the Hawaiian Way of the Adventurer.* New York: Fireside, A Division of Simon & Schuster, 1990.

Kraig, Donald Michael. *Modern Magick: Eleven Lessons in the High Magickal Arts.* St. Paul, MN: Llewellyn, 1988

Bibliography

Lyn, Jamie. *Earth Design: The Added Dimension*. Miami Shores, FL: Earth Design, 1995.

McCubbin, Chris W. *GURPS: Cuthulu Pink*. Austin, TX: Steve Jackson Games, Inc., 1995.

Melody. *Love Is in the Earth*. Wheat Ridge, CO: Earth-Love Publishing House, 1995.

Morrison, Grant. *The Invisibles, Vol. I*, nos. 1–25. New York: DC Comics, 1996–2000.

——. *The Invisibles, Vol. II*, nos. 1–22. New York: DC Comics, 1998–2000

Peschel, Lisa. *A Practical Guide to the Runes: Their Uses in Divination and Magick*. St. Paul, MN: Llewellyn, 1989.

Sanchez, Victor. *The Teachings of Don Carlos*. Santa Fe: Bear & Company, 1995.

Sams, Jamie, and David Carson. *Medicine Cards: The Discovery of Power through the Ways of the Animals*. Santa Fe: Bear & Company, 1998.

Telesco, Patricia. *Urban Pagan: Magical Living in a 9-to-5 World*. St. Paul, MN: Llewellyn, 1995.

Thorsson, Edred. *Northern Magic: Mysteries of the Norse, Germans and English*. St. Paul, MN: Llewellyn, 1992.

Wright, Machaelle S. *Perelandra Garden Workbook: A Complete Guide to Gardening with Nature Intelligences*. Jefferonsonton, VA: Perelandra, Ltd., 1993.

Yin, Amorah Quan. *The Pleiadian Workbook, Awaking Your Divine Ka*. Santa Fe: Bear & Company, 1996.